"An extraordinary story of a nearly forgotten ⌐....
pion, wonderfully told. Michael Cochrane brings to life the ⌐.
Torontonian George Lyon winning the gold medal in the 1904 Olympics
in a compelling re-creation that is literally impossible to put down."

DAVID MILLER, former Mayor of Toronto, 2003-10

"An amazing book. All sports fans—whether golfers or not—will enjoy
the masterful job Cochrane does of making you feel you are right there
beside Lyon on his journey to Olympic gold in 1904."

DAN FERRONE, Canadian Football Hall of Fame, 2013 · Toronto Argonauts,
1981-92 · President, Toronto Argonauts, 2003-4 · President, Canadian
Football League Players Association, 1992-2001

"The story of George Lyon is inspirational and encouraging to golfers at
all levels. It reminds me to continue to be true to myself and to compete
with passion no matter what the perceived odds are. In a time of my life
when I struggle with the physical demands of winning, Mr. Lyon's story
will motivate me to persevere."

FAREEN "FAR" SAMJI, 2012, 2013, 2014, and 2015 ILDC Canadian
Women's Long Drive Champion · 2013 ILDC World Team Champion, Team
Canada 1 · 2015 ILDC International Women's Long Drive Champion

"Who knows the Canadian sports pioneer who won an Olympic gold
medal in 1904? In golf? Michael Cochrane knows, and now he tells the
story of the Lyon before Tiger—plus some surprising golf history and
some fondly told golf stories."

CHRISTOPHER MOORE, historian, author, and two-time recipient of the
Governor General's Literary Award

"I absolutely loved *Olympic Lyon*... Once I started reading it, I didn't
want to put it down. It gave me a personal connection to a vitally important period in golf's history, evolution, and spirit that goes back to the
beginning era of golf in North America. After reading *Olympic Lyon,*
1904 doesn't seem so long ago. I found myself totally connected to
George Lyon's story. [Michael Cochrane's] writing is a lovely gift to the
game of golf. Thank you."

DICK ZOKOL, 1981 Canadian Amateur Champion · NCAA Team Championship, 1981 · Founder/Designer/Developer Sagebrush golf course, BC, 2009

"I felt transported to another time and particularly enjoyed the settings [Michael Cochrane] described and the conversations he imagined. [Cochrane's] book is an important contribution to the game's literature as we move toward the Summer Olympics."

LORNE RUBENSTEIN, columnist, *SCOREGolf* Magazine · author of *Moe & Me: Encounters with Moe Norman, Golf's Mysterious Genius; A Season in Dornoch; Mike Weir: The Road to the Masters;* and *The Natural Golf Swing* (with George Knudson)

"As a great-grandson of George Seymour Lyon, I grew up being quite familiar with 'some' of the folklore surrounding Canada's defending Olympic gold medalist in golf. Michael Cochrane's page-turning story of GSL's midlife adoption and ultimate mastery of golf resonates with me as a golfing descendant, and I'm sure will make good reading for all golfers. Cochrane's voice paints a realistic accounting of George Lyon's rise to golfing fame, and his palette and tone have created a down-to-earth rendering of the character that was George Lyon as well as that of the great man's character. Well done, Michael—a page turner, indeed."

ROSS WIGLE, great-grandson of George Seymour Lyon

"I had heard many stories of my great-grandfather through my grandmother and mother, but *Olympic Lyon* delves much further into the man and his times, and his remarkable accomplishment in winning golf's only gold medal. Michael Cochrane's book provides a marvelous picture of early twentieth-century life and introduces us to the man, the athlete, and the civic leader who shocked the golfing world. As golf returns this year to the Olympics, it is timely and fitting to recognize its current defending champion, to learn about the challenges he faced, and to revel in his personal achievement of his victory at Glen Echo.

"Michael Cochrane weaves a wonderful tale, and *Olympic Lyon* is a must-read for all golfers, historians, and anyone else who appreciates a great story."

SANDY SOMERS, great-grandson of George Seymour Lyon

OLYMPIC LYON

OLYMPIC
LYON

The Untold Story of the Last Gold Medal for Golf

MICHAEL COCHRANE

Jeff,

Hope this inspires golf!

· CARTPATH PRESS ·
AN IMPRINT OF LEGAL INTEL
Toronto

Other Books by Michael Cochrane

. . .

NONFICTION

Surviving Your Divorce:
A Guide to Canadian Family Law

Surviving Your Parents' Divorce

Do We Need a Marriage Contract? How a Legal
Contract Can Strengthen Your Marriage

Do We Need a Cohabitation Agreement?
How an Agreement Can Strengthen Your Relationship

Class Actions: A Guide to the Class Proceedings Act

Strictly Legal: A Guide to Canadian Law

Family Law in Ontario for Lawyers and Law Clerks

. . .

FICTION

The Nightsoil Trilogy (forthcoming)

Gulliver and the Unpainted Tee (forthcoming)

Thunder and Lightning:
Tommy Bolt and the 1958 U.S. Open (forthcoming)

THIS BOOK IS DEDICATED to the memory of those golfers, golf course designers, superintendents, and others who in the last quarter of the nineteenth century were responsible for the founding of golf in North America. The current generation of golfers stands on their shoulders. I believe that understanding the game's origins contributes to an even greater appreciation of this marvelous sport.

It is also dedicated to George S. Lyon, whose victory in St. Louis in 1904 stands as one of the greatest achievements in Canadian golf history. I hope his story inspires other Canadian golfers to leave their mark on the game—perhaps in Rio at the Summer Olympics in 2016. As George Lyon would have said, "There is always room for a dark horse in the race."

Cataloguing data available from Library and Archives Canada
ISBN 978-0-9948545-2-0 (paperback)
ISBN 978-0-9948545-3-7 (ebook)

Cover and text design by Peter Cocking
Cover photo courtesy of the Canadian Golf Hall of Fame
Interior photos courtesy the Lambton Golf and Country Club,
Canadian Golf Hall of Fame, and the Archives of Ontario
Printed and bound in Canada by Marquis Book

Cartpath Press
An imprint of LegalIntel
151 Yonge Street, Suite 1800
Toronto ON M5C 2W7

Contents

Acknowledgments

BOOKS SUCH AS this one do not get written without help. I would like to briefly acknowledge some of those who helped to make it happen.

First and foremost, my wife, Rita, has been a great support and very tolerant of me slipping away for hours on end to work on this labor of love. She also reminded me from time to time as I went down research rabbit holes that it is a book about George Lyon, not a master's thesis. Thanks, my love.

The Canadian Golf Hall of Fame and Museum has been very helpful, allowing me access to their library, sharing photographs of George Lyon, and maintaining Canadian golf history. Visit the Hall of Fame at www.golfcanada.ca and support their work.

Lambton Golf and Country Club (www.lambtongolf.com), the golf home of George Lyon, has been wonderful, allowing me access to their beautiful club to talk with members of their heritage committee, hosting in 2015 an event to celebrate the 111th anniversary of Lyon's win in St. Louis, sharing the club's history, and arranging for me to play eighteen holes with two of Lyon's great-grandsons.

I could not have done my work without relying upon two seminal books about Canadian golf—James A. Barclay's *Golf in Canada: A History* and L.V. Kavanagh's *History of Golf in Canada*. To me, they are important works that merit republication (with updates and corrections).

When I started this work, I had already read Donald E. Graves's book *Red Coats & Grey Jackets: The Battle of Chippawa, 5 July 1814* and was shocked to discover in its pages that Lyon's grandfather was injured in that very battle. I relied heavily upon Graves's book and greatly appreciate his entire body of Canadian historical writing.

I also appreciated and relied upon the book by George Matthews and Sandra Marshall entitled *Images of America: St. Louis Olympics, 1904*. The photographs allowed me to see what participants in those unusual Olympics actually looked like.

Finally, I would like to acknowledge the work of Page Two, whose amazing team helped me prepare this book for publication. Jesse Finkelstein, Megan Jones, editors Gabrielle Narsted and Shirarose Wilensky, and designer Peter Cocking, I could not have done it without your support, advice, and guidance.

OLYMPIC LYON

Preface

A Few Words about Golf

LIKE GEORGE LYON, my introduction to golf came a little late in life. I watched Tiger Woods win the Masters in 1997 and, at age forty-three, thought, "I'm going to give that game a try." Also like George Lyon, I quickly fell in love with the game and found myself staring at marked-up scorecards, saying, "I can shave a few strokes off that." I had my rites of passage as I walked on air after breaking a hundred, sat in quiet satisfaction enjoying a cold beer with my buddies at Lookout Point Golf Club in Fonthill, Ontario, the day I broke ninety, and then amazed even myself when I shot a seventy-seven in a match one afternoon at Markland Wood Golf Club in Toronto. Now in my sixties, on any given day I hover between those benchmarks. And if I hang on long enough, I might shoot my age someday.

My love of golf deepened when I discovered match play. I think in retrospect stroke play is designed to help us get and keep our golf game in good working order. Match play is how we get and keep our golf *head* in good working order. A match play ladder was my introduction to this aspect of the game, and I took to it, winning the 2007 Lookout Point Match Play (B Flight), with my first hole in one along the way. Can it get any better than that?

My wife and I bought a cottage north of Burlington, Ontario, in a lovely little place called Cedar Springs. Membership includes a gorgeous golf course wrapped along the Niagara Escarpment. My wife has taken up the game with enthusiasm, even if she was a little "surprised" by my gift of clubs one Christmas, and we enjoy playing together, whether at home or destinations such as Hilton Head, Florida, Barbados, or Alabama.

In our community, we have a golf ladder, and I managed to win the 2010 Match Play Championship (eighteen and over) as well as the 2014 and 2015 Senior (sixty and over) Match Play Championships. They might as well be the Masters and Canadian Open as far as I am concerned.

My nickname in our cottage community is Cartpath. A few years ago, I sliced a drive on our 205-yard uphill par three. My playing partners and I watched as the ball followed a slow arc. Someone called out, "It's leaking," and suddenly it hit the edge of the cart path, kicked wildly into the air, and spun up the front of the green. You guessed it. Into the hole for a hole in one. The ball, sporting a massive scuff mark, was duly framed for me, with the official card, by my wife.

The next year, I sliced (I know) yet another drive on our downhill par four ninth. I was certain the ball was headed deep into the woods on the right-hand side of the green with the cart path some thirty yards away. Someone in the group thought they heard a click. When we arrived and began to look for the ball, my friend John Willmott said, "You'd better look in the hole. It's happened before..." You guessed it. There was my ball in the hole, with a huge scuff from the cart path. Albatross, hole in one. It was suitably mounted. Now you know that if you play me, this is the sort of thing you are up against.

Golf can be a wonderful way to see the world. Since I took up the game, I have traveled to play some wonderful courses—among them St. Andrew's (New and Old) (where I felt I should lie down and embrace the hallowed ground); North Berwick (the second hole there is called Sea for a reason—I actually played my second shot from the sea back to the fairway); Muirfield (where Jack Nicklaus won the first of his three British Opens, and I came to understand why he chose that name for his course in Dublin, Ohio); Royal Wimbledon (a hidden gem and England's third-oldest club, founded in 1865); New Zealand Golf Club (where my locker was next to the one once used by Sir Arthur Conan Doyle); Woking Golf Club (Bernard Darwin's club, which was originally intended to be a private club for lawyers); Westhill (It was commissioned in 1907 by a woman for her new husband. Think about that for a minute.); Walton Heath (a course opened in 1904 with a match between the Great Triumvirate—Braid, Vardon, and Taylor—and where the 1981 Ryder Cup was played); Royal St. George's (where I enjoyed the hospitality of its members in their magnificent grill room and admired their trophy collection. Note, too, that this is where Walter Travis became the first non-Brit to win the British Amateur, in 1904); Toronto's own character-laden Stanley Thompson–designed St. George's (where George Lyon laid the foundation stone in 1929); Doral, Florida (where the Blue Monster nearly convinced me to give up golf and switch back to tennis); the marvelous Donald Ross–designed Essex in Windsor, Ontario (host of the 1938 Canadian Amateur); and the intoxicating Apes Hill in Barbados (where as we started the back nine, our group could gaze out over the Caribbean to the left and the Atlantic to the right). I think an amazing part of golf is the way in which the courses themselves connect us to the game's past.

In 2015, as I worked on this book, I had an opportunity to play two of Canada's finest courses, located just north of Toronto—the Devil's Paintbrush and Pulpit. It was the twenty-fifth anniversary of their opening, and course architect Dr. Michael Hurdzan and his son and business partner, Chris, were there to celebrate. As if it was preordained, the weather was some of Ontario's best. Over lunch, Chris and I shared a mutual appreciation for what goes into a great course and the importance of remembering the game's origins, the people, and the courses. Golf courses and the game itself are changing to accommodate technology and more athletic players, but that was as true in 1904 as it is today. The game is evolving and some things will change; that is inevitable. But in my opinion, we should hold fast some unique aspects of this great game.

At the turn of the last century, they could not build golf courses fast enough. (See the chronology at the end of the book for the very short period over which Canada goes from having just a few courses to more than five hundred.) Interest in the game was exploding between 1895 and 1915. Today, the game is overbuilt and some contraction is taking place. Younger people are not joining established clubs. There are a variety of reasons for this, ranging from the economic to the length of time required to complete eighteen holes—the pace of play issue.

I would like to address one aspect of this challenge to the game and the solutions that are being proposed. Certainly, pace of play needs to be addressed, and I believe there are ways to accomplish that goal so that a round of golf does not take five hours. However, I think some of the other proposals to attract young people to the game threaten to ruin it more than any new club head design, shaft innovation, or ball construction. Golf and golf courses need to be very careful over the next ten years to build an attraction to the game that is not based simply on what I would call flash. I grew up playing many sports—baseball, hockey, basketball, and tennis to name a few. Golf is different. The future of golf needs to be built on the demonstration to young people of why this game is special among sports and why it is worth the time, the practice, the silence, and the opportunity for personal introspection. If you play golf, you know exactly what I mean. Flash can and will always be topped. But how can you top an opportunity for personal reflection in a simple game based on an honor system and personal integrity? How do we teach that? That is the game's challenge.

I hope this little book about some of the history of the game and one man's life helps in meeting that challenge.

MICHAEL COCHRANE
Cartpath Press, Toronto, 2015

Introduction

IN 2012, AFTER playing a round of golf with my good friend Doug Green at Rosedale Golf Club in Toronto, I noticed a framed gold medal hanging above the counter in the pro shop. Curious, I asked about the story behind this medal. Staff explained that it was the gold medal won by George S. Lyon at the 1904 Olympic Games in St. Louis, Missouri.

Gold medal for golf? Why had I never heard the story of George Lyon and his gold medal? My curiosity was piqued, and I began to investigate. I was under the impression that golf had never been a part of the Summer Olympics. I was wrong.

Golf had been a part of the Summer Olympics in Paris in 1900. The competition was a strange affair with many of the golfers not even knowing that the matches they played were a part of the Olympics. The ladies played nine holes and a winner was declared—she received a porcelain bowl as a prize. It was not until long after her death many years later that she was declared to have won an Olympic gold medal even though no such medal was ever awarded. Twelve men competed in a thirty-six-hole event, and American Charles Sands won with the low round. Although described as the winner of the gold medal, there is no evidence that any such medal was awarded to him. In fact the 1900 Olympics were odd in that medals were generally not awarded. Winners received valuable artifacts instead. Another unusual twist in 1900 was the decision for the men to play an additional round of golf, this time handicapped. A different winner, Albert Lambert of St. Louis, was declared for that event but, again, no gold medal.

Golf returned to the Olympics in 1904 in St. Louis and now not only would there be medals but, true to the new confident America that was emerging, they would be real gold, silver, and bronze ones and there would be magnificent trophies as well. This was to be the beginning of an Olympic golf legacy. But then in 1908, with the Summer Olympics scheduled for London, golf was dropped because of continuous infighting about the rules. As a result, the idea of Olympic-level golf fell by the wayside, and the legacy of golf's gold medalist was lost. After George Lyon, there were no defending or repeat Olympic golf champions; there was no passing of the proverbial torch, like we see in prevailing golf competitions such as the Masters, with its coveted green jacket passed down each year as part of Augusta National's deep heritage, or the presentation of the Claret Jug at the British Open each year.

Alas, it seemed that the story of George Lyon had also been lost along the way.

Now, after hundreds of hours of research—on weekends and days off from my law practice in Toronto—I am excited to tell the story of a Canadian, a Torontonian, who, against all odds, traveled to St. Louis in September 1904 and defeated the best golfers America had to offer.

But this is not just a story about a man playing golf 112 years ago. It is a story about how a man's roots and experiences shaped his character and gave him the skills he needed to meet innumerable challenges. I think golf can reveal a lot about a person, whether it's played for pleasure on the weekend or competitively in a tournament. Golf is about honesty, integrity, perseverance, patience, physical and mental endurance, humility, humor at times, and a certain brand of wisdom.

In the following story, I hope to reveal how George Lyon developed all of those characteristics during his lifetime and how those traits helped keep him on a path to victory at the 1904 Summer Olympics.

There are two ways to tell a story like George Lyon's. I could have written a history book that tells you where and when he was born, where he played golf, what tournaments he won, where he raised his family, when he went to St. Louis, who he played, the final score, and so on. But when I began to immerse myself in research, reading stories about his life, his golf, and his road to victory, I realized that I could convey much more about this amazing man, and the times in which he lived, if I told his story as I imagine it unfolded. Because of course the lives people led more than a century ago were not black and white like the photos we see. They were just as colorful and fascinating as the lives of men and women golfers we know today.

The historical facts to which I refer are to the best of my ability accurate; names, events, dates, places, scores, and, in some cases, strokes taken are correct. As for George's story—I have done my best to make it authentic. I have woven his life and historically correct facts into a work of historical fiction.

You may be struck by parallels between this interpreted history of George Lyon and the ongoing evolution of the modern game of golf. At the turn of the century, when golf exploded in North America, there was much to do to keep up with the leaders in golf from Europe: players learned new skills, developed and debated improvements in equipment, established new clubs, fleshed out new rules and methods of scoring, and resolved issues of amateurism and professionalism, and of course there was the design and construction of many of the classic golf courses golfers know and admire even to this day.

As well, I hope to show you a glimpse of the men he met in St. Louis, some world events that intersected with their lives, a bit of national history, and I hope, a lot about the origins of golf in North America.

Throughout this period there was a keen focus on that one true constant, that which never changes, despite a golfer's age or skill level—fierce competitiveness. George Lyon, standing over a putt on the thirty-fourth hole at Glen Echo in 1904, felt the same burning desire to win as Jack Nicklaus did over his putt at the Masters in 1986 (both men were the same age at the time of their respective wins). Likewise, Tiger felt the same rolling in his birdie on the seventy-second hole to force a play-off against Rocco Mediate at the 2008 U.S. Open. Or perhaps you have felt that burning competitiveness as you made a four-footer to beat your friend last Sunday.

On a very cold Toronto weekend in March 2015, I sat sipping a coffee, alternating between working on this book and watching the final rounds of the World Golf Championships (WGC) at Doral in Miami. Having played the Blue Monster a number of times, I watched the play with an extra level of interest. (One of the great aspects of golf is that we can actually play the same courses as the pros—maybe not from the tips, but we can play the great courses and dream.) That Sunday, Dustin Johnson hung tough and outlasted J.B. Holmes, Bubba Watson, and a few others to win the title—his first since he had taken a few months off to sort out his personal life. Like George Lyon, Johnson is a great natural athlete, and it was satisfying to see him return to all his promise.

During a break in the action, Johnny Miller—one of my favorite straight-talking golf announcers on the Golf Channel and NBC—began to discuss the upcoming 2016 Summer Olympics. During that broadcast Miller went on to say, "Wouldn't it be great to be the first person to ever win a gold medal for golf?"

What?! I spilled my coffee all over my desk as my head snapped around to look at the TV screen. Here, at even the highest level of golf knowledge, George Lyon and his gold medal had somehow disappeared. I cleaned up the mess and got back to work on the book, recharged about telling Lyon's story in time for the 2016 Summer Olympics.

In these upcoming Summer Olympics, sixty men will compete for the Olympic gold medal in golf. That group will be made up of the top fifteen men in the world to a maximum of four golfers from any one country (so while, for example, the U.S. might have five of the top ten golfers in the world, only four of them would go on to represent the U.S). The remaining forty-five spots will be allocated among the highest-rated golfers from other countries to a maximum of four per country. As of the time of writing, in late 2015, we do not know who will be among those sixty men, though we can guess at a few names, such as Jordan Spieth, Rory McIlroy, Jason Day, and perhaps Canada's Graham DeLaet. Women golfers—likely to include, Inbee Park, Stacy Lewis, Suzann Pettersen, and Canada's Brooke Henderson—will have a similar system for qualification and will play the same course for their Olympic medals.

The 2016 Olympic competition will be quite different from the golf marathon held at Glen Echo Golf Club outside

St. Louis in 1904. Those golfers faced a thirty-six-hole Monday qualifier, and then five days of thirty-six-hole match play each day. In Rio, we will be watching a seventy-two-hole stroke play event with, if needed, a three-hole play-off.

Golf course architect Gil Hanse has built a brand-new environmentally sustainable golf course in Rio de Janeiro. The course, which will eventually be public, is just a six-iron from the Atlantic Ocean. It has been carved out of a massive site with what can only be called great patience. It will include two man-made lakes, elevation changes, and two holes that run alongside the Marapendi Lagoon, and it will be affected by what some golfers will probably call a "Texas wind," that is, a wind that blows constantly. (A golfer from Texas once told me, "One day the wind stopped blowing and all the chickens fell over.") It sounds like Hanse's course will present a worthy challenge at the Olympics.

Will the ultimate winner know that they hold not the first but rather the *second* gold medal for golf? Will they know who George Lyon was? What kind of life he led? What type of challenges he faced in winning the first gold medal? I hope this book answers some of those questions and that George Lyon resumes his rightful place in world golf history.

1

Tipcat

OCTOBER 1895

IN THE FALL of 1895, George Lyon, truth be told, had a mild contempt for the game of golf. His sport was cricket. And he was good at it. Known to his friends and fellow competitors as one of the best "wielders of the willow" in Canada, just last year he had set a world cricket record when he carried his bat for 238 innings. As a very active member of the Toronto international cricket team, George had watched oddly dressed golfers as they played in the cow pasture next to the pristine Rosedale cricket fields, crisscrossing the fields as they swatted their little white balls and stepped in occasional cow pies. To Lyon, cricket was a true sport. Golf? Hardly.

But cricket was not his only sport. No, not by any stretch. Baseball was a suitable challenge for him too, and as one of the best amateur ballplayers in the city, he captained the Toronto team in the very competitive Civil Service League. Baseball? Now there was a sport George could play all summer and into the fall and he could do it without interfering with his other favorite summer sports: track and field and football.

And once the leaves had fallen and Toronto's snowy winters arrived, without missing a beat George could turn his attention to yet two more of his sporting loves, winning curling trophies with the Toronto Curling Club and playing hockey. Curling and hockey? Now there were true winter sports. And he had the trophies on his mantle to prove it. They sat right alongside the trophy that he may have held the dearest, the one he won for pole vaulting. He had set a Canadian record in the sport. Ten feet, six inches. It was a very proud day—after all he was just nineteen years old.

So, by any standard of the day, George Lyon was a natural athlete. And for him, cricket, baseball, hockey, football, curling, track and field, and even lawn bowling were the greatest sports at which men could compete and challenge each other—and themselves.

But golf? Not interested. After all, as of October 1895, he was thirty-eight years old. He and his wife, Annette, had been married just four years and had a little girl, Kathleen, at home—the newest addition to their modest family of five. His fire insurance business in Toronto was growing, and his young family needed his attention. His life was busy; his life was full. Certainly his wife would have agreed that he really didn't need to play yet another sport. Especially one that seemed to call for the most unusual dress code. And besides that, when he watched them walking about nothing ever seemed to, well, *happen.*

That is until Friday, October 18, 1895. On that beautiful fall afternoon, Lyon's friend John Dick stood on the first tee of the Rosedale Golf Club with the unmistakable Canadian fall foliage of yellow, orange, and red autumn leaves ablaze around him. As he prepared to tee off, he waved to George, who stood on the other side of the fence, waiting for his cricket teammates to arrive for practice.

As a well-known figure in Toronto sports circles, George was quite aware of the recent growing interest in golf. It seemed incredible, but the Toronto Golf Club—only a few years old—actually had a waiting list. The increasing number of golfers were demanding that more new courses be built. He had heard the stories about some noisy town hall meetings just a few years ago led by a young Presbyterian minister, Reverend White, who championed Toronto golfers' demands to import the finest golf clubs and balls directly from Scotland.

Avid cricketer that he was, George voiced his concerns when he heard that the golf members of his own Toronto Lacrosse and Athletic Association had merged to incorporate all the golfers from the Deer Park Golf Club *and* the new Rosedale Golf Club. The whole lot of them were now being given access to the association's clubhouse. With all these new people they would be chock a block. In fact, that was how he had first met John Dick, John's wife, and their daughter, Muriel. They were a family of golfers. Puzzled, George had never seen a sport where an entire family could play together. "Imagine, competing against one's wife and child," he thought. "For heaven's sake, that cannot be a sport."

But in no time, to meet the demands of their zealous new golfing members, the club had managed to squeeze an entire eighteen-hole golf course into an area just south of the railway tracks and right next to the Rosedale lacrosse and cricket fields. Like the clubhouse it was a very tight fit, and George himself had shaken his head and laughed as he witnessed the good-natured abuse some golfers suffered as they played two of their holes—as they called them—alongside the bleachers that were usually full of a few hundred witty cricket fans.

The golf course had fairways that seemed to crisscross all over the place, and golfers frequently intersected each other as they plotted their way around. George noticed that there also seemed to be a lot of standing around. To make matters worse—and, frankly, more chaotic—a local dairy farmer had retained the right to pasture his cows in those same fields. George had even seen the occasional cow grazing the course while the men played golf. Although the Rosedale membership soon stood at an astonishing 270, George still asked himself, "Golf: How could anyone take it seriously?"

John Dick organized his golf clubs and watched George for a few more minutes. Seeing that his mates were late, he called out to him: "George, why don't you join me for a bit of golf?"

Lyon leaned all of his muscular 180-pound, five-foot, eight-inch frame on his willow cricket bat and frowned. He was about to say, "Tipcat," but his manners got the better of him.

Many years ago, George's Irish mother, Sarah, had taught him the children's game called tipcat. It involved flipping short tapered wooden pegs into the air and then trying to hit the peg with a larger stick. This was followed by noisy debates among the children scrambling to measure how far it had been hit. George remembered playing it as a child in Richmond, Ontario—a small village outside of Canada's capital city. He had fond memories of hopping through the grass, yelling and laughing, and cheering as he hit and flipped the pegs. "Tipcat is a children's game, and perhaps," Lyon thought, "so is golf." But, ever the jovial gentleman, George bit his tongue, waved politely to John, and looked at his pocket watch. His fellow cricketers were already fifteen minutes late.

Not satisfied, John Dick called to him again: "Come on, George, you'll enjoy it! We can share my clubs." He waggled his hickory-shafted club in the air and laughed.

George looked up and down the street, glanced at his watch one more time, clipped it shut, and climbed over the short fence to join a now beaming John Dick on the first tee of Rosedale's course. "What's this golf all about then?" he asked.

Grateful for a new pupil, John pulled a club from his canvas golf bag and began to explain its purpose with enthusiasm. "This club is called a driver, or what we might call a play club. But sometimes we call it a grassed driver." John then began to point to several other clubs in his bag. "This is a long spoon. This is a baffing spoon—I've had it for a few years now, love it. This is a niblick—it's one of my favorites, and so is this brassie. Oh, and this little sweetheart is my putter. This one here is an iron for driving. This one is my lofting iron. This is a cleek, and this last one here is a mashie."

He introduced each one as if they were dear friends, but George's head was spinning trying to remember these strange names. *What kind of sport requires a veritable toolbox to be able to play?*

John, blissfully unaware of George's skepticism, continued, "Personally, I never use more than seven of them on any given day: mostly my brassie, and my driver, my cleek, of course, my mashie, and my putter." John then took his driver, stood at the tee, pinched up a mound of sand, gingerly placed a ball on it, took up an athletic stance, and began to demonstrate to George what he considered to be a model golf swing. "It's easy if you follow some very simple rules," he said. "It is all set out in a wonderful new book called *Golf in America,* written by this fellow named James P. Lee—a direct descendant of the American Civil War general Robert E. Lee, I might add. But there is no need for you to take up reading any books at this point. I can lend it to you later. Now," said John, adopting his golf stance and turning to George, "Lee recommends that you stand square to the ball, put your feet apart about shoulder width—maybe eighteen to twenty inches. Have a slight bend to the knees, feel athletic, hold the club firmly in the palm of your left hand, but let your right hand be loose. Your left thumb should lie along the shaft, like this, and your right thumb can go all the way around, like this." John held the club up to show his grip. "Now, let the club rest for a moment on the ground behind the ball, then take the club back, slowly. 'Slow back' is a good reminder as you begin. Swing the club around your right shoulder and neck but not so far that it reaches back to sit on your left shoulder." John laughed as he said the last part, as if this was an obvious correction.

George took off his tweed hat and scratched his head, watching and trying to remember all of John's instructions.

"Turn your hips, but don't sway back and forth. Always keep your eye on the ball—not the top of the ball, mind you, but the back of the ball, where you'll make contact. Try to keep your head down as you swing through—don't try to *hit* the ball, but rather *swing through it*. But don't swing too hard. Let the club do the work. After you make contact, follow through, all the way around, and pose like this." John held a position for George to observe: his driver held firmly aloft, elbows in the air, and his chin pointed proudly down the course. With those final words of advice, John demonstrated his swing in slow motion. The path of the golf club moved from behind the ball, around his shoulders, then down and through to a final pose. "Oh, and don't grip the club too tight, and keep your head down, and try to keep this right elbow tight against your side, and remember to *swing through the ball*," John listed his final tips off quickly, trying not to forget anything. But noticing the look of total confusion on George's face, he stopped short and smiled at his new pupil. "Will you give it a try, George?"

George furrowed his brow in concentration. "General Robert E. Lee played golf?" he said in a daze.

"No, no, no... his son, or... his grandson wrote the book. It doesn't matter. Just try what I told you."

George stole a quick look to see if his cricket friends had arrived; perhaps he could excuse himself from this nonsense. Alas, feeling as though he couldn't slip away politely, George watched distractedly as John demonstrated one more time in slow motion the so-called model swing. John repeated his instructions, but this time George couldn't hear the words. They fluttered away in the wind like the orange and yellow fall leaves that covered the teeing area where they stood as John now chattered on about the golf ball he was using. A gutter? George thought he heard him say. He dared not ask for any more information.

Then, with a calculated and dignified air, John Dick set up for his real swing and calmly stroked his drive down the grassy fairway about 150 yards from where they stood. "There, that will play," he said, with great satisfaction, to himself as much as to George.

George took a deep breath and leaned his willow cricket bat against the small fence as John handed him the driver ("Is this a mashie?" George thought). His teacher reached down to pinch up a small mound of sand onto which he placed another fresh white ball. He took George by the shoulders and positioned him beside it, trying to arrange George's massive hands on the grip. George scowled as he held the club out in front of him and examined it as if it were some strange foreign musical instrument. One that perhaps smelled bad as well.

"Tipcat," George muttered.

"What?"

"Nothing," he mumbled as he positioned himself beside the ball in the way John had suggested. He rolled and shrugged his shoulders to loosen his wool jacket, tugged his Irish tweed cap a little tighter, and brushed each side of his thick moustache with the back of his hand. George stared down his nose at the ball as he tried to remember John's suggestions, but they had all become a blur. Paralyzed over the ball, arms stiff in front of him, George stood contemplating his next move, gripping and regripping the club. *Where do I begin?*

"George, George, just relax and swing," John said. "Pretend you're hitting a cricket ball."

Well, that was all George needed to hear. He relaxed, spread his legs wider, opened his stance with his left foot, crouched a little, and settled his weight comfortably on his toes. He took the club back about three quarters of the distance recommended by John, and then brought it down through the ball, as if swatting a dusty carpet. He held the follow-through, pointing his club to where he wanted the ball to go, rather than wrapping it around into a pose as John had demonstrated so elegantly. It was not what could be described as a classic golf swing by any stretch of the imagination, but the ball sailed out, straight over and past John's ball. It landed with a sharp kick that sent it rolling a further ten yards down the grassy fairway. The ball settled nicely in the center, about two hundred yards from where they stood.

George winced and turned to look at his friend, frustrated. "Sorry, John. Is that what you meant?"

John, stunned, stared at the ball on the fairway and, turning back to George, slowly took the club from his friend's hands and slid it into his cloth golf bag. "Good Lord, George."

"Listen, I'm sorry to be so awkward, John. But it was an awful lot to remember. It is my first time after all."

"Sorry? Those suggestions I gave you about the golf swing—"

"Yes, I know. I'm sorry..." George interrupted.

John put his arm around George with a broad smile. "Forget what I said. Forget it all!" He laughed. "Swing like that and you'll be fine, my friend, just fine. Now let's play some golf." And with that they started down George's first fairway.

As the two men played nine holes of golf that afternoon, George forgot all about his cricket match. On each hole, George, as if swinging a scythe, would fiercely swat his ball off the tee and down the center of the fairway, well past his friend's ball, delighted at John's stunned reaction to each powerful drive. But those other parts of the game did not come so easy for him, and he soon began to realize why so many people considered this a sport, not just a game. He often lost track of the number of strokes and putts he needed to close out each hole. John seemed so much better than him. His short game needed work, a lot of work. And putting? Well, there were no ladies nearby, so George's language could be excused.

While they were finishing the seventh hole that sunny fall afternoon, John held up a hickory-shafted iron and pointed out three golfers who were playing ahead of them. "We should buy those gentlemen a drink when we have an opportunity," he said. George, never one to pass up an opportunity for a fortifying drink and a bit of socializing, asked who these men were. "Why, just last spring those gentlemen, Mr. Cronyn, Mr. Edgar, and Mr. Carter, were convicted felons!" explained John.

"Good Lord! Convicted? Of what?" George exclaimed. *What kind of sport is John Dick getting me into? Who have I been rubbing shoulders with in the clubhouse?*

"All three were convicted of no less than a charge of..." John paused for effect, "playing golf on a Sunday, contrary to the provision of the Lord's Day Act!" He laughed, tipping his hat and waving to them as they walked past and down the leaf-covered fairway of the eighth hole.

"Golf on Sunday is illegal?" George was mystified that such a seemingly harmless walk in the park could be considered a breach of the Lord's Day Act. "And they were actually convicted?"

"It was illegal, indeed, and they were duly convicted, but we dedicated golfers rallied! With the help of the Toronto Golf Club, we appealed their conviction, and a year ago this very month, Appeal Judge McDougall reversed the trial judge's decision and threw out their conviction. The *very wise* judge said..." and here John lowered his voice to capture a sense of judicial authority, "'Golf is not a game of ball similar in any sense to the games enumerated in, or intended to be prohibited by, the Lord's Day Act. Golf is not a noisy game'—at least when he played it," added John with a grin, "and especially when he played it on Sundays!—'This game of golf is not a game within the meaning of the law. It attracts no crowds. It is not gambling. It is on a parallel with a gentleman going out for a walk on Sunday, and as he walks, switching off the heads of weeds with his walking stick.' And that was that. So ever since his decision, we've enjoyed glorious Sunday golf."

"Well, may the good Lord bless them all," George added with a laugh, thinking how ideal it might be to have a sport for Sundays, when baseball, football, cricket, and other sports were banned. He must not mention this to Annette, though.

Two hours later, after nine holes of golf on that glorious afternoon, the two men walked off the final green. John tallied up their scores: George sixty-five, John forty-four. As he slid his golf bag over his shoulder, John folded and tucked the scorecard into his vest pocket.

Noticing this, George asked, "Say, John, I wonder if I might take a look at that scorecard?"

John passed it to him with a knowing smile. "Certainly, keep it as a memento of your very first round of golf. Use it as a benchmark against which you can measure your improvement—of course assuming you want to play again sometime." He looked at George out of the corner of his eye for any telling reaction.

George pursed his lips together tightly as he looked closely at the card; then he folded it and tucked it into his own vest pocket. As he picked up his cricket bat and headed for the streetcar home, he thanked his friend for the lesson and for the very pleasant walk that fall afternoon. John noticed that not ten steps away, George had pulled the scorecard back out of his pocket. He was already carefully replaying each hole, re-creating the game in his mind, shot by shot. He would do so all the way home.

The next day, George Lyon asked to be proposed as a member of the Rosedale Golf Club. He had caught golf fever.

$=$ *2* $=$

Match Play

GEORGE LYON THREW himself into golf. He had a new sport to which he would devote himself. Cricket and his other favorite sports would be set aside that summer as he learned his new craft. With strong hands and powerful forearms and keen hand eye from cricket and baseball, he realized that he could drive the ball great distances. But now he was determined to master what John had described to him as the "short game." George soon understood that while driving the ball came easy to him, the closer he got to the hole itself, the more important—and difficult—the stroke seemed to become. He practiced. He played. He practiced more. The other members of Rosedale would often find him crouched at the edge of a green as dusk turned to darkness, chipping and putting with a midiron, over and over again.

George was a gregarious man, and he wasn't afraid to ask for advice from more experienced members. He spent hours at the course probing other golfers with questions about golf. *Which clubs do you think are best? Where can I purchase that new club everyone is talking about? What are the advantages and disadvantages of the various balls? What are the recommended techniques for hitting irons? Where can I find tips on putting? Where can I find a putter that feels right?* No aspect of the game escaped his attention.

One member, stumped by many of George's questions, approached him one afternoon and set down three slim volumes. "George, read these," he pleaded. "These men have thought about golf more than any man at Rosedale. All your questions will be answered. And perhaps then you can share those answers with all of us."

George immediately flipped through the pages and saw the names of the authors who would soon become household names to him: Horace Hutchinson's *Famous Golf Links,* Willie Park's *The Game of Golf,* and a book by James P. Lee, *Golf in America: A Practical Manual.* "This is the book that John Dick has read so closely," George said, remembering his first day on the course and his ridiculous thought of General Robert E. Lee playing golf.

"Yes, it's fairly new off the printing press, published just last year. American, of course. The way John has been playing lately, perhaps he should read it again," replied the fellow golfer with a laugh.

That summer, George inhaled the advice in these books and any other upon which he could lay his hands. He was determined to master the game.

Later that week, as he stood on the green at dusk, hitting dozens of practice putts, Mr. M. McLaughlin, President of Rosedale, approached him: "George, I say, you have taken this game to heart."

George laughed. "I'm afraid it's worse than that, my friend. I'm embarrassed to say that I am starting to fear that my fire insurance brokerage will begin to suffer. I've neglected a few clients these last few weeks. But I feel that I'm improving my game. It is starting to feel somehow more comfortable."

"Oh, don't let that comfortable feeling fool you. It can disappear with one bad stroke just like that." He snapped his fingers and laughed. "The reason I came over to disturb you, George, is that I have arranged some match play between our club and the Toronto Golf Club—something to kick off the season. We'll have ten men from each club go head to head, man to man. I think you'll enjoy it, and it will be good experience for you. John Dick is off his game and suggested you as a replacement. I would be delighted if you would join us."

"Match play?" George hesitated. He had only played golf by counting strokes.

"Right, right, you haven't played a match yet. Well, when you're done practicing, join me for a drink, and I'll walk you through the rules. Pretty straightforward really but there is a little strategy involved," he added, as he turned to walk back to the club.

"No time like the present," George called back, picking up his clubs and practice balls. "In match play, how many holes does one play?"

"As many as we decide at the outset. It could be nine, eighteen, even thirty-six, if the weather holds and our wives and children don't miss us too much. The important thing is to win more holes than your opponent. You play it hole by hole, you see. Strokes only matter for the hole you are playing. If you score a four and your opponent scores a five, you win that hole. Now you're one up and you move on to the next hole. If you score five and your opponent scores five, that hole is halved. It's called 'no blood,' as we like to say. So you're still one up. On the next hole, if you score a three and your opponent scores a four, you're two up, and so on. Whoever wins the most holes wins the match. If you are up three holes but there are only two holes left to play then the match is over. We would say you won, three and two."

They had reached the clubhouse just as night fell, sat down at a table, and ordered some drinks. George soaked up the rules easily, but it was the strategy that truly caught his attention.

McLaughlin continued. "Let's assume you've played twelve holes of an eighteen-hole match, and your opponent has won the last hole, No. 12, drawing you into a tie, or as we say, you're 'all square.' There are six holes left to play. He will have the honor of teeing off on the thirteenth hole. Let's imagine that he hits his drive poorly into some trees on the side of the fairway, leaving him an impossible shot to the green. Let's assume he cannot possibly be on the green in two. When you step to the tee, what is your play?"

George laughed. "I'd hit that little devil of a ball as far as I can, get on in two if I can and try to beat him with a three—"

McLaughlin interrupted his student, "What will your *opponent's* likely score be on this hole?"

George hesitated.

"You haven't asked me if this hole is a three, a four, or a five. This will matter, will it not?"

George nodded.

"Let's assume it's a five and he won't be on in two. His likely score?"

George thought for a moment. "We can assume he chips it out of the woods to the fairway, then hits two fine shots, and is on in four. If he makes a one-putt, his score will be a five. Six if he two putts."

"What score beats five?"

"Four."

"What score beats seven?"

"Six."

"What score beats nine?"

"Good Lord!" George laughed. "An eight!"

"So you can see that getting into the hole in regulation is not as important as ensuring that you're patient George, patient, strategic, and that whatever your opponent scores..."

"I am one shot fewer." George smiled.

"Aye, one shot fewer." They raised their glasses in a toast.

Some late-night stragglers had finally made their way back to the clubhouse, and the room was getting full with chatter and clinking glasses. George rose and called his new friends to attention with his glass held high. "Gentlemen, it is a beautiful summer evening, won't you join me in a song?"

"Aye!" they called, raising their glasses.

George took a sip of his beer, cleared his throat, and began to sing "My Wild Irish Rose." After only a few lines, everyone joined in, full throated, and their voices could be heard roaring across the golf course and cricket field. It would be the first of many songs led by George Lyon, not just at Rosedale but also at innumerable golf courses around the world.

That weekend, on the morning of the competition between Rosedale and Toronto Golf Club, McLaughlin posted the list of challengers that would be paired together. George was anxious to see whom he would meet in his first match. He ran his finger down the page to the name, J.D. Edgar. McLaughlin looked over his shoulder and said, "Ah, Edgar is a serious fellow who has golfed for several years."

"Is he not one of the fellows who was charged with playing golf on Sunday?"

"Yes, yes, that's him. And he hasn't paid for a drink since his conviction was overturned." McLaughlin chuckled to himself.

"Well, I look forward to playing with him and hearing the story of his trial."

But it seemed that Mr. Edgar didn't necessarily share George's feelings. Later that morning, as players mingled and introduced themselves at the first tee, George overheard a group of Toronto club members grumbling about their pairings. One serious, well-dressed fellow in particular complained that he had hardly expected to be matched with a neophyte. It was J.D. Edgar.

"I came expecting a challenge. Does McLaughlin fancy this match-up as an insult to me because I bested him last month?" Edgar proclaimed to his colleagues.

George stepped forward and introduced himself. "I'll be looking forward to a pleasant afternoon with you, Mr. Edgar, as I'm still a student of this game."

A member of the Rosedale club overheard George's modest claim and called out to the group, "We shall always be students of the game, Mr. Lyon. She can be a humbling mistress!"

George laughed, but Mr. Edgar, unamused, pretended not to hear. "Yes, well, let's get out there, shall we?" he said. Without any further words, Lyon and Edgar teed off for what would be George's first round of match play.

Two hours later, they were back where they started to report their scores.

"I have never seen greens in such rough shape," Edgar muttered.

"Aye, they were a tad shaggy," George agreed.

"And the rough ... My goodness, it was terrible."

"True, the rough was ... well, very rough." George nodded.

McLaughlin stood by with a large pencil and a chart in hand, waiting to take their scores. "Gentlemen, enough grousing. Do you have a result that I can post?"

Mr. Edgar hesitated and then said under his breath, "Six and five … for Mr. Lyon."

McLaughlin glanced at George with a smile and carefully recorded the numbers. "Humdinger. Well done, George."

"It was an excellent match. Thank you, Mr. Edgar," said George, extending his hand for a firm, now respectful, handshake from Edgar. He had won his first golf match and fallen a little deeper in love with the game.

3

Laying Foundations

IT WAS OCTOBER 1902 and George's favorite time of year. He had a lot for which to be thankful. His family life was happy, and business was good. The Boer War had been over for months now, and the 8,300 Canadians who had gone to fight were coming home, many back to Toronto, minus of course the 135 killed by fighting or disease. The violent three-day strike at the Toronto Street Railway had ended, thanks to mediation by the board of trade, not to mention the calling up of some 1,400 troops in case the workers destroyed any more streetcars. "What a waste!" George had fumed back in June. George's company, Sun Fire Insurance, had a busy summer season; Toronto's business community was growing rapidly. With Niagara's hydroelectric power finally tapped, 10,000 horsepower of electricity was now being diverted to Toronto over special pole-mounted wires. Business owners needed insurance, and George was only too happy to oblige. There was also a boom in Toronto real estate sales, and the newspapers estimated that as many as 2,000 families were looking for places to rent, but no one was building for the tenant market. Rents had soared and it was now difficult to find a place for less than twenty-five dollars a month. On top of Toronto's prosperity, pioneers were pouring into Northern Ontario. There were waiting lists for potential farmers to take government-sponsored train trips to look at farmland in the North. Times were good and young men no longer felt they had to travel to the United States to look for work.

As George made his way north along a crowded Spadina Avenue in the early evening, he wondered why his fellow Toronto Golf Club member and close friend Albert Austin had left several messages that he had something important to discuss. He had suggested that George meet him at Albert's home. *Interesting. Why not the club?*

George had decided to walk to Albert's home at the top of Spadina to give his forty-four-year-old legs a good stretch and to have some time away from the bustle of the office to reflect on his golf game. Typical of George, he started with the positives. In the six years since he had first held a golf club, George had transformed himself, through sheer self-discipline and practice, from a golfing neophyte to a force to be reckoned with on the course. Just one year after taking up the game, he had shocked the Canadian golf world by defeating Stuart Gillespie—the defending 1896 Canadian Amateur champion no less—in the first round of the Amateur Championship at Royal Montreal Golf Club. And the match had not even been close, with George dispatching the reigning champion seven and five. Golfers had taken notice of this new man and his unusual style. Although George had been knocked out in the third round of the 1897 championship, the competition had only whetted his appetite for the 1898 championship that was held at the Toronto Golf Club. Two weeks of daily practice had paid off as he trounced his competitor, James Pattison, in the final match, twelve and eleven. Within just three years of taking up the sport, George Lyon had become the 1898 Canadian Amateur champion. It was an unprecedented rise to the height of the sport.

After that victory, Lyon was a sought-after golfer and looking for ever more challenging matches, so the next year he had taken up an invitation from his friend and mentor Andy Smith—or Curley to his many friends—to join the Toronto Golf Club. He enjoyed the new club and their competition so much that he promptly won the club championship in his first year.

Not satisfied with one Canadian Amateur Championship, George had traveled to Ottawa in 1899. It was a tough field that year and he nearly won it again, losing a close match to bank manager and Rosedale club mate Vere C. Brown. George's reaction? He had vowed to practice even more.

Undeterred by that loss, Lyon roared back in 1900, winning his second Canadian Amateur Championship, this time defeating Gordon MacDougall of the Royal Montreal Golf Club. That match had looked like it was out of reach for George when he found himself standing four down with nine holes to play. Never before had he fallen so far behind in a match. But with a huge crowd following them, George reached deep inside himself and claimed the next four holes to square the match. It stayed square through the next five holes. After thirty-six holes of golf, the two men were tied, and it would need to be settled with sudden death. The thirty-seventh hole was halved, and on the thirty-eighth, Lyon drained a long putt and then stood at the edge of the green holding his breath as MacDougall set up to putt. He needed to make it to halve the hole. The crowd hushed and he rolled his putt only to see it stop a quarter of an inch from dropping. George had won the Amateur Championship again—not to mention the civic bragging rights that seemed to alternate between the golf adversaries from Toronto and Montreal. After all, the Montreal Shamrocks had defeated the Halifax Crescents two games to none back in March to win the Stanley Cup. Toronto needed something to brag about.

In these early years, George had also been honing his skills playing in international competitions for three consecutive years against the U.S. Granted, the Canadians had been drubbed in the first year, 1898, losing by twenty holes, and they had been absolutely slaughtered the next year, losing by a humiliating ninety-three holes, but by 1900, the Canadian team seemed to have found their game, going down by only five holes. For George Lyon, the international experience would be invaluable, and he loved the opportunity to meet golfers from the U.S. These Americans were a different breed.

George stopped on his walk to buy a fresh fall apple from a fruit market and thought back to what had perhaps been one of his greatest lessons. It had come in 1900, when he had had the opportunity to play against the great Harry Vardon, who was on a promotional tour for the newly designed golf ball, the Vardon Flyer. Vardon was sponsored by Spalding Sporting Goods and had traveled North America promoting the new golf ball in exhibition matches at dozens of courses. Although it had been a home game for George and his partner, Vere Brown, Vardon, playing against the better of their two balls, still clipped the wings of their Rosedale team. They had gone down five and four in front of an estimated three to four hundred spectators. True to form, that day Vardon set a course record for Rosedale with a seventy-two.

As he climbed the last leg of Spadina Avenue, George reflected on these positives. He had achieved so much in such a short time, and he had taken all of these experiences to heart: playing against the Americans had been an eye-opener, having the opportunity to analyze Vardon's approach shots, short game, and putting had been a veritable clinic that George wouldn't soon forget, and winning the Canadian Amateur title twice had been extraordinary. There were many positives.

But. There was always a *but* with George Lyon and golf.

He picked up his pace as he thought about the 1901 Amateur Championship match. It had been a hard loss for George, watching as Archie Kerr—a Toronto lawyer and member of the Toronto Golf Club—took the Amateur Championship. George's confidence had been at an all-time high as he went into the championship that year. He had won not only the Toronto Golf Club championship but Rosedale's as well. He had felt unbeatable. But as every golfer knows once on the course, every day is a new day, a new game, and Kerr, another all-around athlete, an excellent rugby player, and a man who excelled at tennis and hockey had been waiting for him. Kerr had been to the Amateur finals before, winning in 1897, five and four over T.R. Henderson of the Royal Montreal. Kerr wasted little time and knocked George out in the semifinal round. Granted, George had been suffering from a terrible fever during that match, but he had offered no excuses. He would simply work harder.

He had vowed that the 1902 Amateur Championship would be different and spent the summer focusing on his golf. He was determined to address any shortcomings in his game to get his precious Amateur trophy back. He was striking the ball well and had even won a long drive contest at the competition in Niagara-on-the-Lake. Driving the ball was never an issue. Recently, he was trying a new putting technique recommended by the famous amateur American golfer Walter Travis and using a putter given to him by Tom Morris. Travis was a bit of a hero to George. In fact, both men had started their golf career in much the same way. George had even heard a story from Albert Austin that Travis, like George at one time, was known to have a mild contempt for the game before his friends convinced him to give it a try. Travis had been a tennis player, a hunter, and a fisherman. And above all, he loved the latest craze: bicycling. But golf? Travis was not interested. That is, until a friend persuaded him to give it a try one afternoon.

Per Travis's instructions, George had practiced putting into much smaller holes so that in a match, the real ones seemed as big as paint cans. It had worked, and George's putting became a stronger part of his game.

Just last month, in September, Lyon had felt ready for all comers as the Amateur Championship approached—to be held at Royal Montreal again. But, but, but. There had been just one problem—unfortunately his thirty-three-year-old brother-in-law, Fritz Martin, had designs on the Amateur Championship too. A lawyer from Hamilton who had only taken up golf two years after George, Fritz was another natural athlete who fell for golf. Whether it was rugby, rowing, or even cricket, he was a competitor. And his golf game had come together very nicely indeed. He drove the ball a long way with a pretty swing, and he was an excellent putter. Some said he was the greatest left-handed golfer in North America.

And now, as George walked up Spadina Avenue to call on his friend, he replayed that Amateur Championship in his mind. *How, after all that work, all that preparation, did I let my brother-in-law take it all away from me? Fritz, with one of his typical electric games, outplayed me. How?* Although he had tried not to let on, their train ride home together from Montreal had been torture, and now Fritz would make family dinners intolerable for another year. George would need to find something to occupy his mind until he could start practicing for next year. *Perhaps the curling season will bring a pleasant distraction.*

It was a little unusual for George's Rosedale friend Albert Austin to invite him to his home, especially in the later part of the evening. George climbed the steps to Austin's estate on Spadina Road. Its white bricks seemed to glow in the soft light of dusk. Lamps blazed in several windows of the magnificent home, and George could see an electric light on in the billiard room. Before he could ring the bell at the stately front door, he heard Albert's voice call from around the side of the home. "George, I am back here. Come and join me before we lose the light."

George walked around the side of the mansion to the huge landscaped gardens, where Albert was practicing his putting at the edge of his private golf course. Albert's father, James, had been the founder of the Dominion Bank and Consumer's Gas and was, to put it mildly, very successful in business. Albert had joined him on the board of directors for both companies and, like his father before him, was enjoying a very prosperous life in Toronto. When Albert's father acquired the large estate in 1866, he had a grand Victorian-style home built, with twinned bay windows, detailed Italianate features, and an elaborate glass-roofed porte cochere at the front entrance. The buff brick mansion called Spadina House sat like a beautiful white cake at the top of the hill near Spadina and Davenport ridge. When Albert had inherited the home after his father passed away five years previous, in 1897, one of his first orders of business had been to construct his own golf course on the northern portion of the estate.

"Albert, can you even see anything out here?" George asked.

"Oh, I just wanted to practice my putting a little more. We won't have much golf now that the leaves are flying, will we George?"

"No, I suppose not," George said glumly.

"I hope you are not still moping about the Amateur." Albert was always to the point.

"Well, as a matter of fact I *have* been thinking about what I might have done wrong... or differently and of course Fritz will not let me forget it either."

"Oh, fiddle-faddle. We have much more important things to discuss," said Albert, waving away George's look of concern.

"Business?"

As he hit one last putt, Albert said, "Something more important than business. It's about Rosedale. It's simply too crowded. The membership has swelled to 270. It cannot carry on like this. Do you not agree? Come inside where we can discuss it over a glass of something that will take this fall chill away."

As they made their way through the house, George could not help but marvel at the lavish design and furnishings. They passed through the billiard room and into the jaw-droppingly beautiful palm room that overlooked the gardens and terraces. *This is how the wealthy live.* George thought of his own modest middle-class home in Rosedale.

Albert listed the faults with Rosedale Golf Club, as they settled into chairs with glasses of sherry, and George suddenly realized where the conversation was going. "Albert, you're not thinking of starting another golf club..."

Albert Austin was famous in Toronto circles for his talk of establishing new golf clubs. He had gently pestered his friends to join him in founding his own golf course, the Spadina Golf Club. But even that had not been enough. Developers were buying up local farmland, and Austin knew the Spadina course would soon be squeezed out.

"If my hunch is correct, George, golf is here to stay in Canada. And it's destined to be popular, bigger than even cricket. Golfers will want a serious club, with a serious course, and a very serious country club atmosphere..."

"Rosedale is serious—"

Albert cut him off. "Not crammed into that space, with golfers crisscrossing fairways and avoiding cow piles. I'm surprised no one has been killed. We need a serious course and a serious clubhouse. You've heard of what the Americans have done in places like Shinnecock and Newport..."

"Albert, you—*I* am not one of the Astors, the Belmonts, or the Havemeyers of the world. Those kinds of people can afford that posh country club lifestyle and those lavish clubhouses designed by famous architects."

"But we can do it, too! I know we can."

"We?"

Albert sat across from George and looked him square in the eye. "I want you to be a founding member of a new club with me. Leave Rosedale and come to the new club. I have identified a beautiful piece of property west of the city near Lambton Mills. There are 150 rolling acres and the Humber River cuts right through the property, along with a small creek. With its four tiers dropping down to the river, it would be perfect for us to develop a truly challenging course."

"Us?"

"And it gets better, George. There is even a CPR line at the southern end of the property. We could have a direct link by train to Union Station. Imagine."

"We?"

Albert ignored George's hesitation. "I have been putting together a provisional committee with some members from High Park, Rosedale, and even Highlands. I've done the business plan, and if we offer one-hundred-dollar shares, I am confident we can raise enough for what I have in mind." Albert was on the edge of his seat looking intently at George.

"*We?*" George couldn't help but look at his friend with a blank stare. He couldn't afford the same dreams as Albert.

"We need to sell three hundred shares at a hundred dollars apiece."

George let out a low whistle and shifted in his seat at the thought of that unprecedented amount. Golf courses were struggling financially; a few like those in Kingston and Brantford had even folded after a few years. Where would they find golfers with a hundred dollars to spare? But then, Albert always thought big.

"The clubhouse will have lounges, dining rooms, a reception area, good kitchens, and rooms for members to stay the night if they wish. I even imagine a nine-hole course for the ladies, eventually. With all the women taking up golf nowadays, that will be a selling feature."

George knew that there was probably little point in debating this new adventure with Albert; he was an entrepreneur with a track record for success. Twenty years previous, as a twenty-four-year-old, Albert had gone to find his fortune in Winnipeg. Once there he established the Winnipeg Street Railway Company, electrified it, sold his holdings ten years later for a rumored 5,000 percent profit, and then returned to Toronto to join his father's bank on the board of directors. George had total confidence in his friend's business acumen. That was not the problem.

"Albert, I have to be honest. I am not in a position, financially, to be starting such a venture. I appreciate the offer, though."

"George, old boy, I'm not looking for a financial investment." He chuckled, as if his intentions were obvious. "I want *you*. You're the attraction. You do the legwork and sell the shares at a hundred dollars. People have confidence in you. They will want to play where two-time Canadian Amateur champion George Lyon plays."

George smiled a little doubtfully and glanced at the clock on the mantel. It was getting late and Annette would be wondering what he was up to at that hour. "I will give it serious consideration, Albert, and thank you for thinking of me. I should be on my way. I promise to give it some thought." He rose to leave.

"I have already spoken with a course architect," said Albert coyly. He knew of George's growing interest in course design.

George's interest was piqued, and he sat back down slowly. "An architect already? Who? Albert, you need to understand that any design will need to be able to accommodate the new rubber core balls. It will need to be a long course, longer than we are accustomed to... and the bunkers... all bunkers must be strategic..." This was serious business after all.

"Willie Dunn will be our architect. I was hoping you would be able to help him with the design," said Albert with a satisfied grin. He knew George would be more than a little interested. Dunn had become, along with Tom Bendelow, one of North America's prolific golf course architects. He had come from Britain in 1893 to design and lay out most of the new courses in the U.S. But then in 1900, the year of George's second Canadian Amateur win, Dunn was offered the job of redesigning the Royal Montreal course. It was during that project that Albert Austin had sowed the seeds with Dunn of coming to Toronto to develop a truly first-class golf course.

Willie Dunn's name was all George needed to hear. He would join Albert Austin as a founding member of Lambton Golf and Country Club. Within a year, golfers were lining up to pay, not $100 but $250, for a share in the new course. It would be the base from which George would launch his Olympic challenge, and it would come to be his home course for the balance of his golfing life.

4

The Prevalent Craze

FEBRUARY 12, 1903

GEORGE AND ALBERT Austin worked hard through the fall and winter of 1902. Between working on Lambton's course layout, selling shares, and collaborating with an architect on a worthy clubhouse, launching this new golf club was turning into a full-time job. As George sat in the card room of the Victoria Club on Adelaide Street on February 12, 1903, he could hear the shouts of competition from the two sheds that housed the Toronto Curling Club's eight curling rinks. The club was the envy of curlers across the province and as far away as Montreal and even Scotland. After his visit to Toronto, the well-known Scottish curler James Brown, vice-president of the Royal Caledonian Curling Club, had lamented that although outdoor curling as they enjoyed it in Scotland had more charm, he was envious of the "sumptuously housed" Toronto Curling Club. Scotland envious of Toronto? After all their lording of their golf courses over

North American courses, George found the fact they envied Canada's curling quite to his liking.

George certainly understood what James Brown meant about their club though. In winter, they curled comfortably indoors; in summer, they had as many as ten lawn-bowling rinks in action, and members also enjoyed their own card room and a billiard room. In fact, George and Albert had turned it into a home away from home during the harsh winter days as they worked on Lambton matters.

As if he didn't have enough to do between selling insurance and selling shares in Lambton, George had serious curling matters on his mind this particular February afternoon. The railways were charging rates that actually discouraged curlers from traveling to and from matches outside the city. The Grand Trunk Pacific Railway was now coast to coast and profitable, but their rates made it simply too expensive for curlers to pay full fare when traveling to and from a friendly match. One suggestion was that the railways charge one-and-a-third fares return for anyone "going a-curling." George had suggested another option—two cents a mile if there were more than eight curlers traveling to a match. As a result of his work, a committee had been dispatched to try to persuade the railways to give a special rate that would encourage curling competition and railway business at the same time.

As if that wasn't enough to keep him busy, another very serious matter now concerned him as well. There were complaints circulating among curlers about—of all things—their "competitive spirit." In fact, an executive committee of the Ontario Curling Association had recently issued a report strongly expressing the view "that the practice of playing for trophies and prizes had now been carried to dangerous lengths and was transforming the game of curling from a friendly rivalry, which produced recreation and amusement and promoted friendships and good fellowship, into fierce struggles for victory."

George had been aghast when he had read the committee's conclusions: "The prevalent craze for winning trophies was a degrading prostitution of the grand old game and not to be distinguished from professionalism."

"Fierce struggles for victory? Degrading prostitution? Comparing the competitive spirit to professionalism? Good Lord," he thought, "those were harsh words. It was only curling, after all. A bit of competitiveness is exactly what people were looking for. That was a far cry from being insulted with accusations of professionalism. Surely, playing for trophies and prizes had not degenerated to that extent."

George of all people was well aware of the treatment of poor Jack Carmichael two years previous this very month. That pot had boiled over in the Toronto community, and the sports associations and athletic clubs were still abuzz with gossip and strong opinions. Carmichael, a young man in his twenties, had made the unforgivable mistake of accepting a fee for playing in a hockey game. George knew him and had played against him many times. He was a good fellow but showed poor judgment in accepting money from a team for playing one night. His punishment? Not only did his former hockey friends refuse to play with him, but he was now shunned from all organized athletic activity and social events associated with those sports in Toronto. Persona non grata at even George's own curling club. He was a sports pariah, and to add insult to injury, he lost a very good job offer because of his slip in judgment. George could not forget seeing the poor lad's picture splashed all over the front page of the *Toronto Daily Star.* For many in the sports community, amateurism was next to godliness, and so said many a Catholic priest. But professionalism in sport? Disgusting.

As George sat struggling with these concerns, Albert slipped a strategically folded copy of the previous day's *New York Times* onto the table beside George's cup of tea. Albert said nothing and simply walked away into the billiard room. It was a little routine the two of them played with each other if they thought there was something of interest in the news. It could be a story about the outcome of a sporting match in another city, an account of some military adventure in Russia or Africa, or merely interesting local gossip. Just last summer Albert had found an article in a Halifax newspaper about some women golfers who had been criticized in a sermon by their local Anglican minister. Their crime? Swearing on the golf course. According to the story, when the women demanded the minister retract his remarks, he refused and noted with even greater concern that he heard they also smoked on the course! As he reached for the *New York Times,* George smiled recalling his hearty laugh with Albert over that one.

George glanced at the headline, expecting, almost praying, that Albert had found some much-needed humor to distract him from the harsh words of the curling report. Instead it read: "ST. LOUIS GETS OLYMPIC GAMES." A smile crossed his face and he waited until Albert was out of sight before picking up the newspaper to read the whole story. Beneath the head-line it read, "International Committee Sanctions the Change for the World's Fair in 1904."

"Interesting," thought George. "Very interesting." He read on: "St. Louis, Missouri, February 11, 'Everything settled. You have Olympic Games,' is the wording of the cablegram received today from Michel La Grave, Wold's Fair Commis-sioner at Paris, France, by the Louisiana Purchase Exposition officials. The meaning of the cablegram is that the Olympic Games, which were originally intended to be held in Chicago in 1904, will be held in St. Louis during the World's Fair, the international committee having so decided."

George grimaced at the typographical error that sat like an ugly inkblot in the middle of the page. "Wold's Fair?" Here was a mistake on the front page of the *New York Times,* for heaven sakes. But still, typographical error aside, this was very interesting news. George had never been to the World's Fair and had certainly never played in the Olympics. Although he had won the Canadian Amateur Championships in 1898 and 1900, by the time he learned of the poorly publicized Paris competitions, he had missed his chance to compete.

"Well, well, well," he thought. "Summer Olympics next year in St. Louis, Missouri?" He smiled more broadly at the prospect of Olympic golf in North America and couldn't help but notice Albert watching him from across the room. Albert was smiling, too. *What did he have up his sleeve now?* The bitterly cold February day suddenly seemed a little warmer.

5

Westward Ho

COL. GEORGE MCGREW had been waiting, watching his mail for a very important package. It was August 1903, and although the Olympic Games were still a year away, there was much to be done. As the co-founder of Glen Echo Golf Club, along with his son-in-law, Albert Lambert, he had a huge stake in ensuring the golf competitions of the 1904 Summer Olympics were a success. Albert had become somewhat of a sports celebrity upon his return from winning the golf event at the 1900 Summer Olympics in Paris, and the two of them had immediately set about founding their own golf course the following year. In May 1901, they had proudly opened not only St. Louis's first course but also the first eighteen-hole golf course west of the Mississippi. With that mission accomplished, the two of them had immediately begun work on hosting an international golf championship at Glen Echo.

McGrew had followed—from a safe distance—the very heated battle that had been waged between Chicago and St. Louis to host the 1904 Summer Olympics. Missouri Governor David Francis had been desperate to host the World's Fair ever since he lost out to Chicago in 1893. He had seen what a splash Chicago made on the world scene with its famous White City, and he had been determined to see his state do likewise. His opportunity arrived when St. Louis won the bid to host the 1903 Louisiana Purchase Centennial Exhibition. But not satisfied with merely hosting the World's Fair, he had then set to work finding a way to boldly top Chicago's hugely successful effort. His plan? He would add the Summer Olympic Games. St. Louis would host the World's Fair and the Summer Olympics—at the same time.

There had been just two details that Governor Francis needed to resolve, and they were not small details by any stretch of the imagination. First, the St. Louis World's Fair had been scheduled for 1903, and the Summer Olympics were already scheduled for 1904. How could that time be bridged? Second, and even more challenging, Pierre de Coubertin, the very powerful founder of the International Olympic Committee, had favored Chicago for the Summer Olympics—if they were to be held in North America at all.

De Coubertin had single-handedly revived the Olympic Games, working tirelessly for them to be staged successfully—and symbolically—in Greece, in 1896, before an estimated forty thousand spectators, and then again in Paris, in 1900. But Paris had been quite a different experience, and de Coubertin had no intention of repeating what he considered that complete fiasco. He had been allowed to stage the Games there only if he agreed to pair them with the already planned Exposition Universelle. By the time the Games began, not only was their identity lost in the larger fair but they were also spread over two months and not a single program bore the word "Olympic." No, if the Summer Olympics were to be held in North America he would work to keep control of them as best he could.

De Coubertin still had uncomfortable visions of Buffalo Bill's Wild West and Congress of Roughriders of the World that had settled into fifteen acres beside Chicago's World's Fair. He had heard the stories. The show had been able to fill an eighteen-thousand-seat arena day after day, detracting from even the fair. He had seen the carnival-like sideshow for himself in London at Windsor Castle when Buffalo Bill came to entertain the Royal Family. It was disgusting to watch the Prince of Wales being hauled about in a stage-coach while Indians pretended to attack it. In de Coubertin's world, the Olympics were supposed to be the main event, not carnivals.

But Governor Francis was a determined man, and with a special petition to the U.S. Congress and a hard-nosed lobby-ing effort, he received permission to postpone the St. Louis World's Fair a year. With that delay secured, he dispatched his secret weapon—a French count—to Paris. Count Henri de Penaloza was a personal friend of de Coubertin, and he just happened to be married to one Marie Fusz, the daughter of Louis Fusz, a prominent St. Louis businessman. Of course, Governor Francis and Fusz were both members of the pow-erful Merchants Exchange Club, and it was there they had met to hatch a plan. The Count, eager to please his father-in-law (and to see France again), had been dispatched in April 1901 to Paris with an unofficial request from Governor Fran-cis. Francis's ploy had worked, and by February 1903, he had pulled off his coup—the Olympic Games intended for Chicago would be held in St. Louis during the World's Fair. De Coubertin's wish to control these Games would be another matter, though.

With the Olympic Games now committed to St. Louis, Colonel McGrew and Albert Lambert rose to the occasion and offered to convert their planned international event into the Olympic golf competitions at Glen Echo Golf Club. Best of all, Lambert would have a chance to compete in the Olympics again and this time they would have medals and trophies.

It was all coming together beautifully. But. With McGrew there was always a but. McGrew sought perfection. He had invited the esteemed Walter Travis to survey the Glen Echo course. Here was a man who, in his forties, had won the U.S. Amateur Championship three times in the last four years, most recently this very year. He understood the nuances of what made a great golf course and was now offering his services as a golf course architect.

He and Travis, each with golf club in hand and a few of the latest Haskell golf balls, had walked the Glen Echo course for hours earlier in the spring. McGrew, extremely proud of the course, had been anxious to hear Travis's thoughts about the layout. But as they toured it, Travis, with a reputation for being what some would call prickly, had said very little. Perhaps that was a good sign, McGrew thought.

After their walk, and standing on the large wrap-around porch of Glen Echo's beautiful clubhouse, McGrew turned to Travis and asked, "Walter, you have golfed every major course in the U.S. I expect that my course will be a challenge worthy of the Olympics. Am I not correct?" It had come out more a statement of fact than a question.

Travis had remained silent, took a long pull on what remained of his ever present cigar, took off his Roughriderstyle hat, and looked back down the eighteenth fairway, which shared a common fairway with holes fifteen, sixteen, and seventeen. Exhaling a breath of smoke, he had simply said, "No."

Expecting a much warmer endorsement, McGrew was taken aback. "Well, why not? What could possibly be missing?"

Travis, ever the businessman, replied coldly, "My fee for such work is $125 plus expenses for a one-day inspection. If you would like me to redesign either of Glen Echo's nine holes, my fee is $2,000, but," Travis had turned and held out his arms as wide as they would stretch, "I would be prepared to redesign *the entire course* for $3,000. And for $4,000, I would be prepared to redesign the course to play eighteen holes in either direction." He had then pulled another long black cigar from his vest pocket, lit it, and waited for McGrew's response.

McGrew was speechless. It was preposterous to think that Glen Echo would be entirely redesigned. But at the same time it was also hard to ignore Travis's frank advice. McGrew gathered himself, "I think I could authorize on behalf of the Glen Echo Club Executive fees for your inspection and recommendations for some changes, but certainly not a . . . *redesign.*" McGrew had barely been able to say the word.

"Excellent. I will begin immediately." And with that, Travis set off alone to walk the course again with a golf club and a few balls in hand, this time in reverse.

For hours, McGrew had watched from the clubhouse's second-story balcony as Travis crisscrossed the course, hitting balls, making notes in a small black book, stopping occasionally to pour a drink from a thermos he seemed to carry everywhere. At one point, McGrew saw Travis sit for nearly an hour on a hill, overlooking hole No. 8, Alps. *What is he thinking?*

McGrew had walked him to the streetcar station later that evening. And Travis promised to send McGrew his report and recommendations as soon as possible. That was four months ago, and still nothing had arrived.

Until now.

A thick white package arrived at the clubhouse by special delivery that morning. Travis's New York return address gave away its contents. McGrew closed the door to his office and told his secretary he was not to be disturbed. He sliced open the envelope to find Travis's neatly handwritten report entitled, *Glen Echo: Olympic Event Changes.* He pulled the covering letter out of the envelope and read.

Dear Colonel McGrew,

I apologize for the delay in getting this report to you. It has been a very busy year to date. In the enclosed report you will find my recommendations for improvements to Glen Echo's course. It is a fine course, but I believe the changes recommended herein will make it a suitable challenge for the next generation of golfers. We both know well the driving prowess of these young men who have taken up golf. For example, Jerry Travers is only seventeen, and Chandler Egan not yet twenty. They drive these new golf balls long and straight. They have been playing since childhood, taught by experienced professionals, and have an abandon with the game that only a young man could know or enjoy. Changes must be made if those prodigy golfers and international players from over the pond are to be challenged.

And then, with his usual bluntness, Travis added a concluding paragraph.

There is no need to correspond over this report, or to discuss which of the changes you approve or disapprove. Either make all of the changes as recommended or none at all. Whichever you prefer. It really makes no difference to me. My account for the work is enclosed. Thank you, and I look forward to participating in the Olympic competition next year.

Yours truly,
Walter Travis

McGrew looked up from the report and scowled at the ultimatum. He and the Glen Echo executive members would be the ones deciding which changes would be implemented, if any. He read through Travis's list of recommended changes as set out in a neat schedule. They were accompanied by several carefully drawn sketches of each hole's proposed new layout. Clearly, Travis had put considerable thought into these recommendations.

No. 1 Lilac Way: This hole currently measures 245 yards. It must be lengthened to at least 276 yards to put it well out of reach for the competition, or else you shall see golfers driving the green on their first shot. Unacceptable.

No. 4 Long Drive: This hole measures some 550 yards. I took a club and played a ball to the large bunker that crosses the fairway at about 500 yards. I reached it in two. That is a good test, but I fear none of the competitors will reach the green in three, never mind two. I recommend that you pull the tee forward on this hole, turning it into a 538-yard hole offering a reward for those who choose to challenge it.

No. 7 Boomerang: This hole is currently set up at 330 yards. The green is much too close and must be moved up the hill a further 150 yards to make it a meaningful challenge.

No. 8 Alps: I assume you have named this hole in fitting tribute to No. 17 Alps at Prestwick, a spectacular blind hole. It was very tough when the British Open was played there in 1899. Glen Echo's hole plays at 345 yards. It is a par four, but once a golfer drives over the crest of the hill, they are left almost every time with a hanging lie. Totally unacceptable. The tee must be moved back 133 yards and made into a par five at 478 yards.

McGrew was feeling light headed. No wonder Travis had sat so long looking at this hole. *Convert Alps to a par five? That proposal will never be approved by the members.* He took a drink of water, wiped his glasses, and read on.

No. 11 Hillside: This hole currently plays at 265. It is too short for a par four and must be lengthened to 271 to present a challenge to these young golfers. I remind you, too, that our foreign friends will expect a challenge. As is, the hole will not present one. Change it.

No. 12 Westward Ho: Named, I assume, for Devon. We have the same issue here as No. 11. This hole is simply too short to be any sort of challenge for today's players. It must be lengthened from its current 355 to at least 496 yards. With this alteration, the hole could be a match changer.

No. 13 Echo: The lake extends across the bottom of the hill in front of the tee area. At 280 yards, it makes a very challenging par three. However, this hole is supposed to be a par four. The tee area must be pulled back and the hole length-ened to 317 yards.

No. 15 The Lake: This hole should remain as is, with two exceptions. It is a magnificent test, and I extend my com-pliments to its designer, Mr. Foulis. Well done. However, 280 yards for a par four will not do. Extend it to 360 yards. Also, something must be done with this green. Its undula-tions are far too severe, particularly if the weather is hot and dry. I stood on this green for nearly half an hour, drop-ping balls from all angles just to watch them simply roll off. A new green that can be held with a good approach shot is a must. I see this hole as a potential match changer as well.

No. 17 Old Hickory: I am not sure what the original design-ers were thinking here. Add 35 yards to make this hole play properly as a 400-yard par four. I need not explain why, as I am sure it is obvious from the enclosed sketch.

No. 18 Sweet Home: A finishing hole that brings the player back to the clubhouse must be a signature hole that leaves lasting memories of his round. At the current 355 yards, I fear all he will remember is that this hole—and therefore perhaps the whole course in retrospect—was not much of a challenge. Add 50 yards. Leave the dogleg untouched, finishing uphill. Now you will have a memora-ble final hole. I imagine a huge crowd around this green to watch a winner declared.

Exasperated, McGrew shuffled through the sketches. He didn't know what to do with Travis's advice. Ten holes would need to be redesigned; it would mean profound changes for the course. And the expense.

Glen Echo had only been open for two years. Designed by Robert Foulis and his brother James, the winner of the 1896 U.S. Open. They were both respected course designers. Robert Foulis was a professional golfer, born in St. Andrew's, Scotland. His father was a foreman in the golf shop of legendary Old Tom Morris himself. Foulis learned golf at the knee of a master and was renowned for his powerful drives—sometimes in excess of three hundred yards. In 1895, at the age of twenty-five, he traveled to the U.S. and took a job at the first U.S. club to have an eighteen-hole course, the Chicago Golf Club. Eventually, his brothers joined him to run a golf shop of their own. Foulis was an established figure in golf and golf course design. *Travis proposes to upend his work?*

As he flipped through the sketches again, McGrew recalled how he and the Foulis brothers had labored that wet spring over the 138 acres of land set aside for the new course. The property was a gem, with a beautiful stream cutting across it from north to south and a railroad stop within walking distance of the second tee. The elegant Southern-style, two-story mansion already on the property was easily converted to a first-rate clubhouse that rivaled the best in the U.S. The Foulis brothers sought and got authorization to import large trees—not just any trees but trees from France—to line the main fairways. The course was first class, and McGrew had expected to hear as much from Mr. Travis. This report was an unexpected turn of events.

He called for his son-in-law, Albert. As the reigning Olympic golf champion, not to mention President of Lambert Pharmacal Co.—manufacturer of Listerine—McGrew respected his opinion.

"Albert, take hold of Mr. Travis's sketches and walk with me."

McGrew, with a club and balls in hand once again, and Albert by his side with the sketches, walked all of Glen Echo for hours that afternoon. As they stood at each hole, they imagined the effect of implementing Travis's recommendations and took turns striking balls from the proposed positions of new tee boxes. Three hours later, they returned to the clubhouse and called for a meeting of the Executive.

The following evening, in a smoke-filled room, amid the shouts and groans from many of Glen Echo's disgruntled members, McGrew and Albert presented the proposed redesign of their precious golf course.

When they were finished, Albert called for quiet, and order was returned to the meeting. "It is Colonel McGrew's and my joint recommendation that we move for immediate implementation of *all* of Mr. Travis's recommendations."

There was stunned silence, and then McGrew moved a motion for approval. There was no need to count the hands. The motion was unanimous. Work would need to begin immediately.

Glen Echo would be ready for its Olympic challenge.

6

The Thistle

"**M**ERDE. C'EST DE LA MERDE!**" The jewelry designer had clearly had enough. After an hour of meeting with Colonel McGrew, it was clear that the colonel would not be persuaded to change his mind. And it was probably best that he did not understand French.

Colonel McGrew had left course development in the capable hands of Walter Travis, while he turned his attention to a more personal artistic interest. He fancied himself a designer and had made several preliminary sketches of what he thought the Olympic golf medals should look like—after all, no one had ever designed an Olympic gold medal for golf before. He had tucked his designs into a worn leather briefcase and made his way across town on foot to the finest jeweler in St. Louis: Mermod, Jaccard & Co.

The president of the company, Monsieur Lemieux, and one of his most skilled jewelry designers sat at a long ornate carved mahogany table ready to unveil their own designs for what promised to be a most prestigious and lucrative contract—America's first Olympics. However, things were off to a very poor start.

"Monsieur McGrew—forgive me—*Colonel* McGrew, please just give my designer the opportunity to at least present some designs for your review. He has been trained in France and has the highest qualifications. He has been considering this very important matter for weeks: a variety of sketches and preliminary designs have been made specifically for your personal consideration." Lemieux was struggling not to sound as if he was pleading, but he was.

Even the mention of France irritated the colonel. He was a Yankee through and through. *What could be better than American know-how?* "Not necessary. Waste of time and money. I have prepared these designs as a good starting point. Your people can work with these, add some polish." As he spoke, he set his fat cigar on a marble ashtray and spread out two large sheets of high-quality parchment paper on the table. Each had roughly the same basic design. At the top it simply said "1904." Underneath that date, on a banner, he had printed the words "Universal Exposition, Olympic Games St. Louis," and then beneath those words, on a crest, appeared the words "OLYMPIC CHAMPION." A crudely drawn golf bag with six clubs was set at an angle and hovered above the word "GOLF." McGrew ran his hands over his sketches, pleased with his artistic renderings. The designers looked at each other in horror as McGrew explained his design.

"Here. You see this?" he pointed to what looked like flowers with golf balls on their ends as blossoms. *"That* is thistle, the national flower of Scotland." He paused for effect. *"That* is where golf was invented."

"Vraiment?" the designer said sarcastically. He looked at the company president, exasperated, and stood to leave. "I'm sure you do not need me then," he said in a heavy French accent. "Au revoir, et bonne journée." Lemieux gestured to him to get back in his seat.

Colonel McGrew leaned forward, ran his hands over his designs again, and said softly, "You have a *bun journey,* too." Without looking at Lemieux, he said, "I could take the project to Tiffany. Their people in New York City have been calling me. If your people cannot handle it, we can move the work there, but I need to know soon... I would prefer to keep the work here, in St. Louis, in our fine state of—"

Lemieux leapt from his seat. "No, no, Colonel, that won't be necessary. Your designs are more than appropriate. They have a certain, shall we say, *dignité* in their simplicity."

"Precisely my thought. *Dig-na-tay.*"

"We want to work with you, Colonel. Truly we do."

"Well, Lemieux, I'm from Missouri, sir. You have got to *show me.*"

Lemieux knew this debate was over. "Exactly how many medals will we need to make for you, Colonel McGrew?"

"Well, there will be one gold medal for the champion—no pottery bowls like Paris..." Lemieux glanced at his designer and shrugged as if to say, "Pottery bowls?"

McGrew continued his list. "There will be participation medals for each of the registrants, silver medals, bronze medals, not to mention the trophies that will be needed for the putting contest, the driving contest, trophies for the team competitions, and of course the trophy for the champion." He handed a list to him. "I have a few ideas for the trophies as well. I have arranged for each trophy to have its own local sponsor. I suppose the sponsors may have some ideas for designs as well." The jewelry designer fell back into his chair and stared at the ceiling.

By the end of their meeting, Mermod, Jaccard had an order for enough medals and trophies to keep them busy for several months if not a year.

McGrew plugged his cigar back into the corner of his mouth. "I want everything done and ready by July 1, 1904."

"But, Monsieur Colonel McGrew, I understand the competition is not until September."

"That's correct, but I want everything available months in advance. There can be no margin of error." He turned and looked off into the distance imagining a special day months away. "I want this to be the most impressive collection of medals and trophies ever presented for Olympic golf. Lemieux, you must understand these will set the standard for all golf medals and trophies at future Olympics. The trophy is going to be passed from champion to champion for generations of golfers."

Colonel McGrew held up his design for the gold medal to the light and smiled. "Imagine winning the first gold medal for golf." He was already thinking of the day he would announce the winner and hand that medal to him. Little did he know he had designed what would be the last medal awarded for Olympic golf for 112 years.

═ **7** ═

A Dark Horse:
An Old, Dark Horse

APRIL 1904

EVEN THOUGH HE had read and reread the March 4, 1904, issue of *Golf Illustrated* a dozen times over the last month, George sat at the desk in his library reviewing the article and his notes once again.

His wife, Annette, a voracious reader, sat close to the fire, pretending to read Jack London's latest novel, *The Sea-Wolf.* Her thoughts wandered, however, to her husband, and she knew that even though it was still a frosty April Toronto night, George already had golf on his mind. She noticed him look up from his study to consider the trophies on the mantel. *What is he plotting this time?*

George set the article out in front of him—"The Olympic Golf Championship at St. Louis"—and turned to the portions he had noted previously. Understanding these rules for the competition could make all the difference to George if he was going to travel to St. Louis in September. The competition was just five months away and he knew that he needed to start planning and practicing now. His work schedule needed to be efficient this spring and summer; he needed to schedule matches and challenges to keep himself sharp.

Since 1896, the Canadian Amateur Championship had always been played in September, near the end of the season, when Ontario and Quebec teams also had the opportunity to play their hard-fought interprovincial matches at the same time. This year, though, George had already heard that the Amateur would be moved to the week of Dominion Day of all things. The Royal Canadian Golf Association had decided to go the way of the U.S. Golf Association and include an Open competition for the professionals at the same time. And both would be held at the Royal Montreal. It was a course he was familiar with, and George smiled softly at the memory of his victory there in 1900 over G.W. MacDougall, and the putt that just refused one last revolution. *What a match that had been.*

But switching the championship to July would proba-bly mean more competitors. It would be hot. And Montreal meant travel. He would need to practice even more than he had already imagined. It would be a very busy spring and summer.

And on top of all that, George was finding more than ever that he needed to stay abreast of the latest developments in golf equipment. There were always rumors at Lambton that the most successful players were now using some new iron, or a livelier ball, or the new Pyralin drivers. George would take advantage of any new information—any new technology—he could gather. The game was changing, and he would, too.

He set aside his golf magazines and lined up four different golf balls along the edge of his desk—a Haskell, a Spalding

Wizard, a Spalding Flyer, and a Kempshall Click. He had read the catalog notes and the promised results of each ball. He rolled them in his hands, held them up to the light, compared their covers, and studied them.

The first he examined was a Haskell. He knew the story of its invention: tightly wound rubber strands wrapped in a hardy cover gave it liveliness off the tee. He also knew that a couple of years ago in the 1901 U.S. Amateur, twenty-four out of twenty-seven competitors had played the Haskell. Walter Travis himself had won the championship that year playing a Haskell. That was quite a vote of confidence. But then George had also heard stories that some found the Haskell was too unpredictable. The Brits called it a "Bounding Billy," like a goat, because it was a little too lively when one got near the green, and touch was all important. However, one night in the Lambton grill room he had also heard from a golfer visiting from the States that James Foulis claimed to have accidentally brambled a Haskell and cured these deficiencies. *Hmm, Brambled? Interesting. I will need to look into that.* George set aside the Haskell and picked up the Spalding Wizard.

George had followed the newspaper accounts that said Spalding had sued Haskell, claiming they were infringing on Spalding's method for manufacturing their famous baseballs, baseballs that George knew so well. George laughed at his recollection of the judge's reported way of dealing with that patent challenge. He had put it to rest with the simple pronouncement, "Golf balls aren't baseballs. Case dismissed." So Spalding had changed course, licensed the Haskell special rubber winding process, and then brought out their own version: the Spalding Wizard. It had a gutta-percha and balata cover, and they guaranteed that the cover would not crack or break. This was probably a thinly veiled shot at

Haskell, because it was well known that poor Sandy Herd's Haskell had actually broken during the 1902 British Open. *Good Lord. Imagine that. But is the Wizard the latest and greatest ball? Perhaps it will be my ball by fall.* He set the Wizard aside.

George picked up and looked over another Spalding ball that had become famous through advertising and endorsements. He had seen this ball up close and in action. *Was it three years ago already?* The Spalding "Vardon Flyer" had been played by Harry Vardon in their match that day at Rosedale, and he had played it at more than seventy-two different courses during his North American tour. He had broken records at nearly every course with that ball—not just at Rosedale. George recalled the very precise short game Vardon had displayed with the ball the day he beat George and Vere Brown. It would be hard to ignore the Flyer.

Picking up the Kempshall Click, George remembered hearing that Walter Travis had also played this ball. The catalog said it was "the embodiment of all that was excellent in a golf ball … waterproof and practically indestructible."

"Catalogs," George thought scornfully, "can say anything."

Travis, however, had said he found it was softer and better for chipping, pitching, and putting. Given Travis's putting skills, that was quite an endorsement. But it also seemed to have helped increase his driving distance. The ball apparently gave off a distinctive click sound when struck.

"That might be a distraction," George thought. But still he would give it a try this spring.

Cost was a factor, albeit a minor one; it was performance and feel that he really needed from a ball. Haskells were $6 a dozen. George had heard a rumor that although the Brits complained about the Bounding Billy, many of them paid

$7.50 *a ball* under the counter. The Silvertown balls, which George could find nowhere in Toronto, were $5 a dozen. The regular Spalding balls were reduced to $4 a dozen to make them competitively priced for average golfers. George would not let a few dollars this way or that decide the issue.

He sat back and looked at the array of choices. *Will any of these balls be better than the good old-fashioned gutta-perchas that I've been repairing, remolding, and in some cases, repainting? They have served me well, to date. Why change now?* He had played one in last year's Amateur Championship at the Toronto Golf Club, when he took sweet revenge on Fritz, knocking him out in the first round. With him out of the way, George had cruised to his third championship victory. *So why change my ball?* He answered his own question. *Because the game is changing, George. The game is changing.*

As soon as the snow was gone, he would take each ball out for a trial run. There would be time to experiment over the spring and summer. Then he could make a decision based on evidence rather than catalog promises and fancy endorsements.

For now, he would concentrate on more immediate matters, so he tucked the golf balls away and turned back to the article on his desk.

This important contest, which will be held at the Glen Echo Country Club, of St. Louis, next September, is in no sense of the word a World's Fair championship, or a contest for merely pot hunters. It is the Olympic championship of the world, and the winner will receive the Olympic gold medal, given by the Olympic Association. While there will be minor subordinate events, under different control, to hold the interest of those who fall by the wayside in the championship contest, the star attraction will be the struggle for the Olympic golf championship of the world.

George sat back in his chair and contemplated those words once again: "Olympic championship." *Is it possible? Could I do it?*

A special American committee—divided into subcommittees for the various sports—has been appointed to conduct the Olympiad at St. Louis, and for the first time in history, golf has been added as one of the branches of athletic sport. This notable addition and recognition of golf is due to the untiring energy of Col. George S. McGrew, president of the Glen Echo Country Club, over which course the contest will be held, but whose grounds will be in the charge of the Olympic committee during that period.

We have champions of various countries, sectional champions, and minor champions every year, but golf has never had an Olympic champion. It should mean something to even the best of the British players to be able to hand down to posterity, as an heirloom, the Olympic championship medal, the first and only one of its kind in the world.

George leaned back again in his chair and thought of his three children: Kathleen; Marjorie; and his only son, George Seymour, who was just six years old. *Imagine, a gold medal as an heirloom for my children.*

George hardly needed any more motivation, but these thoughts stirred something deep inside him. He thought of his grandfather Capt. George Lyon, who had arrived from Scotland nearly a hundred years ago to fight in the War of

1812. *Could he have ever imagined the lives of his grandchildren turning out this way?*

The program has been well arranged and consists of a qualifying round of thirty-six holes medal play—the best thirty-two to continue at thirty-six holes match play rounds. Any golfer who wins all his matches at thirty-six holes will be fully entitled to the coveted honor. The qualifying round is intended merely to eliminate those who really have no chance to win at match play, and while it is possible that some sterling good golfer may, through poor play at a hole or two, fail to be among the distinguished thirty-two, still a thirty-six-hole qualifying round is a good test of anyone's ability, and those who fail to qualify should not complain.

The Glen Echo course is a good test of golf, requiring a great diversity of play, and one where the player must use his head as well as hands, and is one of the best golf links in the Western states. It is of generous length, being 2,055 yards going out and 3,171 yards coming in, with holes varying from 148 to 538 yards. It is an interesting course, and one in every respect that may properly be designated as a championship course. There are some changes to be made in the disposition of the bunkers, all of which tend to make the course more difficult, and true straight play more necessary.

George had heard that the members of Glen Echo had retained none other than Walter Travis to make changes to the course in preparation for the Olympic event. He tried to imagine what Travis might do to a course to make it even more challenging. George smiled at the thought of standing on the first tee of that course, admiring Travis's handiwork. It occurred to him, though, that Travis would now have an advantage in the competition, with intimate knowledge of the course's secrets. George made a mental note. *Perhaps I should arrive early and play a few practice rounds.*

It is to be hoped that some of the very best of the British golfers will consider the honor of winning the Olympic championship medal grand enough glory to be a sufficient inducement for them to make the journey and compete. 'Tis the mere glory of winning a coveted title and of being the proud possessor of the distinguishing badge, not the intrinsic value of the prize itself, that makes the true amateur sportsmen so keen to win it. The title of Olympic golf champion should certainly be as eagerly fought for as that of amateur champion of Great Britain or amateur champion of the United States. Even the glory of lasting to the semifinals and securing one of the Olympic bronze medals should be tempting enough to attract the very best of our amateurs. The date is late enough to find all our American golfers at the top of their game, and the weather at St. Louis in September is generally very delightful. Aside from the Olympic medals, a generous list of prizes has been provided.

This bit of the article stuck in George's craw, as his father would say. George would be the first to admit that British golfers have a great deal more experience over North Americans, but there was no reason to assume that they would dominate these Olympics.

Any amateur in the world is eligible to compete. The Maori Chieftain Kuropa Tareha, who is amateur champion of New Zealand, or some crack young golfer who has learned the game on a public course is just as eligible as the proudest titleholder in England or America. Possibly a dark horse in the person of some golfer hitherto unknown to fame may win the coveted honor. But what a battle royale it would be should the semifinals be between two crack English players against Americans, fighting it out between them for the final in the championship of the world.

"And what of Canada and her titleholders?" George thought. It appeared to him that Canadian golfers were not being taken seriously. "More fuel for the fire," he said to himself. That's what his Irish mother would have said.

Annette looked up from her book. "George, what are you muttering about?"

"Nothing, my love. I'm just reading this article."

"From the way you're sighing and groaning, may I assume that you're rereading the part about the Maori champion from New Zealand?"

George turned to her and smiled. She knew him well. "As a matter of fact I am. Fuel for the fire, my dear. Fuel for the fire."

"You know, sometimes the dark horse has the advantage, my love."

"That is very true. I shall be a dark horse. An old, dark horse."

Again, George turned to look at the trophies, cups, and tankards on his mantel and felt a swell of confidence. His first Canadian Amateur victory held a place of prominence. George Seymour Jr. had been born just six months before that victory, and George had practically burst with pride, holding the cup in one arm and George Jr. in the other. He had added another Amateur victory in 1900, after a hard-fought battle. And of course, there was the Amateur from last year when he had won the cup back from Fritz. It was perhaps the sweetest win of all.

Fritz had been nagging him that he was past his prime. It was true that George was forty-five years old, but the dark horse had showed them differently. Last summer, he had played an international tournament in Niagara-on-the-Lake and he not only won the tournament, but he also shot the low gross score with a seventy-seven, won the long drive contest, and won the approach and putting contest for good measure. *Some dark horse.*

George Lyon's mantel was full, and his life was full. He had a good wife, three healthy children, a successful career in the insurance business, and now an opportunity, perhaps his last, to add something extraordinary to his achievements. *Olympic golf. At this age, do I dare dream about another trophy and a gold medal?*

The April night turned a little chillier, and a light snow began to fall in Toronto. After looking in on his children one more time, George returned to the library and opened his calendar to review the dates for the competition.

The amateur golf competition for the Olympic championship, open to all amateur golfers of the world, will be played on the course of the Glen Echo Country Club, St. Louis, Missouri, Monday, Tuesday, Wednesday, Thursday, Friday, and Saturday, September 19th, 20th, 21st, 22nd, 23rd, and 24th, 1904.

The rules of the United States Golf Association will govern all competitions. Entry shall close at 6:00 p.m., Monday, September 12, 1904. An entry fee of five dollars will be charged, the payment of which makes the entrant eligible to all events, and subject to the rules governing this competition. No entry fee will be charged for the team competition. Competitors for the Olympic championship who

are members of a golf club shall enter through the secretary
of their respective clubs; those desiring to compete who are
not members of a club must prove their amateur status to
the satisfaction of the committee.

George had already spoken to Albert Austin and the secretary at Lambton about what would be required to ensure his
entry arrived on time. Although it was only April, he wanted
to confirm that the necessary paperwork was in order. He
would need to guarantee that his work calendar was open for
extended practice over the summer and clear for most of September as well.

George put another log on the fire and told Annette of his
plans. The competition was just five months away. He would
be busy preparing. She needed to know that he would be off
to Montreal for the Canadian Amateur in July, and then to
St. Louis for a week in September. They were not used to
being separated that long or at such a distance. But Annette
watched his eyes light up when he described to her that he
would be meeting the best golfers from around the world.
Ireland, Scotland—"the home of golf," he reminded her
again—the best from the United States, and even some of his
club mates from Canada would be competing.

He rhymed off the names of those he expected to meet:
the great John Ball, winner of the British Amateur five times;
Harold Hilton, winner of the British Open back to back in
1900 and 1901 at the great courses of Muirfield and St.
Andrew's; Charles Hutchings, winner at Liverpool in 1902;
and Robert Maxwell, winner in 1903.

"It will be glorious," George said. "Glorious."

Maybe it was the thought of glory that turned George's
mind to poor Frederick Tait at that moment. The Scotsman

was a formidable driver of the ball, and they said Tait had once driven a ball 341 yards at St. Andrew's. Granted, part of it was over frozen ground, but it was said the ball carried nearly 240 yards before it began to roll. With his powerful drives, he had won the British Open in 1896 and again in 1897, and led it on other occasions. George would have loved to meet him on the course, but it could never be. Frederick Tait fell in action February 7, 1900—a month after his thirtieth birthday—during the Boer War's battle of Koodoosberg. *What a waste of life.*

As he had grown older and considered the future welfare of his own children, Lyon's views on war and glory softened. *Certainly some wars were necessary, but the Boer War?* He wondered if Prime Minister Robert Borden, who had lost his own son in the Boer War, felt the Empire had been well served by that conflict—by that loss of a son. *Glory? Where was the glory once dead? For the living? True, Victoria Crosses had been awarded to three Canadian soldiers for their bravery in action during the Boer War, but medals were not as good company as sons. To whom would that kind of heirloom be passed on?* Lyon prayed his son, Seymour, would never face such obligations for his country.

Annette could see his mind had wandered to something that troubled him, and she knew there was little point in debating this trip. She remembered how disappointed he had been to miss the Paris Olympics four years ago. The competition had not been publicized, and no medals or trophies had been awarded, but still he wished he could have been there. He was Canadian Amateur champion, after all. He should have been there, he said. She knew that meeting the best in competition was what thrilled him; she had heard endless stories about the golfers he wanted—*needed*—to meet on the golf course.

"Will Mr. Travis compete?" She didn't look up from her reading.

George smiled. Annette evidently knew the names of some of his likely competitors.

"Ah yes, Mr. Travis." George looked up at his bookshelf. All of Travis's books were there. *Practical Golf* was now two years old, and George had the first and second editions. He had read it a dozen times. He had Travis's most recent book, *The Art of Putting,* on order, and he prayed that it would arrive before the summer.

"Yes, I imagine Mr. Travis will be there," he said brightly.

"And Mr. Lambert?"

"Certainly, I think Mr. Lambert will be there to defend his Olympic reign. Glen Echo is his home course. Imagine if he were to make two Olympic wins. He will be highly motivated, I would think. This time there will at least be medals and a trophy." George knew, though, that St. Louis would not be Paris. The rules had been different in 1900; matches had been handicapped in Paris. He had heard stories that the field had been weak. And there was no gold medal or fine trophy awarded. St. Louis's would be golf's first gold medal.

But it was really Walter Travis whom George was impatient to meet in St. Louis. There would be others, no doubt, and great golfers among them, but none who could rival George's utter admiration for Walter Travis. They called him the Old Man; he was the true competition. Travis was forty-two, reigning 1903 U.S. Amateur champion, and George would turn forty-six in a few months, reigning 1903 Canadian Amateur champion. If they thought Travis was the old man, what would they think of George?

Annette closed her book and rose to go to bed. "Coming?"

"You go ahead, my love. I have some reading to catch up on." He reached up to his shelf for the well-thumbed copy of Travis's *Practical Golf.* As Annette climbed the stairs of their Rosedale home at 13 Dunbar Road, she could hear George half-singing, half-humming his favorite song, "My Wild Irish Rose." She knew that he was already playing against Mr. Travis in his mind, and that if he came to bed in an hour, he would thrash about as he dreamt of the match.

But little did they know, as they kissed goodnight, that in a matter of a few hours, George Lyon's Olympic dreams would nearly go up in flames.

8

The Fire Call Box Rings

EORGE LYON WOULD never admit it, but he was sound asleep in a chair in his library when the telephone rang at 10:00 p.m. on April 19, 1904. A telephone call at that hour could mean only one thing: an emergency, or at least certainly bad news. It was his former army mate in the Queen's Own Rifles and now business partner, Higginbotham. He was breathless and shouting into the telephone.

"George, thank God I got through. I have been trying for the last thirty minutes, but all the telephone lines are jammed, or they're out altogether. I'm at the office... the city... it's in flames! I've moved as many files as I—" The line went dead.

In the wee hours of the next morning, George and Higginbotham huddled at the corner of Wellington and Bay Streets with a dozen other Toronto businessmen, looking over the burnt shells of building after building. They walked along the few portions of the street that had not buckled from the heat, their mouths covered with wet handkerchiefs as they stared in disbelief at what had once been the business district of downtown Toronto. It was nothing more than smoldering ruins.

More than 104 buildings had been destroyed as the fire raged for nine hours through the night, consuming twenty acres of the once-bustling wholesale district. The men looked west along Wellington and saw through billowing smoke and steam nothing but blackened shells of buildings, half walls, and water-soaked streets of absolute devastation. George turned and looked east toward 15 Wellington Street East, where their own office building stood. Miraculously, the fire had stopped a hundred feet from their office, and it had been spared any damage. The hundreds of client files—insurance policies that secured their clients for precisely this type of catastrophe—were safe.

In a city of some 200,000 people, this fire would be a terrible hardship, George thought. More than 5,000 people worked every day in those ten blocks of buildings. Hundreds lived in the area. *Where will they work now? Where will they live? This fire will mean hard times for many families in Toronto.*

As he looked around, George was reminded of the horrible fire in Montreal only a few months previous. That blaze had destroyed the Mount Royal Club at Stanley and Sherbrooke Streets. Better known as the Millionaires Club because of its wealthy membership, it was now gone. Thankfully, only two men had been killed in that terrifying inferno: a young fireman, crushed by a falling granite cornice, and the night watchman, who was trapped inside. George was certain the death toll in Toronto would be much higher, given this fire's wider path of destruction.

A soot-faced fireman approached the group, his arms spread wide as if to herd them off the street.

"Gentlemen!" he shouted. "I'll have to ask you to move out of this area. There is still work to be done." He lifted his arm and pointed at a building from which thick black smoke still billowed. "Gutta Percha and Rubber is still burning, as you can see. So I have to ask you to move along before someone gets hurt. We have more fire wagons coming right through here."

George and Higginbotham looked at each other; they recognized the company name of one of their best clients, once run by their friend and fellow golfer Andy Smith. Curley had been one of Canada's finest golfers, taught at St. Andrew's by Young Tom Morris himself. He had come to Canada from Scotland nearly twenty-five years previous, with a golfing reputation that was already well established. After being moved a few times by the Scottish bank for which he worked as a clerk, Smith ended up in Toronto. He was secretary treasurer of the Toronto Golf Club the day George first picked up a club. They became good friends through their love of golf and met in many a hard-fought match over the years.

In 1895, Andy had traveled to Rhode Island to the Newport Golf Club to compete in the first U.S. Open. George recalled his proud return to Toronto, having tied for third with fellow Scotsman James Foulis, and how Andy had regaled George and his mates with tales of the wealthy American golfers and their posh life in Newport.

It seemed like only seven or eight years ago that Andy had gone home to Scotland on a long vacation and returned as the representative of a prosperous company, Gutta Percha and Rubber Manufacturing Company. For more than fifty years, the company had sourced leathery, water-resistant latex from trees grown in Malaysia, material that was used in golf balls. With their Canadian head office situated in the heart of downtown Toronto, Andy immediately turned to George for his fire insurance needs.

Sadly, Andy had passed away suddenly, just three years ago, and George was grateful the Toronto golf community had acknowledged his contributions to golf in Canada when they had the chance. A year before his death, he had been honored as the "Father of Canadian Golf." During his speech that evening, George had described Curley as a role model and mentor, and as one of the prettiest players he had ever met. And now the business he had so carefully managed was burning before their very eyes—destroyed.

George turned to the exhausted fireman and asked, "Do you know what caused the fire?"

He stepped forward and removed his helmet. His face was framed by frozen sweat, and his hair was frosted in sharp points along his hairline. He shouted a response as a horse-drawn fire wagon raced by him. "From what we can tell, the fire started about 8:00 p.m.—at least, that's when Call Box 12 rang—trouble was first seen over at 58 Wellington: Curries, the neckwear company. It could've been a stove left unattended or maybe an electrical fire. We will probably never know, because that building is gone now. It looks like the fire shot up the elevator shaft. The whole building sat smoldering for hours before we knew anything was amiss. We couldn't get the ladders up because of all the telephone, telegraph, and electrical wires on the clusters of poles around the buildings." He mopped his face with a blackened rag. "The Chief will be on the warpath again. He warned them."

As insurance brokers, George and Higginbotham were well aware of the Toronto Fire Chief's blunt warning to the citizens of Toronto and the city council last year. If the city would not invest in the fire department, deal with the growing mess of tangled wires that now surrounded every building, and upgrade Toronto's building codes, then the entire city would be at risk for another year. He said that if a major fire broke out, he could not guarantee that his men could handle it. The Chief had even pointed to the Kilgour Brothers Building at 21 and 23 Wellington Street West as a model for construction of any new buildings in the business district. That building stored cardboard, but its owners had the foresight to install two large gravity-flow water tanks and a sprinkler system. The fact that the Kilgour Building didn't burn had actually stopped the fire from going farther east to Yonge Street. It was a testament to the Chief's warnings. The devastation would have been far worse had it not been for the Kilgour Building.

It was hard for George to imagine anything worse than what he now surveyed.

The Fire Chief's warnings last year had made headlines but still they went unheeded. "Too expensive," said the building owners. "We are too busy to stop work and make the changes."

"And now everyone's worst nightmare has become reality," George thought. "Now there will be no work at all for some time." Except, of course, for George and Higginbotham, who would now need to process hundreds of fire insurance claims over the next few months. Thinking of the work that awaited them, George was just about to turn back to the office when he noticed something strange. "What the devil has happened to the Queen's Hotel?"

The group turned to look at Toronto's finest hotel and landmark of the downtown business district. The hotel, with the Union Jack flying proudly overhead, stood seemingly untouched by the fire. But with every chilly gust of wind and every wave of the Union Jack, a wall of pale-green blankets also flapped stiffly from every window.

The fireman laughed. "The guests at the hotel had the brilliant idea to soak their blankets in the bathtub and hang them out the windows to make sure the sparks and flames from the fire didn't catch onto the hotel. After an hour, the blankets were frozen stiff as boards, but they certainly did their job." The fireman pointed north from the hotel toward King Street. "It also helped that the hotel was upwind from the fire, protected by that large garden on the north side."

"Good Lord, it would've been a catastrophe for the hotel," said a man beside George who had been listening.

"True enough. The first thing the hotel staff did was move out all the ladies—and of course, the hotel silverware. They moved to a safe place farther west of the hotel. But apparently, several of the out-of-town provincial members of Parliament who are regular guests at the hotel stayed behind. They formed a bucket brigade under the leadership of Mr. James Whitney, and I must say, they helped save the hotel and many surrounding buildings."

"Whitney? The provincial MP for Morrisburg?" George asked.

"Yes, that is the man. Quite a hero, if you ask me."

George knew of James Whitney. Morrisburg was close to George's birthplace, Richmond, just outside of Ottawa. George's family was very active in local politics. His uncle had been Mayor of Ottawa in 1867, the year of Confederation. "Whitney's a good man. They say he could be Premier of Ontario someday."

"I'll leave that for others to debate, but those politicians helped save the hotel and stop the fire from spreading farther south along Front Street."

"Thank God the Legislature was in session!" one of the businessmen called out.

"You don't hear people say that very often," another shouted to laughter.

A team of steaming horses pulled a fire wagon up beside the group, and the driver called out to the soot-faced fireman, "More trouble at the foot of Yonge and Front, the Bank of Montreal! Some men and wagons have come from Buffalo by train. They've started to help fight the blaze!"

"Well, gents, it's back to work, and I would ask you again to move out of the area now." He pulled his helmet on and climbed onto the side of the fire wagon as it lunged forward.

The group of men dispersed, and George and Higginbotham made their way through the slippery, frozen, water-soaked streets to their office, where they spread out a fire insurance map of downtown on the boardroom table. George pulled file after file from the cabinet as Higginbotham called out municipal addresses and corporate names. An hour later, a large stack of insurance policies sat at the corner of the boardroom table.

"We have our work cut out for us, George."

"Indeed we do, but the future of our brokerage may well rest on how well we service these clients. Let's try to make sure that Sun Fire's insurance policy is the gold standard in this disaster. We shall do our best."

Higginbotham smiled. He had been George's lieutenant in the army years ago and recalled that it was one of George's favorite sayings. "Yes, we shall do our best."

Over the next few days, the shocking details of the losses were tallied and blared in newspaper headlines. More than a hundred buildings were lost, 220 firms were destroyed, twenty acres of downtown looked like a disaster zone, and 230 firemen had poured 3 million gallons of water onto the blaze. Miraculously, although there had been twenty injured, George's worst fears had not come true: there had been no deaths. Not one.

The total losses for buildings alone were more than $2 million and an additional $8 million for their contents. But insurance would only cover about $8 million of those losses. The Toronto insurance community pulled together and formed a loss committee, created standard loss forms, and agreed upon a system for adjusters. A salvage company was set to work, and for the most part, the people of Toronto were generally optimistic about rebuilding their city.

Far worse than the loss of buildings was the impact on employment. Overnight, the three hundred people who had worked at Currie Neckties were now unemployed. The Minerva Manufacturing Company and Kilgour Company employees were deeply affected as well, with 280 and 200 respectively being told not to bother reporting for work. There was no employment insurance or welfare, and the suffering spread quickly.

And of course those businessmen who had had no time for building improvements a year before were now paying 75 percent more on insurance rates. But now, as an incentive, insurers offered a discount if the building construction included sprinklers.

There was however, one exception. George saw in the *Toronto Daily Star* that businessman G.R. Cockburn would not rebuild his factory in downtown Toronto because, as he said, "There is too much socialism!" George laughed as he read it—he didn't know that a fire could have political preferences.

As George sat at his boardroom table late into the night, reviewing policies and damage claims, his dreams of Olympic golf in September, of the Amateur Championship in just a few months, of *any* golf during the spring and summer, for that matter, seemed to be just that—only dreams.

9

Another Fire Still Burned

GEORGE UNDERSTOOD THAT selling insurance was always about the "what if" and the "next time." While his clients began to rebuild their businesses and the Toronto core, others had already seen the damage and were determined to have fire insurance coverage in place. So while George's business was booming, his golf was suffering. His trip to Montreal at the beginning of the month on Dominion Day for the Canadian Amateur had brought defeat at the hands of Montreal stockbroker Percy Taylor, who had the advantage of displaying his deadly accurate short game on his home course, the Royal Montreal.

Their final match had been hard fought; they were all square after the morning's eighteen holes. George went for a much-needed lunch in the clubhouse, while Taylor decided to head home for a meal with his wife. When Taylor returned a few hours later, he was in a fresh suit of clothes but in a sour mood. When the typically buoyant George asked why he was so miserable, Taylor explained that when he arrived home, tired and hungry looking for a hearty lunch, his wife had insisted he first row out to the middle of the lake to fetch some fresh water. In his haste on the way back in to shore he had tipped the boat over for a head to toe soaking. He spent the lunch hour drying off and finding another suit. However, the sourness didn't seem to hurt his game, because after the twentieth hole, he was up one and went on to win three and two. George came home empty handed. Golf's bragging rights were given back to Montreal.

But today was July 27, George's forty-sixth birthday, and he stood in the men's grill at Lambton Golf Club enjoying a well-deserved break from the office. His fellow club members had plied him with enough Scotch that he finally climbed up on his chair to lead his friends in a full-throated version of "My Wild Irish Rose." The clubhouse shook with the sound of fifty well-oiled, out-of-tune men as they sang, "You may search everywhere, but none can compare with my-y-y wild Irish rose!"

After cheers, laughter, and hearty applause had died down, George spilled into a chair next to Albert Austin.

"Did you hear about the Winnipeg Shamrocks?" Austin shouted over the noise. "They've won the gold medal for Canada at the Olympic lacrosse game yesterday, in St. Louis."

"Well, let's raise a glass to those lads!" George appeared ready to resume his position standing on the chair. His repertoire of songs was well known, and it would not have taken much to get the room to join him again.

Albert sat him back down. "George, you realize that this is the very first gold medal a Canadian has ever won at the Olympics. It's magnificent!"

It was also the first time Canada was competing at an Olympics under the Canadian flag. In the Olympics held in

Athens in 1896, and Paris in 1900, national flags and teams were not yet part of the Olympic format. There were no grand marches as teams entered opening ceremonies; men and women competed as individuals through their local clubs and sports associations. In 1904, in St. Louis, that changed, and many athletes gathered as teams for their country.

"Magnificent, indeed..." George was glad they had won, but his thoughts were suddenly on other matters.

It was obvious to Albert the Montreal loss and worries about his own Olympic efforts were still on George's mind. He needed a distraction to cheer him up, so Albert unfolded the *Toronto Daily Star* and placed it on the table between them. "Not only did Canadians win the gold, but look at this, a team of Mohawks from a reserve near Brantford, Ontario." Albert pointed to the black-and-white photo. "They've won the bronze as well! And look at their names: Black Hawk, Snake Eater, Almighty Voice. Here's a chap named Man Afraid of Soap. I'm surprised they didn't frighten off their competitors with names like that!"

"You're making this up." George grabbed the paper from him and read for himself the list of men on the team. Albert wasn't joking. Black Eagle, Flat Iron, and Red Jacket were among the other names of the Mohawk lacrosse players.

"I would take that fellow's name to competition in a flash: Red Jacket Austin." He chuckled as he imagined it. Albert was very fond of his red golfing jacket and wore it around the Lambton clubhouse regardless of whether he was playing or not. He cut quite a figure in it. "What would your name be, George?"

George thought for a moment and said with a growling laugh, "I would be Olympic Lyon, of course!" He raised his glass to Red Jacket and handed the paper back to him.

Albert turned to golfing matters. "I see that this Chandler Egan chap has won again with his Harvard golf team."

George turned serious and craned his neck over Albert's shoulder to get a glimpse of the article. "Egan has led his team to their third consecutive college golf championship," he read. "That makes it 1902, 1903, and now 1904. Three years in a row. Unbelievable."

"I've read that his cousin is quite the golfer as well."

As busy as he was with work, George had been following the Egan careers. "Yes, Walter Egan. He and Chandler seem to be real up-and-comers." George told Albert that he heard Chandler Egan grew up with his very own golf course. "Apparently, it's not just rich Toronto businessmen who have their own golf courses in their backyards."

Albert was used to George's good-natured teasing about his wealth. "The truth of the matter, George, is that I checked into that rumor and learned that in actual fact young Egan had taken up golf as a *twelve-year-old* and had built his own course across his neighbors' lawns. It wasn't until his family summered at Lake Geneva that he received formal training and had the chance to play on their course designed by none other than James Foulis."

"Imagine being trained and playing from such a young age."

"And then when they returned to Chicago he grew up playing at his father's course, Exmoor. Whatever he has done has seemed to work. They say he's favored to win the U.S. Amateur this year."

"And beat Walter Travis? Not a chance." George snorted. "How old is he?"

"Goodness, George, he's only nineteen."

Both men sat in silence for a moment to consider that sobering fact. George did a little arithmetic and realized that as he sat there celebrating his birthday, he was now twenty-seven years older than Chandler Egan.

"What were you doing when you were nineteen, Albert?"

"Filling inkwells for my father at the Dominion Bank," said Austin with resignation. "They're coming for us, George. They're coming for us."

George, who was not quite ready to concede defeat, raised his glass. "And we shall be waiting for them."

But even as he said it, George was not entirely sure he would be in any position to travel to St. Louis in a few months. His family came first, his business came second, and golf? Well, there was much more work to be done at the insurance office before there would be any golf.

Albert said good night, and after he left, George picked up the *Toronto Daily Star,* found a quiet corner of the Lambton clubhouse, and read the story about Winnipeg's Shamrocks, Brantford's Mohawks, and their Olympic medals. The people of Winnipeg had chipped in to raise enough money to send the Shamrocks to the Olympics. The team traveled from Winnipeg to St. Paul, Minnesota, then on to Chicago, and finally St. Louis. Although the team had been unhappy about being asked to play an exhibition match along the way—it was on a Sunday, after all—they relented, played, and tied. But that would be the last time they tied a match, as they soundly defeated all comers—including the local favorites, the St. Louis Amateur Athletic Association—to win their Olympic gold medals. George thought about how proud they must have been as they strutted about the World's Fair with their medals pinned to their chests. *It must have been quite a day.*

Toronto's Great Fire may have burned out, but George Lyon's desire to compete at the Olympics had not. It was his birthday, and his friends were calling for another song, but instead, he finished his drink and headed back to the office. If he was going to compete in the Olympics in less than two months, there was work to be done first.

10

The Train to St. Louis

GEORGE WAS GRATEFUL that Albert Austin had made the travel arrangements to St. Louis. The Grand Trunk Railway would take him, Albert, and Albert's son, Bert, from Toronto to the top of Lake Michigan, and then on to St. Louis. To George's delight, Albert had chartered a private railway car. He was a man who knew how to travel in comfort and style; just last year, he had chartered a private railway car to take some of eastern Canada's finest women golfers to an invitational tournament at Philadelphia's Merion Golf Club.

Even though George and the Austins were off to the Summer Olympics, they were able to take advantage of the rates that railways established for those traveling to the World's Fair. The Grand Trunk had reduced rates through the summer to encourage tourists: a fifteen-day pass from New York to St. Louis was $26.25, and even less from Chicago or Atlanta—one could travel for a full week for $20.85. Some 4 million people traveled to the World's Fair that summer and fall, adults outnumbering children in attendance twenty to one. And thousands more were expected to come just to compete in and watch the Olympic Games that summer. In 1904, St. Louis was the place to be.

Albert had also managed to reserve rooms for the three of them in the well-appointed Glen Echo clubhouse itself. He ensured that every detail—from meals to clean clothes to daily hot baths—was confirmed in writing, and then confirmed again for good measure. Both men were well aware of the disgraceful treatment Walter Travis had received while playing in the British Amateur at Royal St. George's earlier in the year.

As reigning 1903 U.S. Amateur champion, Travis had announced his plans to go to Sandwich, England, to compete for the British Amateur in May. That spring, he had journeyed to England with three other American golfers, but when they arrived, they were shocked to discover that no rooms or lockers had been reserved at the Royal St. George's hotel for Travis or the members of his group. This hotel housed all other competing golfers that year—except the Americans. It did not bode well for the rest of the week.

Between matches, Travis had been forced to change his clothes in a public hallway, while the English and Scottish golfers enjoyed a shower and lounge area. None of the usual courtesies had been extended to him; no locals would play practice rounds with him to share a little course insight, and he had been assigned a caddie who Travis insisted actually did more harm than good. All this occurred after those same English players—members of the Oxford and Cambridge Golfing Society—had been treated like royalty during their exhibition tour of America just nine months before.

During that tour in September of 1903 Travis and his fellow American golfers had arranged a dozen events that would take the Brits to the finest courses in America, with a final match play event at the mountainous Ekwanok Country Club in Manchester, Vermont, a course that Travis himself had designed.

Although the experienced English and Scottish players had dominated almost all the American events, and probably were not impressed by the competition, they *had* been impressed by one thing: the gracious hospitality of their hosts. Travis had ensured that each guest received fine accommodations, attended lavish dinners, and had more than enough opportunities for a social drink. But all that hospitality had been conveniently forgotten when Travis and his party arrived to compete in England.

Travis had struggled with his game under this mistreatment—his nerves were off and his erratic putting was hurting his chances of winning. It didn't matter the distance—twenty feet, ten feet, two feet—Travis the great putter couldn't make a putt to save his life. His companions on that trip worked to raise his spirits with nightly doses of stout and lively games of cribbage but it was not enough until a lucky stroke. An American businessman and golfer who had been traveling through England at the time, and who had decided to take in a few rounds of the Amateur, gave Travis the one thing he needed: a piece of golf equipment unlike anything Travis had seen before. Watching Travis struggle on the green, he had asked if Travis would consider giving his Schenectady putter a try. Travis, desperate for help, said he would try anything, so the American dashed back to his hotel to retrieve it.

It was an odd-looking putter that was designed and patented by Arthur Knight and had just been released in New York. A scientist, engineer, and avid golfer, Knight was also working on an idea to replace the traditional whippy but sometimes unpredictable hickory shafts on golf clubs with a revolutionary steel tube shaft that might produce a more stable swing and better contact.

Knight had spent months testing, measuring, and tweaking his design for what he described as "the perfect putter." It was center shafted, more like a croquet mallet than a traditional putter, and was based on Knight's scientific conclusion that the perfect pendulum would produce the perfect stroke and, therefore, the perfect putt. Every golfer's dream awaited.

Travis took the odd putter to the practice green, where fellow golfers and the public gawked as he made a two-footer, then a ten-footer, then a twenty-footer. Travis turned to his new American friend, and a smile crossed his face for the first time all week. The Schenectady putter had ignited a fire in Travis that would help him bear down, forget his mistreatment, and beat the best English and Scottish players. In a controversial victory, British golf had been turned on its head; a foreigner—an American, for heaven's sake—now held their precious amateur trophy. And he had done it using some bizarre new putter. Travis might as well have stolen the trophy. And as such, his win was barely acknowledged at the victory dinner that followed.

As Travis stood to accept the trophy that evening, he was the 1903 U.S. Amateur champion and the 1904 British Amateur champion. It had never been done before. To the Brits, it was an outrage. Although the name of that putter had been heard around the golf world, and Arthur Knight couldn't manufacture them fast enough, the Royal and Ancient had different ideas—they immediately banned it in the U.K.

So as a result of Travis's well-known mistreatment in England, George and Albert had expected the worst as foreigners attending the Olympics. Would they be subjected to

American retaliation? They could take nothing for granted. But Albert had assured George, "I will take care of all the details. You take care of the golf."

On a sunny but brisk Friday morning in September, the Lyon family stood on a railway platform at Union Station, in downtown Toronto, and watched as the porters loaded George's luggage and golf clubs onto the train billowing steam. George was dressed in his usual tweeds: a thick black-and-gray three-piece suit, a stiff-collared white shirt, and a simple black tie. His gold watch chain and fob hung from a vest button. Although he wore his tweed cap, even from a distance Annette could recognize his gray-haired temples and still-dark moustache. After years of marriage and three children, she still found him handsome. She and the children would miss him over the next week.

Before climbing aboard, George made his way down the platform to give Annette and the children one last hug goodbye. "I have asked Fritz to look in on you from time to time while I'm away," he said.

Although Fritz was sometimes a friendly thorn in George's side on the golf course, he would be forever in Fritz's debt for introducing him to his beautiful sister one lazy summer afternoon at a cricket match. Knowing she was watching him closely that day, George played the game of his life, setting a world record for runs scored. It would be the first of many times that thoughts of her made him raise his game.

"We shall be fine. You concentrate on your golf. Remember to send us a postcard or a letter from time to time, my love."

"I'll write as often as I can."

"And George..." Annette pulled on his sleeve as he turned to leave.

"Yes, my love..."

"Please give my regards to Walter Travis. I feel as if he has been living in our library for the past year." She laughed. "And that Maori champion from New Zealand, too."

"I shall pass on your warmest regards, but none of your Irish luck. That's all mine." He smiled, kissed her one more time, and with a wave, he was off.

The day-and-a-half train ride to St. Louis was long but pleasant. There was a tinge of something new in the air. Along the way, George could see more and more people crowding platforms and filing onto the trains on their way to the World's Fair. Their excitement, conversation, and anticipation filled the train stations and railway cars. George got up to stretch his legs when they stopped at a small town outside Chicago and walked into the next car.

A group of young women, huddled near the back of their car, sat chatting and laughing. George, always a friend to ladies, made his way toward the group to see what all the excitement was about. He greeted them warmly and enquired of a young woman about the group's excitement. She unfolded a copy of *Woman's Home Companion* magazine to show him the headline: "Free Trips to the Great St. Louis World's Fair."

"I had until September 15 to enter the greatest number of subscriptions to the magazine." She pointed to the full-page advertisement and practically read it from memory. "'The winner is allowed to remain at the fair for ten days, and it will not cost a cent from the time they leave home until they return.' And I won!" The group let out a shriek of excitement. "We're off to the fair, all expenses paid!"

A woman beside her flipped open *The Sketch* magazine for George to see pictures of the fair. "That's the famous Ferris wheel from the 1893 Chicago World's Fair, which they've

FREE TRIPS
to the Great St. Louis
WORLD'S FAIR

where you may view the sights, scenes and wonders of all the nations of the earth—the greatest exposition the world has ever beheld. Nearly twice as large as the great Chicago World's Fair, with the improvements and inventions of the last ten years added. You can be earning good wages, and at the same time secure a visit of ten days to the World's Fair, including all your expenses—every necessary cent—from the time you leave home until you return.

THE GRAND LAGOON—FESTIVAL HALL AND THE CASCADES IN THE DISTANCE

You will be surprised to learn how easily you can obtain one of these grand trips without cost. If you don't want the trip, you may have the equivalent in cash.

You will be allowed to remain at the fair for ten days, and it will not cost you a cent from the time you leave home until you return.

O EACH one of the five persons who send the greatest number of subscriptions to the WOMAN'S HOME COMPANION before September 15, 1904, the WOMAN'S HOME COMPANION will give a free ten days' trip to the great St. Louis World's Fair during the month of October, paying all expenses, including railroad fare, hotel bills, admissions, and all necessary expenditures from the time they leave home until they return.

The regular cash commission is allowed, and the trips are given free. It will not take very many subscriptions to win the prizes.

You will be surprised when the time arrives to see how easily these magnificent trips to the great St. Louis World's Fair were won, and what a very small club, comparatively, it required to secure these prizes. Now, don't think some one has a better chance than you—you have as good a chance as anybody. Don't stop to study over it, but get right out and hustle a little, and you may wake up to find yourself one of the lucky ones. Be quick.

CONDITIONS

1. Any person can enter this contest.
2. All subscriptions to the WOMAN'S HOME COMPANION must be taken at the regular price.
3. The regular cash commission will be paid for each subscription sent in by contestant; this is in addition to the free trips. Get your friends to help you.
4. You must mark each list you send in "World's Fair Contest," so that no mistakes are made in crediting the same to your account.
5. The contest is limited to the United States only.

6. Each successful contestant will have ten days at the fair during October, all necessary expenses paid from the time they leave home until they return.
7. Contest closes September 15, 1904.
8. In case of a tie, the prize will be one hundred dollars and equally divided.
9. If you don't want to take the trip, you may have the equivalent in cash not to exceed one hundred dollars.
10. Subscription agencies, publishers and wholesale dealers are not included in this contest.

No one connected with our establishment, either directly or indirectly, and no one living in Springfield or Clark County, Ohio, will be permitted to enter the contest, and the contest will be conducted in the fairest manner possible.

WRITE TO-DAY FOR FULL PARTICULARS · **Address WOMAN'S HOME COMPANION, Springfield, Ohio** · WRITE TO-DAY FOR FULL PARTICULARS

4*7,000 Copies of the WOMAN'S HOME COMPANION WERE PRINTED FOR THE JULY ISSUE, GIVING MORE THAN TWO MILLION READERS

moved to St. Louis. And beside it is the Festival Hall, and then the Jaffa Gate from the re-creation of the Old City of Jerusalem, and then an authentic Chinese village, and a real Swiss village, and the Temple of Mirth, and the Creation Exhibition Hall, and . . ." She continued breathlessly, pointing excitedly at the photos as her friends and other curious travelers crowded around them.

George finally stepped away, wishing them a wonderful excursion, and returned to his private car. As the door closed behind him, he could still hear their excited conversation and joyful laughter. He looked out the window at the crowd of people on the platform climbing aboard the train.

"Albert . . ."

"Yes, George?" He didn't look up from his paper.

"I'm beginning to think that we should spend a day at the World's Fair."

Bert Austin, who was just sixteen, sat bolt upright in his seat.

Now Albert looked up, but it was with a frown. "George, we need to get to the course, get settled in, get in some practice rounds, familiarize ourselves with the course. There are driving and putting competitions that we shouldn't miss. And what about the evening social, George? You don't want to miss that! All the international golfers will be there." Albert knew George loved any opportunity to socialize. He was the life of any party, and as many golfers and curlers would attest, "Wherever George Lyon sits is the head of the table."

"But Albert, when will we have another chance to see the World's Fair? I need to be back in Toronto no later than September 26, so there will be no time after the tournament. Unless, of course, we're out in the first round. Then we can spend a whole week at the fair." He winked at Bert. George stopped the young porter as he passed. "Excuse me, good sir, what would be involved if we disembarked at St. Louis to see the World's Fair?"

"Well, I couldn't help but overhear your conversation, and I can tell you that you would be missing quite an experience if you take a pass on the fair. I've been three times, and I'll go again if I get the opportunity."

The porter reached into his pocket and pulled out a billfold containing a carefully protected photo. "I have a bit of a fascination with the Wild West, Buffalo Bill, and the Indian people. That's a photograph of the great Indian Chief Geronimo, and that's his mark." He pointed to a signature scrawled across the bottom of the photograph. "He's an attraction at the World's Fair. I met him and he signed this photo for me. It cost me fifty cents."

He took back the photo but stopped to consider it before putting it back in his pocket. "I met Geronimo," he said to himself, as if he still could not quite believe it.

Bert fell back in his seat and let out a breath. "Geronimo." Bert had read fantastic tales of his battles with the American army as it had marched relentlessly across the West. The Wild West seemed as far away as the moon.

George clapped his hands together. "It's settled then. We're off to the World's Fair!" Albert shook his head silently in protest, but he knew the matter was settled. Olympic golf could take the back burner for at least one day.

And they were glad it did. They had no idea of the wonders they were about to witness.

$$=== 11 ===$$

A Day at the World's Fair

SATURDAY, SEPTEMBER 17, 1904

"LOOK OUT!" GEORGE grabbed Bert by the collar and pulled him out of the path of an automobile that roared past them and shuddered to a stop in a cloud of dust. Two men, both in white straw hats, jumped from the back of the chugging vehicle and began yelling at a young man with the number twenty on his shirt. He was half-running, half-walking and looked near collapse. Bert had been standing in the middle of the bustling street among hundreds of other new arrivals pouring off streetcars. They simply stood, mouths agape, staring in awe at the ornate gates to the St. Louis World's Fair. They had not even entered the grounds and they were speechless, George albeit for different reasons.

Lyon turned to one of the men, angry, and said, "What on earth is going on? You nearly ran over us."

The man sounded as if this was of no real concern to him. "Get out of the way!" he shouted. "Make way for the Olympic marathon runners! They are coming through." No sooner had he called out than several official-looking men arrived on the scene to hold back the crowds. As they extended their arms to clear the street, a team of a half dozen runners from Greece sprinted by, all wearing numbered shirts, heading to the Olympic Stadium near the fairgrounds. They were immediately followed by a dozen people on bicycles cheering them on.

It was easily ninety degrees, and the sun broiled anyone not under a hat or in the shade of a tree. The man who had nearly run over Bert was holding a bucket of water that appeared to have been heated on the steam boiler of their vehicle. He pointed at the runner who stood bent over gasping for air, and then turned to George and Albert. "That is Tom Hicks from Cambridge, he's leading the Olympic marathon. There are just seven miles to go." He leaned over the dehydrated-looking man and began to squeeze water from a sponge onto his head.

"I have to lie down!" The man cried out. "Let me lie down!"

"You can't now, Tom. Come on. You can make it!" But as he poured water over him, an official pushed the sponge away.

"No water! No drinking water! You may only wet his lips!" The official moved again to hold back the crowd as more runners appeared. A barefoot runner being chased by a barking dog veered off the street, practically knocking over George as he ran into a shop to escape the animal.

With the official distracted by this new chaos in the crowd, the moaning man's handler pulled a small bottle from his pocket and offered it to Hicks. He stood and leaned back, prepared to pour anything into his mouth for relief. He gulped from a bottle what appeared to be a thick white liquid. Within a few seconds, he stood upright and with a look of fiery determination in his eyes bolted off in a full sprint like a horse let loose from a barn.

"What did you give him?" George asked. "I thought no water was allowed." Lyon was a stickler from the rules in sports—written and unwritten.

The man looked from side to side to ensure no one overheard and said slyly, "The official said we are not allowed to give the runners *water*," as if somehow that allowed every other form of liquid. "I gave him some egg whites, with brandy... and a sixtieth of a grain of strychnine."

"Rat poison? You're going to kill him!"

He laughed. "Well, that was his second dose, and it seems to have worked. He is going to win this race, come hell or high water. They just caught a fellow cheating, some guy from New York." He said New York as if it were an evil place. "Actually rode in a car for ten miles, ran into the stadium, and accepted the trophy from Roosevelt's daughter, Alice. He was disqualified. The crowd was furious. Damn cheater!" And with that ironic pronouncement, he ran to jump back into the waiting car and roared off to catch up to the poison-fueled Tom Hicks.

George turned to find Albert and Bert in line at the ticket booth. "What was that all about, George?" Albert asked.

"You wouldn't believe me if I told you."

Once they were through the turnstiles, Albert, ever the organizer, said, "Now, we only have a few hours. I would say about three before we need to get back to the train station if we are to make it to Glen Echo by tonight. It is about twelve miles outside of the city. The train can drop us near the course, but we will still need a taxi for a few miles."

"Thank goodness you are looking after us, Albert. Bert wants to see Geronimo, so perhaps we should start there. What do you think Bert? Bert..."

But, lost in awe again, Bert had not heard a single word. Instead, his eyes were cast high up, watching the giant Ferris wheel, 265 feet tall, with three dozen boxcar-sized carriages filled with people turning slowly before his eyes. "Look at that!" he exclaimed.

"I must try to find a stereoscopic card of it for Annette," George said in awe.

"I heard that they moved it from Chicago. Took it apart after the World's Fair, packed it onto trains, and moved it here. Amazing, isn't it?" Albert said.

George tugged at Bert's sleeve to get his attention. "Bert, look." They turned to see a man calmly stroll by with a giraffe on a long leash.

"I think we may need more than three hours," Bert exclaimed.

"Well, let's get moving then." Albert was already concerned and went to a man selling maps of the grounds for advice. "We have limited time. What would you suggest?"

The man looked as if he had been asked that same question a hundred times a day. "Folks, there are millions of things to see at the fair, so pick a few things and plan to come back. You can't see it all in a day. If I were you, I would get some travelin' help," and he pointed to a huge wicker rickshaw-like carriage. "I would suggest you hire a college student to carry you around in a wicker chair. They can tell you a bit about the sights and save your legs, gentlemen." He looked at Albert and George as if they were elderly people who might fade in the heat. "Or the fair has its own railway. There are seventeen stops, and you can jump off and on as much as you like. Either way, you will need a map."

Albert paid the man and thanked him for the advice. "I say we take the wicker chair."

When the student asked where they would like to begin, Bert cried out, "Geronimo-o-o!" And with that, the three of them climbed in to see the sights.

As they passed by a massive water fountain, the young man explained that Scott Joplin's new ragtime song, "The Cascades," had been composed in honor of it. Albert made a note to add that to his sheet music collection when he got home and perhaps buy a recording for his new Gramophone. Next, they passed by the long lines of people waiting to enter the Lincoln Exhibit. A large sign proclaimed that inside one could, "Visit the log cabin in which Lincoln lived as a boy!" Forty years after his assassination, Americans had turned him and his life into a popular legend, some of it actually true.

"I heard that he built the cabin in which he was born with his own two hands," George remarked with a smirk. Albert laughed and Bert frowned as he pretended he understood the joke.

After a few minutes fighting through the crowds, they pulled up to Geronimo's carnival-like tent. They could see the great man sitting solemnly under a canopy with a long line of noisy excited people waiting to shake his hand or have their picture taken with him. A neatly painted sign said, "Signature: 10 cents, Photograph: 50 cents." Two soldiers stood nearby.

"He's technically an American prisoner of war," the college student explained. "He has been for over twenty-five years. And even though he's seventy-five years old, he's still guarded seven days a week by American soldiers."

"Good Lord," Lyon exclaimed. "Just when I think the world is moving forward, I hear something like that."

The young man continued with his story. "I actually spoke to Geronimo one day when they escorted him for a ride on the Ferris wheel. With his guards he climbed into the box-car—or what he called 'a little house'—and off he went for the best view of the fair. When he got off, he turned to me, and you know what he said?"

"What did he say?" Bert waited for some profound words from the great chief himself.

"He said, 'I should never have surrendered.'"

"I understand completely," George noted dryly.

Albert could see the long lineup. "Bert, why don't you get in line, and George and I will search out something exotic to eat."

As Bert joined the line, a man passed him, exclaiming in a strange foreign accent, "I bought Geronimo's hat! I bought his hat! It cost five dollars, but it's Geronimo's hat!" His friends rushed up and surrounded him before they swept off to explore another exhibit. Bert leaned out of line to see Geronimo calmly reach into a box underneath the table in front of him and pull out another hat, identical to the one the man had just purchased. He pulled it on over his long gray hair and waited for the next person in line as if nothing had happened.

When Bert reached the front of the line, a young native woman introduced herself in well-rehearsed tones: "I am Lena Geronimo, daughter of the Chiricahua Apache leader Geronimo." She took Bert's money and walked him to meet the once-mighty leader. Bert looked into his eyes but was surprised to see only sadness.

"Do you want a signature or a photo?" she asked.

"No," Bert said timidly, "I only want to shake his hand." He reached across and took the old man's hand in his and smiled.

When he returned to the wicker chair, George and Albert were waiting. "How was the great warrior?"

"Not what I had expected," Bert said, as he climbed in for the next leg of their journey. Albert could see his mood had changed. He knew that such disappointments could be felt more sharply when one is young.

"Let's see something a little more cheerful, shall we? Try this, Bert." His father passed him a slice of thick bread covered with brown paste. "I can understand why they say it isn't good for people with poor teeth but I think it's delicious."

Bert took a bite, scowled, and stuck out his tongue. "What is it?"

"It's new. They call it peanut butter."

With his mouth full, Bert muttered, "I'm not sure this will catch on." He swallowed and looked around for something to drink. When he climbed out to use a water fountain, a young girl passed by eating what appeared to be a huge pile of pink fluff on a long paper roll. Intrigued, Bert asked her, "What are you eating?"

"It is called fairy floss."

Bert turned to his father. "Forget peanut butter, I want to try that!"

With fairy floss in hand for Bert, they carried on with their tour of the grounds, passing the Irish Village that featured life-sized models of famous Irish landmarks Blarney Castle and St. Laurence's Gate at Drogheda. Celtic music filled the air around the exhibit. Nearby, they insisted their guide stop outside the mysterious-looking Chinese Pavilion. Made entirely of bamboo and teak, it was the first mandarin-style structure any of them had seen. "Inside," their guide explained, "is a genuine prince from China called Prince Pu Lun. He holds court with visitors."

"Prince Pu Lun," Bert repeated his name as if in that palace resided a visitor from another planet.

As they toured, they passed pavilions from Bulgaria, Denmark, Hungary, and Portugal. They passed the Russian Pavilion and the Japanese Pavilion. It was well known that Russia and Japan had been at war all year over Korea and Manchuria. Russia's naval fleets had suffered terrible losses, and the Japanese had defeated the Russian army in battle after battle. The bloody conflict showed no sign of an end, yet remarkably, both countries had put aside their differences to build exhibits at the World's Fair a few hundred yards from each other, without incident.

Their tour guide carried on with George, Albert, and Bert marveling as they passed the exhibits from Egypt, Ethiopia, Turkey, Colombia, Haiti, Peru, and even Australia and New Zealand. They had never seen anything like it in their lives.

A quick stop at Hagenbeck's Zoological Paradise and Animal Circus allowed them to wander for a few minutes among hundreds of harmless but beautiful domesticated animals and birds. But that was nothing compared to the protected area in which they could see through high fences wild elephants, lions, tigers, zebras, and even polar bears and mountain goats. They had only ever seen pictures of animals like these before. George and Albert made a pact to come back with their whole families.

As they pulled away from the zoo area, George noticed a large crowd around a smaller exhibit. "What's going on there?" Their guide pulled the wicker chair to a stop, and the men pushed their way to the front of the laughing crowd.

A man with a speaking trumpet barked at the crowd: "Step forward ladies and gentlemen, and children of all ages! See this amazing horse, Jim Key, The Educated Horse. He'll perform mathematical calculations, count money, and even tell time. He can answer any question you have. Step closer, folks. He won't bite. After all, he's an educated horse! Who will be the first person to ask Jim a question today?"

Conscious of the time, Albert called out, "What time is it, Jim?" The crowd laughed and everyone looked at the clock hanging on the side of Jim's stall to see that it was in fact two o'clock.

The horse's handler, with dramatic hand gestures and great flair, asked the horse, "Jim, what time is it?" The horse turned his head, looked at the clock on the wall, then turned back, and selected a wooden block with the number two on it. His handler announced proudly, "Jim has correctly told us that it is two o'clock!" The crowd burst into applause. Other members of the crowd began to shout out questions to spell simple words like "cat" and "fair."

It wasn't clear if he wanted a cold drink or was testing Jim, but Bert called out "root beer!" Without so much as a stumble Jim spelled each word flawlessly with his wooden blocks.

One wisenheimer called out, "Jim what's three times six, plus five, minus nine?" The crowd groaned as if surely the horse could not be expected to answer this question. The handler held up his hands and asked for quiet. Slowly and dramatically, he repeated the calculation to Jim. The horse turned his head, selected two blocks, and placed them on the table in front of the crowd.

"Jim has correctly selected the answer fourteen!" The crowd again burst into applause, and someone called out, "Jim for President!"

Albert stood looking at his pocket watch. "Bert, George, I think we need to consider working our way back to the train station." The trio climbed back into the wicker cart, with their guide telling them that they would need to return to the fair and excitedly listing the many things they were missing.

"Now, when you return you must go watch the reenactment of a full battle scene from the Boer War. They stage it where the Brits are chasing a Boer General through the jungle, and it comes to a dramatic conclusion as the General rides his horse off a thirty-foot cliff—well, a stage that looks like a cliff, really—into a huge pool of water. And every day at noon, there is a reenactment of scenes from the Old West, as a Pony Express rider delivers mail while under assault by hostile Indians. And in the fields over there, you can watch as hundreds of Indians and soldiers reenact Custer's Last Stand. Will Rogers portrays a dying Custer. It is really something to see. Every day at four o'clock."

"Sounds like we would need a week to see it all, but it's getting late. If we have time for one more stop, what would you recommend?" said George to the driver.

The college student thought for a moment, and then said they had some choices: "On the one hand, I could take you to the very popular Under and Over the Sea exhibit. They pretend to take you on a submarine ride to Paris to see the Eiffel Tower and on a balloon ride over New York City. You're really just looking down on very detailed miniature models of cities, but the effect is quite realistic. On the other hand, the Anthropological Exhibit is quite an eye-opener, and it's on the way back to the train station. Shall we stop there?"

"Sounds wonderful—and practical," said Albert.

"Wait! Can I get one of those before we go?" pleaded Bert, pointing to a vendor's booth with a long line in front. "I saw someone eating it in line at Geronimo."

"What are they selling? Looks popular," George said.

Before the student could answer, Bert called out, "Ice cream!" and leapt from the wicker chair to get in line.

The guide explained that it *was* ice cream but served a whole new way. "It was something invented by accident. That vendor was selling ice cream, but one hot day, business was so good he ran out of dishes, and he was going to close up early. But that fellow over there," he pointed to another food vendor, "a Syrian fellow, was selling waffles. He got the idea of folding a waffle into a cone shape and then putting the scoop of ice cream in it. Eat the ice cream *and* the cone. People have been going crazy for ice cream cones all summer." Before Albert could say a word, George jumped out of the cart to stand in line with Bert.

Ice cream cones in hand, the men set off to the Anthropological Exhibit. As they approached the area, their guide said in a hopeful voice and as if on a safari, "We might be lucky and catch some of the primitives in action. Sometimes they have them competing in games in the afternoon."

Albert and George looked at each other. "Primitives? Where were they being taken?" wondered George.

"We might even be able to see the cannibals from the Hamatsa tribe. I heard a rumor that at night they sneak out of the fairgrounds and catch local dogs for dinner. I hope that is not true, of course."

"Cannibals?! Eating dogs?! What on earth are you taking us to see?" George exclaimed.

No sooner had he uttered those words than their wicker chariot rolled up in front of a full Philippine village. Forlorn-looking, half-naked men, women, and children huddled near huts watching them approach. The driver slowed their cart, and they were not ten feet from the enclosure when he began his tour speech. "These primitives were brought here to the fair so people could see how they live in their part of the world."

The driver moved on slowly to the next enclosure where more solemn figures silently watched as they passed. "Over there, we can see some of the Patagonian giants brought in from South America." He pointed to a group of tall, bored-looking, half-naked men behind a fence, who stood holding what looked like spears. "Yesterday, a Negrito won the pole climbing event. They're very good at throwing spears and rocks, even shooting arrows. The fair organizers had a one-mile race for them and an Indian won it, a man called Black White Bear. When they win a competition, they're given a small American flag as a prize—"

George, mouth agape, had heard enough. "Stop. Stop. For heaven's sake. What are you talking about? What have you brought us to see?" he said, shifting in his seat. "This is outrageous. I cannot bear another word." George felt he was looking at people behind bars. To him, their enclosure seemed no different than Hagenbeck's Zoological Paradise for animals that they had visited only moments ago. "Please carry us out of here. Can we go?" said Albert.

Shocked, the young man brought the chair to a stop. "I'm not sure I understand. I'm just showing you the exhibit—"

"This is no exhibit. This is no more than a human zoo! How dare they create something like this?" George was furious.

The guide, feeling as though he had said something wrong, tried to explain himself. "It's been very popular..."

"Indeed," George said. "It's a wonder there hasn't been an uprising by these poor people."

"Actually, the only people who have really caused any trouble during the fair have been the Negroes. They have been complaining that the organizers didn't give enough of the jobs building the fair to them. There was supposed to be a special Negro Day when they would have been allowed to have their own parades, concerts, and shows."

"A special day?" George was aghast.

"Yes, but it all had to be canceled. The Eighth Illinois, the all-black army regiment, was supposed to march in the Negro Day parade. But then they wanted to pitch their tents on the fairgrounds. My gosh, that would've meant nine hundred black men camping at the fair. When the fair organizers said no, there would be no camping on the fairgrounds, well, the regiment canceled their appearance in protest. In the end, the organizers just canceled the whole Negro Day."

"I wonder how George Poage felt about that." George said, almost to himself.

"Who?" the young man asked.

"George Poage, from the Milwaukee Athletic Club, and a student at the University of Wisconsin. How would he feel about that?"

The student looked at him puzzled. "I don't know him."

"Mr. Poage has been the first black American to compete in these very Olympics. He has been the first to compete in any Olympics. He has been here in St. Louis, competing. He was the first black American to win a medal at the Olympics. He took the bronze in the two-hundred-meter race and competed in the hurdles. Have you not heard of him?"

"I didn't know that. I never heard anything about him." The student seemed dumbfounded.

"No, I guess you did not. Gentlemen, I think I have seen enough. Shall we head for Glen Echo?"

"I think that would be a good idea, George. Let's not let this last bit spoil our visit. We have seen some wonderful things."

"Yes, we have."

They carried on in silence through the crowds back to the front gate. But no sooner had they arrived and paid the student for his services than a group of men scrambled by in a panic carrying another man on a stretcher. They tried desperately to load him into an automobile where a doctor waited for him. A man's straw hat blew off and landed at George's feet. When he handed it back, George immediately recognized the man he had spoken to at the gates when they arrived. The man with the rat poison/brandy potion.

"Have you killed him with that rat poison?" George asked.

"No! He won! He won the marathon ... and a gold medal! But he is too exhausted to accept the victory trophy from Governor Francis. We are taking him to the Physical Culture Building to recover." And with that, the man jumped into the car and it sped away in a cloud of dust.

"What was that all about, George? Is that fellow all right?"

"Albert, I wouldn't know where to start ... Perhaps we should go back and ask Jim, the Educated Horse."

12

Youth Will Not Be Denied

EORGE, ALBERT, AND BERT arrived after dark at the train station near Glen Echo following their half day at the fair. They were still overwhelmed by what they had seen during their excursion, and they were tired. Albert had called ahead to make sure a cab was waiting to pick them up at the train station. Although it was late, the cab driver was excited to see them.

"Gentlemen, welcome to St. Louis and the Glen Echo Olympics," he said, as he put their clubs into the storage box on the back of his six-wheel Toledo Pullman. "But it's a shame you missed the opening contests. Even with the rain, it's been quite a day today."

Bert couldn't contain himself and began to rhyme off the sights and sounds of the World's Fair to the cab driver; it had been an unforgettable, eye-opening day for him. "What have we missed that could top that adventure?"

"Well, there was the driving contest this afternoon," the cabbie explained as he opened the back door for them. "Each golfer had to tee off from the clubhouse onto a checkerboard grid. And depending on where he landed on the grid, he was awarded points."

"It sounds like we missed a bit of fun, George," Albert said, nudging him.

"The shortest distance by any golfer was 175 yards. Douglas Cadwallader from Illinois had the longest drive of the day—some 238 yards—but it was just off the grid, so he didn't get any points. I guess the longest drive didn't even count."

"He must have been disappointed," George said, as the cabbie pulled onto the road.

"He was, indeed, and then a golfer put *two* long drives on the grid, at 202 and 234 yards. Imagine, 234 yards, straight as an arrow! I was standing right beside the fellow when they announced that he'd won. They're giving him a silver cup for longest drive."

"Who was it? Who won?" Albert asked as he leaned forward through to the front of the cab.

"It was that Chandler Egan fellow from Harvard. You must have heard of him."

Albert turned to look at George, who seemed more interested in the dark scenery on the way to Glen Echo than in long drive contests. George had expected to hear the name Chandler Egan many times over the course of the week. "The young man is off to a strong start from the sounds of it," he thought.

The cabbie continued, "Earlier this evening, they had the putting contest. Wait until you see that setup. They rigged the entire putting course with electric lights so you can play at night." As he drove, the driver gestured enthusiastically with his hands, taking them off the wheel every once in a while as the car veered over bumps in the road.

"Golf at night," said Albert, tickled. "What will they think of next, George? Shall we propose something like that for Lambton?" Albert was already planning, but George didn't seem to notice. He was still deep in thought about things he had seen at the World's Fair.

The cabbie continued his narrative, excited to show off his tour guide knowledge of what had transpired throughout the day at Glen Echo. "The putting contest seemed like a real struggle," he said matter-of-factly. "A Mr. Burt McKinnie from Normandie Golf Club and another man from Exmoor Golf Club—the same club as Mr. Egan—were tied going into the final hole. But McKinnie hung on and scored a twenty-one overall, so he'll take home the putting trophy. This afternoon, they had the thirty-six-hole team events. I could tell that they had a bit of trouble organizing that part of the competition," he said reflectively, "what with the golfers not showing. But they finally got the teams reorganized and out on the course. The western team was led by—"

George snapped out of his daze and cut him off, leaning forward in the cab. "What trouble with golfers not showing?"

But the cabbie was more interested in finishing his story. "The western team was led by Chandler Egan, of course, and they won the event. He's quite a golfer. Just twenty years old. Amazing—"

"But what were you saying about the other golfers?" George interrupted again. "The ones from England, Scotland, France? Mr. Hilton? Mr. Braid? How have they performed? And Mr. Travis? How has he fared?"

The cabbie glanced back over his shoulder at them. "Have you not heard?"

"Heard what?" Albert and George spoke in near unison.

"None of the golfers came from overseas. A boat had been promised to bring them all over together, but something happened and the whole thing fell through. I heard a rumor that some big wig was actually telling everyone the Olympics would be a big flop. But who knows what's really happening."

"You mean to say—"

"The only golfers competing at these Olympics are Americans. And of course now you three. You're the internationals."

George fell back in his seat. "Good Lord, what kind of world championship is this going to be?" He had longed to compete against Europe's top men but hid his disappointment as best he could. At least he would meet and perhaps cross swords with the great Walter Travis. There would be some consolation in that, George thought. "And, how did Mr. Travis fare in the driving and putting contests?" he asked.

"I'm sorry, Mr. Lyon, I'm guessing that you really have missed the news. Mr. Travis withdrew from the competition on Wednesday. He said he had business to attend to."

George looked at Albert, devastated. No Europeans. No Scotsmen. No Englishmen. No Walter Travis. Everything George had hoped and prepared for was disappearing in one bumpy cab ride. They drove in silence the rest of the way.

As they pulled up to the clubhouse, Albert finally asked, "Did Mr. Travis make clear the kind of business he needed to attend to so urgently? Was there an emergency?"

"The papers didn't say. To be honest, sir, some say rumor is it's just an excuse. Since Chandler Egan won the U.S. Amateur last week at Baltusrol Golf Club, well, Mr. Travis might not have the heart to be beaten by a boy of twenty twice in one month. Everyone says he's too old—past his prime. If you ask me, it's a new era in golf—it's a young man's game now—"

George wouldn't hear any more idle speculation about Travis's motives and interjected, "If Mr. Travis said he has business that will keep him from the Olympics, then we should take him at his word. Golfers everywhere owe him a good measure of respect for what he's achieved in golf. How quickly people forget. No other man, young or old, as you say, can claim his legacy." George was tired and sounded stern, which was not like him, but he wouldn't take criticism of Walter Travis lightly.

The driver was a little taken aback. "I'm sorry if I've given offense, Mr. Lyon, but it's all over the papers." He took the local paper from the front seat of the cab as they stepped out. "Mr. Travis is forty-two, Mr. Egan is twenty. It will be a long week of golf, starting Monday. Weather's been a challenge and the upcoming week looks to be bad. I think this quote about sums it up. Page seven." He flipped through the pages and handed it to George. "Here, read this."

George spread the paper out on the hood of the car and read aloud from where the cabbie's finger pointed to a story by sports writer George Westlake. "'Youth will not, cannot be denied.'"

The driver nodded. "Look what happened to Travis at the U.S. Amateur earlier this month. He never got past the second round, losing to that Ormiston fellow from Oakmont, three and one. Then Egan went on to win. Travis lost to that youngster Jerry Travers as well at the invitational tournament at Nassau earlier this year. My money's on the kid—no offense to you gents from Canada, but Egan is unstoppable."

"None taken," said Albert, intervening. He gave the driver a generous tip and shepherded George along to the clubhouse lobby. Despite the cabbie's brashness, Albert thought his information had been useful, and whereas Lyon was disappointed, a shrewd Albert saw a possible advantage in a weaker field.

The three men climbed the stairs to their rooms. "I know you must be disappointed, George. It seems that winning the cup and an Olympic gold medal is a foregone conclusion," Albert said solemnly. "They might as well give it to that youngster from Harvard. As the cab driver said, I guess it's a young man's game." He looked mischievously for his friend's reaction. "I'll make arrangements to get our railcar loaded for the trip back to Toronto tomorrow. It's been a waste of time. Don't unpack the luggage, Bert." He winked at his son. "Let's get a good night's sleep, and tomorrow we will head home. At least we saw the World's Fair."

"All right, Albert, all right," said George, cracking a smile. He knew that his friend was having a bit of fun with him; he had no intention of going home, and the cabdriver's comments about youth had already provided him with some unintended motivation. "You know, Walter Travis's mates goaded him before a match, too. During the British Amateur, they told him that all the other golfers were better than him. That he had little chance. That he was in over his head. Apparently, that teasing—along with copious amounts of stout and games of cribbage each night—kept his head on the golf and his feet on the ground." Albert was laughing, delighted that George had finally caught on. "We will be staying, and we will be staying until the very end. And I certainly hope we enjoy some stout and cribbage in the evenings, as Mr. Travis did." George clapped Albert on the back. "It's been a long day. Good night, gentlemen. I'll see you for breakfast."

The next morning, as the sun struggled to cut through the rain clouds, George stood alone on the soggy first tee of Glen Echo with his clubs over his shoulder. It was early

Sunday morning, September 18, and a light mist hung over the lower portions of the course. He stared down the first fairway and took in those sweet, quiet moments all golfers cherish before heading out to explore. He imagined Travis there beside him.

George took a minute to check his nine clubs: a driver, a brassie, a second lead-weighted brassie, two Forgan irons, a Spalding midiron, a corrugated-faced pitcher, a dot-faced patterned iron, and finally, his putter—his cherished putter, given to him by Young Tom Morris himself. In his bag, he had a half dozen brand-new Spalding Wizards. The ad in the 1903 Spalding catalog had promised, *"Well drove 'twill fly from tee to green. It is not an experiment but a pronounced success."* He had also slipped in a half dozen reliable Haskells, just in case. It would be a long week.

Everything was in good order.

He pinched up a small mound of wet sand, placed down a bright, white Wizard, and pulled his worn but familiar driver from the canvas bag. He settled naturally into his comfortable cricket-like stance, and with a crack that was muffled by the humid air, struck his Wizard into the mist and headed out alone.

Three hours later, feeling refreshed, he joined the Austins for breakfast. Albert had finished a pot of tea and now rubbed his hands in anticipation. "Shall we make our way to the course for a practice round? See the lay of the land, as they say?"

George took a hungry bite of his toast and eggs. "Done, my friend. I played eighteen early this morning."

Albert sat back in his chair with a smile. "You've played eighteen already?"

"Yes, and I'll tell you something..."

"What's that?"

"The course is magnificent. One of the finest I've ever seen. It's a little wet, mind you, especially on the greens, but it will test our skills, there's no doubt." George turned to the waiter, "Can I trouble you for some more coffee, my good man? Thank you."

"Shall we head out for a round, Father?" Bert asked Albert.

"I think you two should definitely play eighteen holes. Especially since your father is expected to play Colonel McGrew for the international Presidents trophy later this week," said George.

"What?" Austin had no idea of his sudden obligations now as the sole international club president.

"I've been puttering about the clubhouse—very pretty, and I may have some ideas for Lambton—and I've reviewed all the postings. This Friday, you and Colonel McGrew will play a thirty-six-hole match for the Presidents Cup."

"Good Lord. Come on, son, we had better get to the course if I'm expected to defend Canada's honor."

As Albert and Bert headed out, George decided to explore the fancy new electric putting practice area. It would be time well spent.

13

Hard Luck

"GENTLEMEN, LADIES, IF I may please have your attention." Colonel McGrew held a speaking trumpet up to his mouth as he stood in front of the Glen Echo clubhouse. Beside him on the porch stood a long table draped with red velvet and beneath the rich cloth sat the Olympic trophies. "As of today, Monday, September 19, thirteen registered golfers have withdrawn or did not arrive, dropping the total registration to seventy-five men who will compete in today's qualifying rounds. As you have no doubt heard, the field is composed of seventy-two Americans and three gentlemen from Canada, Mr. George Lyon, Mr. Albert Austin, and his son Bert Austin, all of Lambton Golf Club in Toronto." The crowd of golfers, spectators, and reporters gave a mild but warm round of applause. "Of those seventy-five men, only thirty-two golfers will compete in the match play rounds for the trophy and the Olympic medals." That statement sent a buzz through the crowd; more than half of those golfers standing there would know before the end of the day whether they had a chance for the gold medal. They would need to give it all or nothing if they hoped to move forward.

McGrew continued, "Those thirty-two golfers will enter their match play events over the next four days. The final round will be played this Saturday. And the winner will be the Olympic champion." He gestured grandly to the table as a young man pulled away the velvet cover to reveal a magnificent silver trophy and a row of freshly minted medals.

George and Albert looked at each other, eyebrows raised. Both of them had seen golf trophies before—George had acquired many fine ones—but neither had ever seen a trophy to rival this one. It was easily two and a half feet tall, with two large handles that swept from near the top of the trophy and curled down to the base. In the center, under ornate leafwork, was a depiction of the Glen Echo Golf Club. The gleaming cup sat on a dark ebony base. A local businessman whom McGrew identified at the edge of the crowd had sponsored it. There was more applause for his generosity.

Before continuing, McGrew took a moment to himself, held his breath, and prayed that these Games for which he had worked so hard would not plummet into any further disaster. He had been shocked and very disappointed when he learned that, other than the Canadians, not a single golfer from abroad had ventured to these Games. *Could the invitation that was published in* Golf Illustrated *have been more generous? More welcoming?* He had even made a point of expressing how exciting it would have been to see England's top golfers face America's in a final. Transportation had been arranged. Yet none had registered, and none had made the journey. Not even the Maori champion of New Zealand. Now was not the time for recrimination, but he vowed privately that he would get to the bottom of this snub after the Games.

McGrew lifted the speaking trumpet to his lips again and called the first golfer to the tee. "I have asked Mr. Havemeyer of Deal Beach, New York, to open the qualifying round of the 1904 Olympic Games golf competition. If he could please make his way to the tee."

George turned to Albert. "Did he say Havemeyer?" George and Albert immediately recognized the name of the man who had founded the U.S. Amateur Golf Association, the very man who had donated the U.S. Amateur Championship trophy, the Havemeyer Cup, the man known in business circles as the famed Sugar King.

Albert strained to see the man at the tee. "Theodore Havemeyer passed away a few years ago. I think it was the same year as my father. I would love to have met him. I have heard so much."

George, Albert, and Bert squeezed to the front of the crowd, and George turned to the man beside him and whispered, "Excuse me, but the gentleman about to tee off. Is he of the famous Havemeyer family?"

The man who stood with a notebook in his hand and a pencil behind his ear turned to George, pulled a cigar from his mouth, and said, "He is, indeed. Are you competing?"

"Yes, I am. We all are." George introduced himself and the Austins.

"Ah, you gentlemen are the internationals." He said this as if it was of great interest. "I am George Westlake of the *Chicago Evening Post*. I will be covering the games. We *must* have a word..." But before they were able to speak, McGrew called for quiet on the tee. Havemeyer stepped forward and, without any undue delay, hit a modest 180-yard drive down the left side of the fairway of Glen Echo's first hole, Lilac Way. The gallery now showed its appreciation with a much more enthusiastic burst of applause. The competition was finally underway.

As Colonel McGrew smiled, let out a sigh of relief, and raised his speaking trumpet to announce the next golfer, his son-in-law, Albert Lambert, tugged at his sleeve and whispered something in his ear. The next scheduled competitor was nowhere to be found. McGrew frowned, stood up straight, and called out firmly.

"Dr. Shaw. Will Dr. Wallace Shaw please make his way to the first tee? You are away, sir." He repeated it one more time for good measure, turning his trumpet toward the clubhouse. There was no response. Members of the gallery began to mutter, and murmurs of Shaw's name spread through the crowd. Suddenly, from around the corner of the clubhouse, a man came running—luggage in one hand and golf bag in the other.

"I'm here. I'm here." The poor man was breathless as he arrived at the first tee. "I'm sorry..." he puffed, "the train was delayed, and I've just arrived." He dropped his bag and began to wipe his forehead with a handkerchief. "I've been on the train continuously since Friday afternoon. It was a dreadful trip. I'm so sorry..."

"Mind the gentleman's luggage," McGrew called out hastily for someone to remove it from the tee box and leaned over to speak to the late arrival. "Doctor, you're scheduled to tee off. Take a moment to compose yourself and please join the competition." With that he turned to Albert Lambert and said, "Get the poor man a caddie." He then raised the trumpet one more time and called out: "Next on the tee, Dr. Wallace Shaw of Westfield, Massachusetts, from Tekoa Golf Club."

Dr. Shaw fumbled in his bag for a ball, pulled out a club, and walked to the tee. Those close to him could see that the doctor had not quite caught his breath, and he was sweating profusely. George watched Westlake scribble notes as the doctor set his ball on a small mound of sand. Two slow and graceful practice swings followed, and the gallery once again held its collective breath. However, any sense of grace disappeared as Dr. Shaw dug in his feet and took his first swing. His arms and shoulders tightened and his face contorted. What followed was more akin to a violent lash than a stroke. The ball shot hard right over Westlake's head, striking a large tree, and bouncing into a hedge on the right side of the fairway.

The crowd let out a sympathetic groan.

Embarrassed, the doctor looked to the heavens and walked quickly to the hedge followed by a young boy who suddenly found himself a caddie. The ball was at the edge and playable. Barely. He quickly took his stance. The next lash sent the ball to the tennis courts adjacent to the clubhouse. The crowd let out another groan amid a few laughs, as the doctor, again, looked to the heavens.

McGrew stared at the ground, embarrassed by this amateurish display from only the second golfer to tee off. "I pray the man is not a surgeon," he thought.

More lashes followed, and Dr. Shaw was now ten yards in front of where he had originally stood on the first tee. He was lying seven. His caddie looked dismayed. His eighth shot would find the rough and draw even more laughs from the gallery. And so it went as he headed down Lilac Way. But, to his credit, Dr. Shaw would not be deterred. He carried on, shooting 107 on his first eighteen holes that morning, and after a good lunch and a stiff drink, 102 on his second eighteen. He would learn later that afternoon that his qualifying thirty-six-hole score of 209 would not be good enough to allow him to move forward into the Olympic match play rounds. He would need to settle for the so-called consolation rounds.

Unfortunately, there wasn't any immediate consolation for the doctor, because that night, as he opened the newspaper, he would find (to his eternal shame and embarrassment) that his first hole was considered newsworthy. He stared at the headline in despair. "OLYMPIAN GOLF IS ON—George Westlake Special to the *Chicago Evening Post*. Dr. W.F. Shaw of Westfield Mass. developed the worst case of hard luck ever seen at a big tourney."

Stroke by stroke, Westlake would recount the doctor's embarrassing start to the day. It would not be the kind of press that Colonel McGrew hoped for his Olympics, and after dinner that night, he would make a point of having a word with Westlake.

Within an hour of Dr. Lake's terrible start, George, Albert, and Bert prepared to tee off in their own qualifying rounds. They had hoped to be paired together, but the random draw had spread them out, so they gathered at the side of the first tee, near the practice putting area, for one last conversation to wish each other well and good luck. Bert looked nervous, as if he feared suffering the same fate as Dr. Shaw. George and Albert each put an arm around his shoulders, and George offered one last piece of advice.

"Bert, remember when we played a practice round at Lambton in June this year? It was just before I left for Montreal for the championship. We stood on the first tee, and I have to admit, I was feeling like my game was not what it needed to be. I remember it because you had the honors and teed off ahead of me that day. I watched how you went through your own special routine before driving. I think you know what I mean: how you select your club so seriously, like a surgeon searching for the right scalpel, and then, as you stand behind the ball, you shake your shoulders like this to relax." George demonstrated, and Bert smiled, unaware until now that George had watched him so closely and could imitate his specific approach to teeing off. "I watched you that morning because it was as if you were imagining what the shot looked like. Visualizing it. Then you stepped calmly into your stance and crushed a beautiful drive out to the center of the fairway. It reminded me of just how important it is to have a routine and imagine the shot. Those are the things that will get one off to a good start. I try to remember that disciplined approach you have during my own games."

Bert swelled with confidence as he heard George's words. "I remember that round, Mr. Lyon. I shot an eighty that day. One of my best rounds ever."

"Remember that approach for every shot, and think of that round for the entire thirty-six holes today. You will do well."

Albert was nodding. "Those are wise words, Bert. Thank you, George. I intend to follow that advice myself. But can you do an imitation of *my* swing routine, too?" With that, the three men burst out laughing and headed for the first tee.

After George had hammered his first drive out to the fairway, he turned to tip his hat to Albert and Bert and shot off in his usual fashion, striding along the course like a man on a mission. Albert and Bert followed in good order with well-struck, confident drives. It would be a long, hard round as they worked their way around the course they had only played once before.

Very small galleries followed the Canadians. The biggest crowds were more interested in the local favorite, Stuart Stickney, and of course, the new reigning U.S. Amateur champion as of the previous week, Chandler Egan. A gallery of more than two hundred followed Egan's every move on the course as he competed in the thirty-six-hole qualifying rounds. Frankly, Albert and Bert were grateful for less attention. It was hard enough plotting one's way without the added pressure of spectators talking and calling out to their favorites, the constant opening and closing umbrellas, and, yes, even the occasional groans or bursts of laughter. Neither of them had played under such conditions, such pressure before.

George was waiting for them as they each arrived at the eighteenth hole. Albert arrived first. He looked exhausted but seemed satisfied with his game. Bert arrived in the next group with a spring in his step. He had played well and enjoyed every moment.

"Your advice served me well, Mr. Lyon."

"Excellent news, Bert. Let's thank our caddies and then shall we head up to the clubhouse and await the final scores? I could use something fortifying." As they sat in the clubhouse, George asked other golfers if they had seen Mr. Havemeyer.

"Why is it so important to meet him, Mr. Lyon?" Bert asked.

"Theodore Havemeyer was a very interesting man. He made millions in the sugar business, hence his handle, the Sugar King. Like many other wealthy Americans at the turn of the century he fell in love with golf. You probably didn't know this, but in 1893, there were only sixteen golf courses in the entire United States. Our clubs in Canada were well ahead—Royal Montreal was the first in North America, of course, but the U.S. quickly caught up. Seven years later, there were more than a thousand. That would not have happened were it not for the involvement of America's rich and powerful businessmen like Havemeyer who had become so intoxicated by golf. Of course, no one knows this better than your father."

George winked at Albert. "I was told that while on a holiday in Pau, France, Havemeyer had tried his hand at golf and, like many of his friends, got what was being called 'golf influenza.' When he returned to America, he enlisted some very powerful friends who summered with his family near Newport, Rhode Island—the Vanderbilts, the Astors, and the Belmonts for starters. There he constructed Newport Golf Club, the first nine-hole golf course in America."

"How do you know all this, George?" Albert was impressed by this sudden history lesson.

"When I played in the international matches, there was quite a bit of talk about Mr. Havemeyer. And to be honest, Harry Vardon was a bit of a gossip when we played at Rosedale a couple of years ago. I was a good listener—for a change. In any event, in December 1894, as interest in golf was exploding across the U.S., Havemeyer was one of nine men who gathered for dinner at the prestigious Calumet Club in New York City—"

"I have been to it. Beautiful club at Fifth Avenue and 29th Street," Albert chimed in.

"The topic for discussion that evening? The future of golf in America, of course. Apparently, that night representatives from the most influential golf clubs in the U.S.—St. Andrew's of Yonkers; Newport Golf Club; the Country Club of Brookline, Massachusetts; the Chicago Golf Club; Shinnecock Hills Golf Club"—George counted them off on his fingers—"formed the U.S. Amateur Golf Association, and their first order of business was to call for a national championship the following year. Well, Havemeyer announced that he would be honored to host the first competition at Newport."

"Havemeyer donated the cup," Albert added, "hence, the Havemeyer Cup. It's apparently worth $1,000."

"And the 1895 Amateur Open was a success. It was won by Charles Blair Macdonald, stockbroker, you may recall. He was born in Niagara Falls, Ontario, so I guess we could count him as a Canadian." George laughed. "He was educated in Scotland and learned his golf from Old Tom Morris. Quite a pedigree. He was the first person to take home Havemeyer's namesake USGA trophy. And very proud of it he was."

The three men leaned in on their elbows, drinks in hand, as George and Albert alternated tossing out historical tidbits to Bert.

"Not only did he fund the cup, Albert, Havemeyer paid the expenses of all eleven golfers who played in the amateur competition that first year. But apparently, that inaugural competition was a picnic compared to the trouble that surfaced for him the next year at Shinnecock Hills."

"Why? What happened?" Bert was keen to learn more about the famous Sugar King.

"That year, 1896, the U.S. Amateur was played in July at the Shinnecock Hills Golf Club in Southampton. Its beautiful, very stately clubhouse had been designed by none other than Stanford White, one of America's top architects. The course itself had been designed with the help of those two Scotsmen, Willie Davis and our own architect for Lambton, Willie Dunn—"

"Mr. Dunn told me a little about that project before I came to terms with him to design our Lambton layout. But he never said anything about Havemeyer..."

"Well, as you well know, Mr. Dunn is a man of few words, and those words are usually only about the golf course itself. Anyway, Shinnecock quickly became the center of a posh social circle of wealthy East Coast society. La-di-da." Albert nodded. He knew this already, as some of his American

George Lyon with his clubs and the cup. *Lambton Golf and Country Club*

ABOVE: George Lyon. *Canadian Golf Hall of Fame and Museum*

FACING TOP: Surveying the devastation of the Great Fire of Toronto (April 1904). *The Archives of Ontario*

FACING BOTTOM: Watching the Great Fire of Toronto from one of many rooftops (April 1904).

ABOVE: The Ferris Wheel at the 1904 St. Louis World's Fair.

FACING: An original postcard from the 1904 St. Louis World's Fair.

OFFICIAL SOUVENIR
WORLD'S FAIR— ST. LOUIS 1904

Entrance Palace of Liberal Arts.

Sept. 9, 04

Dear Elesia!— There are lots
of things here that you would
like.
Eleanor.

SAMUEL CUPPLES ENVELOPE CO. ST. LOUIS. MO. SOLE WORLDS FAIR STATIONERS.

The Lambton Golf and Country Club in 1904.
Lambton Golf and Country Club

Replica of the 1904 gold medal.

George Lyon's "Coal Heaver" swing. *Canadian Golf Hall of Fame and Museum*

counterparts often held court, as it were, with this same high society. "They dress as British Redcoats, with their shiny buttons, wingtip collars on stiff shirts, and checkered caps. It's all standard fare for this golfing crowd. Golf at Shinnecock is a society event."

"It sounds wonderful," said Bert.

"If one can afford it, I suppose it is," said George pragmatically. "The Amateur and Open events had been scheduled back to back that year, with the Open competition more or less a sideshow to the main event played between the amateurs."

"What was the difference?" Bert asked.

"To the USGA, an amateur golfer meant someone who had never made for sale clubs, balls, or other articles associated with golf, never caddied after the age of fifteen or hadn't caddied in the last six years. It included someone who was never paid for a match or to give lessons. This definition effectively excluded virtually every golf teacher in America. You need to understand, Bert, that so many English and Scottish golfers had made their way to the U.S. to teach at all these new courses and clubs..."

"Usually after a paycheck, they invited their brothers or friends to come over as well to find jobs with all these new courses," Albert added with a knowing smile.

"That is true. But these professionals, they needed their own competition. In fact, truth be told, although a stigma may not have applied to their status as teaching professionals, there was what we might say was a mutual tension between the wealthy Americans and these rough-hewn foreigners who taught them. Would you say that is a fair description, Albert?"

"Mutual tension? Yes, quite fair, I'd say."

"The wealthy pupils wanted to keep to their tight social circles as much as the clannish Scottish professionals kept to theirs—"

Albert interrupted. "I think, frankly, some of them looked down their noses at these rich amateurs, not to mention at what they thought were these crude new golf courses. Not like back home, as they would say. The money was excellent, though, far better than anything they could earn in Scotland, but these rich people were not what they considered real golfers." Albert leaned back and reflected for a moment on his own words: had Willie Dunn thought of Austin's family in that light as he worked on Lambton? "Impossible," Albert thought.

"But let me back up first. The 1895 competition at Newport, Rhode Island, was held in October—" George continued.

"Rather than in September, which would have distracted from the America's Cup." Albert was a fan of yacht racing.

"Macdonald won it over Charles Sands. For the Open winner, there would be a $150 prize and a gold medal, and the trophy would go to the winner's club. Nineteen-year-old Horace Rawlins, an Englishman who was the assistant pro at Newport, stunned the field by defeating Willie Dunn from Shinnecock Hills. My old friend Curley Smith from Toronto tied for third with Jim Foulis, who at that time was the pro from the Chicago Golf Club. They each took home $50.

"In 1896 it was moved to July. The amateur portion went off without a hitch, but Charles Macdonald had to turn over the Havemeyer Cup to H.J. Whigham. But the professionals' Open challenge would be another matter. My goodness." George was shaking his head.

"Why?" Bert was hooked on this story.

"The Open competition was scheduled for the next day, but apparently, that evening, more than twenty of the professional golfers held a private meeting and then cornered the Sugar King, demanding that he ban two professional golfers or else they would all boycott the next day's competition."

"Boycott? Why?" Bert was puzzled by all this intrigue around a simple golf tournament

"We *must* meet Havemeyer to see if he has any more details. I'm certain he has a story to tell about that night," said George, looking for him as golfers continued to come through the clubhouse after their matches.

George stopped a young man as he passed. "Excuse me, my name is George Lyon and these are my friends Albert and Bert Austin. We have been looking for Mr. Havemeyer. I was certain I heard his named called this morning by Colonel McGrew when he announced the competitors. Do you know him?"

"I know him, indeed. I am Arthur Havemeyer. My cousin Raymond and I are here competing. Theodore was our uncle."

"Well, this is fortuitous, isn't it, Albert?" said George, quickly rising from his chair to shake Arthur's hand enthusiastically. "We are so pleased to meet you. Won't you join us for a drink? I had heard a story about your uncle's involvement in the controversy at Shinnecock Hills in 1896. He took a very brave stand against a determined group of strong-minded—and wrong-minded—professional golfers."

"Yes, I discussed that Shinnecock evening with my uncle many times." Arthur could see Bert's eyes light up as he sat down to join the group. "I can only join you for a few moments, but let me tell you quickly what my uncle told me. The professional golfers wanted to ban John Shippen, an eighteen-year-old assistant pro at Shinnecock Hills Golf Club, and Oscar Bunn, a Shinnecock caddie. Shippen was black, and Bunn was an Indian. If they played, then none of the professionals would play. That was their ultimatum."

Bert was aghast. "But why?" The men looked at each other awkwardly.

Arthur went on to explain that John Shippen's father, a black preacher, had taught at the Shinnecock Indian reservation and married a native woman. Many of the Indians from that reserve had provided the labor needed to construct Shinnecock's golf course. Both Shippen and Oscar Bunn had been trained as caddies by the club's pro, Willie Dunn.

"We know Mr. Dunn well. He assisted us with the design of Lambton in Canada," Albert added.

"Lambton. I have heard of the course, and that it is a real test. I would love to visit sometime."

"Please be my guest. Consider it an open invitation," Albert offered.

"I will give that some serious thought. Thank you. My business associates and I have plans to travel to Toronto in—"

"But what happened to those boys, Shippen and Bunn?" Bert interrupted.

The men laughed and could see that Bert needed to know the end of the story that George had started. Arthur continued, "Willie Dunn had so much confidence in young Shippen's golf skills that he let him give lessons at the club. In fact, many of the Shinnecock members had encouraged the two boys to compete in the Open. Not in the rarified air of the Amateur, mind you, but why not in the lesser sideshow of the Open? But at this meeting, and with the threat of a boycott on his hands, my uncle listened carefully to the group's complaints, thought for a moment, and then announced his ruling as president of the USGA. He said the Open would go forward the next day, as planned, even if there were only two golfers in it, one named Shippen and the other named Bunn. He then wished them a cold goodnight."

"He risked the entire Open competition. It was a brave stand," George added.

"Those twenty white golfers probably did not know that my uncle and his brother, Frederick—thrice-elected mayor of New York City, I might add—were ardent supporters of the abolition of slavery during and after the Civil War. Both enjoyed a strong sense of justice. The professionals had played their hand to the wrong man."

"Did they boycott? What did they do?" Bert asked.

"The next morning at ten o'clock, my uncle strode to the first tee not quite sure what to expect. As he reached the tee, he saw twenty-four golfers, two of them nonwhite. He had called the professionals' bluff and demonstrated that the Association, not the players, made the rules and that *he* would enforce them."

"Good for him!" Bert was satisfied.

"But remember, they still had to play golf! That morning, my uncle paired the strong golfing credentials—if not strong personality—of past Amateur champion Charles Macdonald with young Shippen for the day. After the first eighteen holes, Shippen, having shot seventy-eight, was tied for the lead with two Scotsmen, Jim Foulis and Shippen's own mentor, Willie Dunn. Although Macdonald felt he had played himself out of the competition with an eighty-three in the morning, he still walked the course with Shippen in the afternoon round for moral support and kept his score. However, after a bad slice and a tough go on the thirteenth hole, Shippen ended up shooting an eighty-one, tying for fifth, and taking home $10. Jim Foulis won and took home the tidy sum of $200."

"Was Jim Foulis one of the twenty golfers who went to Havemeyer that night?" asked Bert.

There was another awkward silence as the men looked at each other. "I don't know, Bert, I don't know. My uncle never said."

"That is quite a story, Mr. Havemeyer. Thank you for sharing it with us." George was so delighted to have heard the tale and felt as satisfied as if he had just finished a feast of a meal.

"Please call me Arthur. I look forward to playing your fine course at Lambton someday." He looked at his pocket watch. "I must beg off, as I promised my cousin Raymond I would be waiting for him when he finished on eighteen. We have our own little competition going. I am sure you understand. It has been a pleasure." And with that, Arthur Havemeyer was off to the eighteenth green.

That evening, a large group of anxious golfers crowded around the veranda of the Glen Echo clubhouse once more, waiting for news on the results of the qualifying round. In the middle of the crowd—sharing an umbrella—stood George Westlake, chatting with the golfers and making notes for his next story.

Colonel McGrew stood on the top steps, out of the light rain that had started to fall, and asked for quiet. "The names of the qualifiers are posted behind me on the wall of the clubhouse. Those who did not make the list will play a consolation round on Wednesday against those who are unsuccessful in the first round of match play tomorrow. Therefore, everyone who has registered for the Olympics will play at least two matches. This Friday, Mr. Albert Austin, the international club president of Canada, and I will compete for the international Presidents trophy." McGrew gestured to the trophy table again, where the same young man unveiled and held aloft another fine trophy. McGrew looked at the trophy as if he had already made a place on his mantle for it.

Catching sight of this, George nudged Albert in the ribs, saying, "I can picture that cup on display at Lambton."

McGrew continued. "We are introducing an innovation to scoring the golf matches at these Olympics. As there are so many golfers on the course over the week, there will be no scorers accompanying players during their matches."

Confused murmurs shot through the crowd. *No scorers?*

"Please, please gentlemen, if I could have your attention. Instead, each competitor will carry *their opponent's* scorecard, and they will sign for their score after each hole. Submitting an incorrect scorecard will result in loss of the match and, therefore, disqualification. So pay attention to your own card and that of your opponent. I wish everyone good luck with their matches tomorrow, and after you have looked at the qualifiers list, I would like to invite you all to join me in the clubhouse grill for refreshments. Thank you all." A rousing cheer went up, and the men pressed forward toward the clubhouse. And the list.

George and Albert found themselves at the back of the line, shuffling forward. As they did, Westlake, notebook in hand, tugged at George's sleeve. "That's quite a golf swing you have there, Mr. Lyon. I am reminded of something, but I cannot quite put my finger on it. Where on earth did you learn it?"

George, not liking his tone, ignored Westlake and answered simply, "From a great friend. It has served me well."

"Indeed. It has served you through two Canadian Amateur Championships. And what about—"

"Three actually." George moved ahead in line.

Westlake was pushed away by the crowd of men making their way to the posting before he could ask another question. "Just as well," thought George.

Eventually, George, Bert, and Albert stood before a bright-white sheet of linen paper on the clubhouse wall. Above it was posted an elaborately scripted sign: "Golf Competition 1904

Olympic Qualifiers." Albert ran his finger down the list. "Here you are, George: 169. Well done! It says that tomorrow you meet a Mr. John Cady from Rock Island Golf Club. I'll see what I can find out about him."

They continued their scrutiny of the scores. "Arthur and Raymond Havemeyer have qualified too, with scores of 178 and 183. Arthur will have bragging rights on those scores. They will be meeting..." Albert ran his finger across the sheet, "Mr. Simeon Price from Normandie Golf Club and Mr. Robert Hunter from Midlothian Golf Club."

"Here is Chandler Egan. 166. That is a fine score." George was impressed.

"His cousin Walter beat him with a 165. That should make for an interesting conversation this evening." Albert laughed at the thought of cousins challenging each other.

However, it was the names of two men that stood out atop the sheet, each with a score of 163. Six shots better than George's 169. They were two local favorites from the St. Louis Golf Club, Stuart Stickney and Ralph McKittrick. "With local knowledge and experience on the Glen Echo course, they will be tough to beat," George thought. As he scanned the list of names, he felt a pang of regret that he did not see Walter Travis's name among the qualifiers.

"Father, I don't see your name on the list. Or mine," Bert whispered to Albert. They looked at the list again, running their fingers up and down. Albert hadn't qualified. And nor had poor Bert. They had missed by just a few strokes, and, like all golfers, both immediately recalled a couple of poor shots or missed putts that had probably cost them the qualification.

George was disappointed. "I'm so sorry, Albert, Bert. I was sure you'd both make it to the final round. I had imagined us playing matches against each other."

"Well, let's look on the bright side. I'll have another match on Wednesday, and it will be an excellent warm-up for the Presidents Cup match. Bert, you will have a consolation match on Wednesday. There is lots of golf ahead."

"That's the spirit," George said. "Let me buy you a drink, Albert." And they set off to celebrate at the clubhouse.

"I'll be heading back to the room. I have had enough for one day." Bert sounded tired and disappointed. Hours later, as he struggled to sleep, he could hear the men downstairs in the Glen Echo clubhouse singing a rousing chorus of "My Wild Irish Rose."

Led, no doubt, by one George Seymour Lyon.

$=$ **13** $=$

The Coal Heaver

WEDNESDAY, SEPTEMBER 21, 1904

EORGE KNEW THAT Annette never had any trouble opening his letters when they arrived at the Lyon home in Toronto. Marjorie and George Jr.'s little hands were always ready to help tear open an envelope if they thought it might be a letter or card from their father. He had only been gone since Friday—just five nights—but he knew that to them it would feel like an eternity. Before George left, Annette had promised to read his letters aloud in the library if the children sat quietly for her. George knew that she would follow the newspaper coverage about the matches in the *Toronto Daily*, and he also knew that she would be waiting for his letters to tell her what was really happening. So when he sat down to write Annette on Wednesday evening, he had in his mind a clear picture of her in front of the fireplace, the children at her feet.

My Dearest Annette (and Marjorie, George, and baby),

I arrived safe and sound at Glen Echo late Saturday evening with the Austins. By now, you should have received my post-cards from the St. Louis World's Fair. I picked the prettiest, most colorful souvenir cards that I could find for you and the children. It was a spur-of-the-moment decision to go, and what a marvelous decision it was! The entrance to the magnificent Palace of Liberal Arts is even more beautiful than the picture on the card. I bought you a set of stereoscopic cards for your viewfinder so that you might see some of the sights more closely, including the Ferris Wheel. With any luck, perhaps we can return together before the fair ends.

The golf matches have been quite a test, I will confess. I got in a practice round early Sunday morning, which made a difference for the qualifier on Monday. I was at least moderately familiar with the course. My only concern was to make the cut regardless of my score. Sadly, Albert and Bert did not qualify, but they are busy with other matches, and they have been excellent friends and supporters these first few days, which, I must say, has been needed at times. I have been grateful for their company.

The weather here in Missouri has been dreadful, with constant rain and wind. I was worried that any hot, humid weather might aggravate my terrible hay fever, like it has the past few weeks, so I have been secretly grateful for all this wet weather. I pray the hay fever will not be a bother later this week, as you know it really can take the wind from my sails.

We play thirty-six holes of golf each day: eighteen holes in the morning. We then have an opportunity for some lunch and a shower, and after that, we are back out on the course for another eighteen holes—unless one can dispatch an opponent *earlier. The course is very wet, muddy, and hilly, and simply walking it requires great effort. I have noticed that almost all the golfers are generally exhausted after the rounds. Ready for a drink and socializing, mind you, but exhausted. I know what you are thinking, my love. Yes, there have been a few sing-alongs and a bit of storytelling. They are all good men, and I have enjoyed their camaraderie.*

On Tuesday, I met a Mr. John Cady in a match: a very pleasant young man from the Rock Island Golf Club in Washington State. I was lucky to defeat him with a score of five and four. After the fourteenth hole was completed, we shook hands and walked back to the clubhouse together for dinner and drinks. I was not aware of it at the time, but we had started with a small gallery following us, and it grew to several dozen over the course of the day. Newspaper reporters among them. They are good fans of golf here and dozens of nongolfers have made their way out from the World's Fair by train to take in this competition. This has added to the traffic on the course, and the noise! Goodness, they sometimes talk and carry on as if they were at a cricket match or a baseball game.

The putting surfaces are unfamiliar and quite wet, so they have taken some getting used to. After Tuesday's match with Mr. Cady, and dinner, I slipped off to use the electrified putting area. You would be amazed at the sight. They have strung electric lights over a nine-hole practice putting course, so I was able to practice for two full hours. It was pitch black all around, but there I was, alone, putting under the lights with music and laughter pouring out from the clubhouse into the humid night. It was beautiful. As a result of that practice, I have become more familiar with the putting surfaces.

Now here is the shocker: Albert, Bert, and I are the only Canadians present, and therefore the only internationals.

Imagine! Not a soul arrived from Europe. No Maori champions either. There has been quite a buzz about mischief, and there have been rumors circulating that it was a deliberate snub of some kind. I have no time for gossip, but it has left a sour taste for some, especially Colonel McGrew, who threw his heart and soul into this competition.

The most disappointing news was that Walter Travis is not competing at these Olympics. I learned that from a cab driver, and I cannot tell you how upset it made me. I nearly asked to be taken back to the train station to return home. He has apparently been kept away by business, though some say that he is off form and afraid to meet the younger golfers. Personally, I do not believe it, and I recall my own disappointment at not being able to attend the Paris Olympics. I intend to write to him when I return home.

You know, my love, that I am not easy to anger, but my good nature was tested this morning when I opened the newspapers to see my victory over Mr. Cady ridiculed. Ridiculed! A Chicago newspaper correspondent who had been following the match characterized my swing as that of a coal heaver! Another paper said my swing was more appropriate for using a scythe than a golf club.

After he wrote those words, George had to smile at the thought of George Jr. asking, "What's a scythe?" He knew that Annette would put the letter down and stand up to demonstrate. He imagined her using her long skirt, swooshing it over the children, who would no doubt be screaming and laughing. He suddenly felt homesick.

I have written letters to both the local newspaper and the United States Golf Association. I told them whether I

play like a sailor, a coal heaver, or a farmer with a scythe, I
never said that I am proud of my form. I only do the best I
can. Competition is all well and good, but it can be spoiled by
unkind, critical comments about the way in which one plays
golf, rather than what is on the scorecard.

Annette would read between the lines and know that George
must have been seething inside, and that he was right when he
said he was not easy to anger. If his competitors were not taking him seriously, they were making a big mistake. George was
well known for preferring—no, *loving*—to be the underdog.

My efforts at practicing my putting paid dividends, as
the next match that I played today was against Mr. Stu-
art Stickney from St. Louis. When I arrived at the first tee
with him, a very large crowd had gathered to see our game. I
assumed it was to see Mr. Stickney, who was the medalist in
the qualifying round on Monday with a score of 163. He is
also a member of the local St. Louis Country Club and nat-
urally a local favorite. You can imagine my surprise when I
learned that many of those gathered had in fact come to see
the Coal Heaver! As I prepared to tee off, some young boys
called out "coal heaver" and laughed. Bert Austin quickly
shushed them, but it was a real insult and made me feel
unwelcome. I thought I saw Mr. Stickney smirking at the
comment too, and for a moment, I got the impression that
he was taking the match for granted. I was reminded again
of Walter Travis's treatment at Royal St. George's in May...

George reconsidered for a moment what he was about
to write. Annette had probably heard enough from George
about Travis's troubles in England earlier in the year. George

would never forgive or forget their treatment of a man he had never even met. After one of his angry rants about it, she had stopped him and said, "Honestly, George, you are like a dog with a bone." And then they had both burst out laughing when little Marjorie began running around the house excitedly calling out, "We are getting a dog! We are getting a dog!" It had taken them both a few hours to break the bad news to her that no, they were not getting a dog. George decided to leave out any further comments about Travis.

. . . and I knew that I would need to bear down for this match, as the crowd would clearly favor the local player. And bear down I did. Mr. Stickney had honors for the match, having won the toss. He teed off and hit a solid ball to the right center of the fairway, and from the applause, you would think he had already won the match. I dug in my feet and swung, and as I did, I could hear a gasp from the crowd as if to say, 'Goodness, what a swing.' But then, my dear, there was absolute silence. My drive sailed out and down the center of the fairway—I think everyone had held their breath—and then one of those same young boys cried out, 'He's driven the green!' That's right, my ball sat at the front edge of the green. I can tell you, the unfriendly remarks about my swing continued for only a few more holes after that. I dispatched Mr. Stickney, eleven and nine. We decided to finish the round. On the first eighteen holes, I shot a seventy-eight and was eight up. On the second eighteen holes, I shot a seventy-nine. Course records!

Annette put the letter in her lap for a moment and considered what joy her husband must have felt at the end of that match. But then the children demanded more news.

My driving was solid, as usual. But what made the differ-ence—as Mr. Travis always said—was putting. My practice the night before was rewarded, as my putting was cracker-jack during my match with Stickney.

Tomorrow, I face the most difficult test to date: Mr. Albert Lambert. He is the last Olympic champion, having won in Paris four years ago in the handicap event. To make mat-ters even tougher for me, he is a member of Glen Echo Golf Club and is very familiar with this, his home course. He had a hand in the changes to the course made by Mr. Travis. We shall see what tomorrow brings.

Writing these words to you has brought me great comfort, and I wish you were here beside me tonight. Please give my love to the children and tell them I picked up a little some-thing for each of them at the World's Fair.

All my love to my sweet Irish Rose,
George

P.S. You must tell the children that I had a meal at the World's Fair the likes of which we have never seen before: we drank iced tea (not hot tea but tea in a glass with ice and lemon juice—delicious on a hot day); we ate what they call a hamburger, which is a fried meat slice between pieces of soft bun with catsup and mustard (you eat it with your hands—no knife or fork!); and for dessert we had ice cream served in a cone made from a waffle. They call them ice cream cones. People walk about licking the ice cream out of the cone, and then they eat the cone as well! It can make a bit of a mess toward the end, but it is fun nonetheless. I confess I had two of them. I have much to tell you and the children about the World's Fair.

George set down his pen and folded up his letter, tucking it into the pocket of his tweed jacket, which hung from his bedpost. He would post it before breakfast the next morning. Exhausted, he climbed into the plush bed and dreamt of one day playing golf with his son, George Seymour Jr. And of eating ice cream cones.

15

Spirit of St. Louis

TWENTY-NINE-YEAR-OLD Albert Lambert was waiting at the first tee for George on Thursday morning. More than two hundred spectators crowded around the tee, and Colonel McGrew took a towel to his damp speaking trumpet. As George approached, he could see Mr. Lambert pacing the tee box from side to side, stopping every now and then to look at his bright gold watch. Immaculately dressed in a dark wool jacket and vest, wearing silver wire-rimmed glasses, with his short jet-black hair parted down the middle with absolute precision, he looked more like an aspiring accountant than a champion golfer. George could tell that here stood—or rather paced—a serious young man. He stepped forward to introduce himself.

"Mr. Lambert, it's a genuine pleasure to meet you."

"Likewise, Mr. Lyon. I'm looking forward to our match today. I've read much about you in the papers recently." George stirred a little inside, as he wasn't sure if Mr. Lambert was referring to the coal heaver reports. Although Mr. Lambert's handshake was firm and businesslike, he was soft spoken, hardly the voice one would expect of a man who was President of the multimillion-dollar company Lambert Pharmaceuticals.

"I hope during our match today you'll indulge me in a few tales from your adventures at the Paris Olympics. It's not every day one gets the opportunity to play an Olympic champion." George gave Lambert a broad smile and a look that invited storytelling. "And please, call me George."

But Lambert brushed off the compliment humbly. "Well, Mr. Lyon—George—you probably know that my victory in Paris was in the handicapped event. I shot modest rounds of ninety-four and ninety-five. It was really only my ten handicap that allowed me to pull through. There will be no handicaps to save me today, Mr. Lyon." He laughed politely and looked at his watch again. "I believe you have the honors this morning."

Colonel McGrew lifted his speaking trumpet and stepped onto a box to bring the noisy crowd to attention.

"Quiet, please. Thank you. We can be grateful that the rain has held off. Perhaps we can get through thirty-six holes of golf without an umbrella. In today's quarterfinal match we have Mr. George Lyon of Lambton Golf Club, Canada, facing Mr. Albert Lambert, co-founder of Glen Echo Golf Club, Olympic golf champion or what the French like to call..." he glanced down at a card in his hand, *"championnat international."* If anyone present spoke French, they would have surely winced at McGrew's pronunciation. "He is also my son-in-law."

There was an enthusiastic round of applause for the clearly favored local boy. Mr. Lambert, evidently a little embarrassed by the attention from his father-in-law, raised his hand to acknowledge their support. He stepped back beside his caddie and looked unconsciously at his watch again,

George stepped forward, teed a ball, and, to a smattering of applause, hammered a drive down the middle, just ten yards short of the green. George realized for the first time as Mr. Lambert stepped up to the tee, that the young man was left-handed. Lambert wasted no time and quickly stroked his drive out to the middle of the fairway. Their thirty-six-hole quarterfinal match had started.

George, famous for his quick pace of play and his tendency to dash off the tee down the fairway as soon as his opponent had hit, could barely keep up with Mr. Lambert. Within seconds, he was several strides ahead of George and picking up speed. George quickened his pace and called out to him, "I see you're a southpaw, Mr. Lambert. My brother-in-law Fritz Martin is a lefty and a very accomplished golfer."

"Yes, I've heard of Mr. Martin. Was he not your Amateur champion two years ago?" said Lambert without looking back. "Some say he's the best left-handed golfer in all of North America."

"Well, he certainly describes *himself* that way." George laughed, now jogging to catch up, his caddie far behind.

Mr. Lambert quickened his pace and strode off to his ball. His own young caddie fairly sprinted to keep up.

"So, tell me about Paris," George called out. He was eager to sustain some conversation. It actually helped his game to have some chatter on the course. "What was it like facing Europe's best? I'm very sorry none of them could make the voyage to St. Louis."

Mr. Lambert hesitated before answering, as if he was judging whether or not to go down that path of conversation. He peered down at his watch again.

"We do have thirty-six holes ahead of us, Mr. Lambert. There's no need to rush," George called out, slowing to a walk.

Realizing that George couldn't easily be ignored and not wanting to be rude, Lambert abandoned his hurried gait. Smiling, he waited for George to catch up to him. "I hope we do manage thirty-six, Mr. Lyon. After seeing that drive of yours, this match might end much more quickly."

"Just a lucky start. An old man like me will probably fade over the course of the day," George said with a wink. But after a short pitch and an easy one putt, George was down in three to Lambert's four, and one up.

The first nine holes of their battle passed quickly, with the two men trading holes, but George remained one up. The golf was good and George could see why Lambert had soundly defeated Walter Egan in the first round. He had then hung tough in his second match to beat Ralph McKittrick one up. And McKittrick was no pushover; he had tied as a medalist with Stuart Stickney for the lead in the qualifier on Monday with his 163. But this was match play, and George knew that he had to take Albert Lambert seriously.

After three and a half hours, the first half of their match had held no surprises. They went about their golf in a workmanlike way. No man made any dramatic moves; no leads were built. Except for their occasional polite small talk with caddies, it had been relatively steady, grinding golf. "At least the weather is a little more agreeable," thought George, as they each went about their work efficiently, "but it's certainly not my idea of a sociable round of golf."

The gallery waxed and waned during their match, drifting between them and the match of Chandler Egan, who was facing Harry Allen of the Field Club. After eighteen holes, George and Lambert were all square. When they came off the last green and the caddies cleaned their clubs, George called over to Lambert, "Will you join me for lunch? You *must* tell me about your golf in Paris."

"Mr. Lyon, I'm grateful for the invitation, but I am very sorry I'll have to decline. I have some important business to attend to over the lunch hour. I assure you that I shall be back within two hours." He glanced at his watch and then walked away quickly to join two young men who waited for him by the clubhouse. They scrambled into a car and were off.

At two o'clock, after a full lunch of a thick steak and roasted potatoes and a fortifying pot of black coffee, George approached the first tee and again found Albert Lambert waiting. But this time, he was neither pacing nor looking at his watch. He appeared relaxed, smiled, and apologized again for missing lunch.

"No need to apologize. I can well understand the call of business, Mr. Lambert. Our golf must always come after our families and our livelihoods. We are amateurs, after all."

"Truer words were never spoken, Mr. Lyon. I believe you still have the honors, but the caddies say we are asked to wait while the first green is swept of water and a few bunkers are drained. The rain that fell over the lunch hour has pooled."

"No harm done if we wait, and I see too that the rain has hurt the size of our gallery. If we have a few minutes, Mr. Lambert, I wonder if I might ask you a question that has troubled me this week."

George could see Lambert look at him attentively, as if to say, "Of course."

"And that is, why no international golfers were able to make the journey from overseas," George continued. "I, frankly, had expected men like John Ball, Harold Hilton, Robert Maxwell, Horace Hutchinson, James Robb, and others to be here competing for the medal and that trophy. What happened?"

Mr. Lambert looked troubled and stepped closer to George, as if their words should be confidential. "In a word, I would say politics. As a Canadian, you're probably unaware of the battle that was waged between St. Louis and Chicago to host the World's Fair and these Olympic Games. Our local and state politicians were engaged in near hand-to-hand combat over the matter for the past five years. It went all the way to Washington and back. President Roosevelt was even dragged into the affair after McKinley's assassination."

"I had no idea."

Mr. Lambert went on to explain how Chicago had initially been awarded the Olympic Games, which was supported, albeit weakly, by the International Olympic Committee president, Pierre de Coubertin. "I met him a number of times and had thought him pretentious but also someone who shouldn't be trifled with. He was constantly going on about how Buffalo Bill would ruin everything."

"Buffalo Bill? What has he got to do with the Olympics?"

Lambert shrugged and carried on. "I have no idea, but when St. Louis was awarded the Louisiana Purchase Exposition, or what became known as the St. Louis World's Fair, Missouri's politicians lobbied hard to pull the Olympic Games away from Chicago. They had stopped at nothing, but when they finally succeeded, it was against the wishes of de Coubertin, and as his act of protest, he has refused to set foot on American soil or attend the Olympic Games in St. Louis."

Lyon realized as they stood in their private huddle that he had opened the proverbial can of worms.

"The head of our Games in St. Louis, Mr. James Sullivan, is what some would call a tough-minded Irish American. He and the IOC have a little history. A few years ago, he actually tried unsuccessfully to wrest control of the IOC away from de Coubertin. I understand that he and Sullivan came to despise each other. It's my belief, though I have no proof of it, that de Coubertin has been telling anyone in Europe who will listen that these Games will be a failure and not to waste time, money, or energy attending."

"Good Lord. Not very sporting at all."

"I believe the English golfing community listened. My goodness, Sullivan and my father-in-law were even prepared to send a ship to pick them all up and bring them to St. Louis. I'm told that overall at our Games we've had nearly a dozen countries from four continents represented. Athletes have come from Greece, Germany, Hungary, and of course Canada. But almost none from Britain and France for the Games themselves, and absolutely none came for the golf."

"Politics and golf."

"Yes, I am afraid these Olympic Games have become very political. But *your* countrymen have done well, Mr. Lyon. The lacrosse team did well to win gold. I was even there the day that fellow from Montreal, the policeman, won the weight throw for the gold medal. Extraordinary."

"Would you believe that the gentleman, Mr. Desmarteau, was the first Canadian to win an Olympic track-and-field event, and the thanks he got was to be fired from his position on the Montreal police force because he insisted on going to compete in the Olympics?"

"No. Why on earth would they do that?"

"Just a working chap who took too much time off work. Of course, when he returned to Montreal with the gold medal, he was a hero, so they gave him his job back. Madness."

Lambert looked down the fairway to see a man waving them on. "I have just seen them give us the signal, Mr. Lyon. We can begin. I think all those European golfers have missed a wonderful competition. Shall we play some golf?" he said almost jovially. It seemed he was quite enjoying himself.

"Well said. Let's play some golf." George was delighted yet puzzled that Mr. Lambert seemed so much more relaxed and open, a totally different person.

Two solid drives later, as they were walking down the middle of the first fairway Lambert finally volunteered details of his golf in France. "I had been in Paris on business in October that year. I was expanding with factories in France and Germany—"

"Your advertising of Listerine has been quite powerful. I have seen the advertisements featuring that young woman shunned for her bad breath. And the ones 'Never a bride' and 'Are you unpopular with your own children?' I confess—thinking of my own family—I bought a bottle!" Lyon chuckled.

"Wonderful. As President, I thank you!" he said with a laugh. "Apparently, Europeans are as worried about halitosis as Americans and Canadians. I was over there with my associate Charles Sands. I think maybe you know of him. He competed at the very first Amateur here in the U.S. Both of us, very average golfers, were there in France when we heard that there would be a golf competition. No one even said it was Olympic golf. In fact, none of the athletic events, which were spread over two months and paired with the Exposition Universelle, were even described as Olympic. I think that must have made de Coubertin furious. Anyway, we were attending a dinner at our hotel and someone told me that the mayor of a little town thirty miles outside Paris was organizing a tournament over three days at the Compiègne Club. We thought it might be fun, so we boarded a train, borrowed some clubs, and went to compete."

"Not at all what I had imagined."

"When we arrived, it seemed more like a huge social event than a sporting contest. Very lavish. I was told by the club captain that a number of princes and viscounts and contessas had come out to watch us play, though I never met any of them. Quite a rarified atmosphere." He said this as if he had no time for putting on airs.

"Sounds interesting, though."

"It was, but truth be told, Mr. Lyon, there were only twelve of us competing in France, and it was only after we arrived that we learned the whole thing was part of the Paris Olympics. We were astonished. There were ladies there to compete as well—daughters of some rich Americans studying art in Paris or vacationing in Switzerland. One I actually knew: Margaret Abbott from Chicago. She went on to win the women's event. They played only nine holes."

"Goodness, I wish I could have been there. It sounds marvelous."

"Oh, it was. Wonderful weather, too. Not like this, I assure you. Charles Sands was a lot like you. He had only taken up golf in 1895, and then went on to play in the finals at the U.S. Amateur three months later. Imagine that! Mind you, he was clobbered by Charles Macdonald of the Chicago Golf Club— twelve and eleven in that match—but still, he played in the final. I have to give the man credit."

George was suddenly impressed with the young man's knowledge of golf. *How does he know when I started playing?* He had obviously done his homework.

As they walked on, Lambert continued his story: "Charles had actually shot the low rounds in Paris to win the gentlemen's event, but for some reason they decided to add a final event that was handicapped. That was the only reason I won. So you can see, George, why I do not think of myself as a *champion international.*" He pronounced it with flair and laughed. "There weren't even medals awarded. Somebody handed Charles some kind of china piece. Not sure what he did with it."

The men played on in their second eighteen-hole match, continuing to trade holes, but after eight holes, George was again one up. As they made their way up the slippery hill to tee off at the ninth hole, Fountain, a par three over the lake to a large green, the two men, who had settled into comfortable conversation, continued to talk about business. "How was your meeting at lunch? I hope everything is all right." When George inquired, Lambert suddenly perked up even more.

"I have to admit, Mr. Lyon, the distraction this morning was not about my current business, but rather what I *hope* my business will be in a few years." Lambert seemed excited by the thought.

George stepped to the tee and hit a solid iron to the center of the green, some 164 yards away. Lambert, who suddenly seemed energized, teed off and flew the green by twenty yards. The men looked at each other.

Lambert burst out laughing. "Now see what you have done, Mr. Lyon, by getting me to think about the future."

As they walked to the green, Lambert became animated as he explained his love of balloons and the growing prospect of genuine flying machines. "I left the course over lunch to meet two brothers with whom I am studying and working, Orville and Wilbur Wright. A Colonel Capper, Superintendent of the Royal Balloon Factory in Europe, has come to the World's Fair to see the new aeronautical exhibits. I arranged a meeting of these gentlemen. I've been taking ballooning lessons from them." His excitement was clear as he raised his arms up to the sky.

"Ballooning?!"

"Yes, but only as a preparation to flying. Last month, the Wright brothers made a flight with their airplane—unassisted takeoff and flight for more than 1,300 feet—with a safe landing."

"I had heard a little about these brothers, but I also read that the papers could not decide if they were flying or lying, as they put it."

"Mr. Lyon, trust me when I say this: they are flying. Just two days ago, the brothers took off, flew a complete circle in their machine—more than four thousand feet. They were airborne for more than five minutes. *Five minutes!*"

"Good Lord. So it's true!"

"Mr. Lyon, the future is up there." He pointed skyward. "These Wright brothers are onto something. There is a race to see who can get one of these machines to stay up in the air for an extended period. They're getting close to a reliable machine, and I'm doing my utmost to help with money and encouragement. One day, I expect that a man will be able to fly an airplane from city to city, over this country, even across the ocean. The whole world will be open." He said this as if flying would liberate the world.

George was fascinated. "Fly across the ocean? Good Lord, I can't imagine. I thought electric streetcars couldn't be topped!" As Lambert looked to the sky, George tapped in a two-putt to win the hole, to go two up.

"Well, I tell you it *can* happen, and it *will* happen soon."

Energized by their discussion, Lambert bore down over the next two holes, halving the 400-yard par five on the tenth hole, Hard Scrabble, and the eleventh—a difficult 271-yard par four, called Hillside. Both men looked at the scorecards they kept for each other and smiled. They were enjoying the match and each other's company, but Lyon was two up with seven holes to play, and Lambert knowing the course's finishing holes well, decided he must press now.

However, as can be the case with match play, he pressed too hard, and George captured the twelfth hole, Westward Ho. The thirteenth, Echo, with the lake that cut across the fairway, was a challenge, but George's powerful tee shot easily carried it. He was on in two and won the hole with a four. He was up four holes with five to play. If Lyon won or halved one more hole, it would be over. If Lambert was concerned, it did not show. They made their way to the tee area for the fourteenth hole, Dewdrop.

"We members here at Glen Echo say this is the easiest hole on the course, Mr. Lyon. You have the honors."

With a smile, George looked at his scuffed Haskell and instead asked his young caddie to find a fresh ball. The boy reached into the pouch and pulled out a Spalding Wizard. He handed it to George, who rolled it in his hands. Brand new. *"Well drove 'twill fly from tee to green..."* Things seemed to slow down as he felt the smooth outward bumps of its surface. For the first time, he became aware of the large gallery that had formed. He searched the faces in the crowd and found Albert and Bert smiling broadly. "When they say it's the easiest hole, you know what that usually means, don't you, Mr. Lambert?"

"I do indeed, Mr. Lyon." Lambert knew he faced elimination. He needed to make a heroic shot or pray Lyon faltered.

George pinched up some soggy sand and placed the new Wizard on it. He looked downhill to the large green with a center pin placement. The little American flag that topped all flagsticks during the Olympic matches flapped gently in the wind. He recalled that any ball landing on this green should funnel down to the center. But the greens were still soggy. *Should I press for the win? Should I go right at the flag?* His mind flashed back to that first lesson he had been given about match play by Mr. McLaughlin nine years ago. *Patience, George. Patience.* He was four up; there was no need to press.

George elected to ignore the flag and simply hit the fat of the green. With his typical, low swing, he clipped the ball into the air and watched it sail 136 yards, hitting the back of the green, where it bit sharply into the soft turf. Satisfied that he was safely on board he turned to hand his Forgan iron back to the caddie. As he did, the gallery began to shout, "It's moving!" He turned to look back at the green, and as the gallery roared, his bright, white Wizard began to trickle down the back of the green, coming to rest two feet from the pin. The gallery burst into applause.

"Wizard indeed," he muttered.

Mr. Lambert teed up and struck a solid shot to the slope on the right side of the green. The gallery held its breath. They waited. *Will it move? Will it funnel down?* No. The crowd groaned as the ball stuck fast in the soft, short grass.

A few minutes later, the two men stood on the green surrounded now by a huge gallery. Mr. Lambert studied his putt. With George facing an easy one putt he needed to make this one and hope that Lyon missed his putt. He rolled his ball toward the hole, but it stopped short. It was not to be. He two-putted. George stepped forward and tapped in for the victory. He had won five and four. As they left the fourteenth green, the men removed their hats and shook hands. George was sorry it was over. He had enjoyed their time together almost as much as the match.

As they walked back to the clubhouse, George continued their conversation. "I hope your father-in-law doesn't give you a hard time about the outcome of the match. I think he had hoped you would repeat your victory."

"Not to worry, Mr. Lyon," he said, patting George on the back. "He's delighted that I even had the idea to host these golf matches here in St. Louis."

"*Your* idea?"

"Yes. As soon as I returned from my trip to Paris, we began work to have an international golf championship at Glen Echo. Our original plan was to have a competition in 1903, but when St. Louis secured the Olympics for 1904, well... We knew we had to petition to allow Glen Echo to hold the Olympic golf event instead. It meant a delay, but that allowed us to make some changes. We spent some $60,000 to prepare the course and the clubhouse. It's been a real labor of love."

"Well then, I guess I have you to thank for this Olympic adventure. I wish you good luck with your balloons and your flying machines. I've seen many things in my life, but if I ever hear that a flying machine has crossed the ocean, I'll know that your spirit of adventure here in St. Louis was its fuel."

Lambert smiled thoughtfully. "Thank you. It's been a real pleasure getting to know you... Spirit of St. Louis? Interesting. You have given me an idea for something, Mr. Lyon."

George met up with Albert Austin and Bert who had been cheering enthusiastically in the gallery. As they walked back to the clubhouse, Albert's arm wrapped proudly around his shoulders, George learned that Chandler Egan had dispatched Harry Allen six and five, and had already left the course for the day.

"George, I have some good news and some not-so-good news. First, the good news: I won my consolation match!"

"Bravo!"

"The not-so-good news is that I followed one of the matches today, and I have to admit you may have your hands full tomorrow."

"Is this young Chandler Egan impressing you, too, my friend?"

"Not Egan. He'll play Burt McKinnie of Normandie Golf Club. You will meet Francis Newton of Seattle Golf Club. Today, he defeated Mason Phelps of Midlothian Golf Club just outside Chicago, two and one. It was a hard-fought match and he is quite a golfer. They call him the 'Scotch Wizard.' Sorry, George, that is all I could learn. Everyone has become a little tightlipped now that we are nearing the finals. They're concerned that it won't be an all-American final. The best I could determine is that he was the Pacific Northwest champion in 1902, and he played on the team with Lambert, Stickney, and Cady in the team matches held earlier in the week. Those three gents weren't willing to divulge any other information."

"Well, that's perfectly understandable." George hummed as they stepped into the clubhouse grill.

"He's a very steady player, George. Quiet and steady."

"Thank you for the intelligence, Albert. It will be very helpful. But tomorrow is another day. Now let me buy you a drink to celebrate. I have just played golf with the most interesting young man. I have a feeling we have not heard the last of Albert Lambert."

And with that, George Lyon moved on to the semifinals. It was Thursday evening. He had played more than 150 holes of golf, and he now stood just one match away from the championship round—and that beautiful trophy and gold medal.

16

The Sphinx

THE NEXT MORNING, Friday, the weather was overcast; rain was in the air again. The golfers and the large crowd of spectators surrounding them at the first tee shivered in the wind. Many, hearing of the Olympic events, had taken the short train ride out from the World's Fair for the day, and most carried precautionary umbrellas as they prepared to follow the men around the sloppy Glen Echo golf course.

Colonel McGrew climbed once again onto a sturdy box to announce the day's matches. "Our first semifinal match this morning pits our remaining international competitor, Mr. George Lyon, of Lambton Golf Club in Toronto, Canada, and Canadian Amateur champion of 1903 against Mr. Francis Newton of the Seattle Golf Club and Pacific Northwest champion, 1902. Gentlemen, if you are ready please prepare yourselves to tee off. Our second match of the day will see Mr. Chandler Egan of Exmoor Golf Club compete against Mr. Burt McKinnie of Normandie Golf Club. They will be teeing off shortly after Mr. Lyon and Mr. Newton. I will then be turning my duties over to my son-in-law, Mr. Albert Lambert, at noon, when I and Mr. Albert Austin from Lambton Golf Club, Toronto, Canada, will compete for the international Presidents Cup. Thank you for your attendance, ladies and gentlemen, for what should be an exciting day, and to the players, play well."

By day's end, everyone would know the Olympic finalists, as well as the winner of the Presidents trophy.

Although he was scheduled to tee off in less than ten minutes, Chandler Egan was nowhere to be seen. He had developed a reputation among the golfers for being deliberately late for his tee times.

George reached across to shake Mr. Newton's hand. He was of average height and wore a crisp white shirt and black bowtie. As they greeted each other, Newton's thick cotton vest beneath his striped wool jacket lifted to reveal a very unusual belt buckle. It was made of fine brass and was engraved with a Sphinx and the word "Egypt." George leaned a little closer and recognized it immediately, and a small fire began to burn in his heart. George waited until they were both safely off the tee and down the fairway before he inquired, "I can't help but admire your belt buckle, Mr. Newton. Do you mind if I ask where you got it?"

"Thank you. I think it was my grandfather's. It was found in an old toolbox, and my father had it fashioned into a belt buckle. A little exotic, isn't it? Egypt, imagine."

"Exotic, indeed."

George bristled and the fire burned a little more intensely at the thought of that buckle that seemed so familiar to him, but for the time being he needed to concentrate on golf. As the two men played their way through the first few holes, he realized that Albert was right about Newton; he was a steady player—a very steady player. Newton had made no mistakes. Even though George was playing well himself, after five holes, Newton was two up and gaining confidence.

On the tee for the 330-yard par four, Boomerang, George watched Newton's strong drive and realized he would not be able to rely on overpowering Newton with his own long drives. Today he would need his full game. The realization made him bear down a little more intensely, and he fought to close the gap. After twelve holes, it was George who was now three up. But Newton was relentless, and he fought back to win the next hole and cut George's lead to just two.

George rebounded, and after fifteen holes he was three up again. It was becoming something of a battle, and as word spread around the course, the crowds that had followed Chandler Egan now swelled into the hundreds around George and Newton.

Throughout the morning, the two men plotted their way around the course with military efficiency. After eighteen holes, George had shot eighty and Newton eighty-one, but the match was all square. As the caddies cleaned clubs beside the eighteenth green, each man secretly considered the other a formidable opponent and felt fortunate to have even a tie.

Lunch that afternoon was a quiet affair as both men strategized with friends for the upcoming eighteen holes. When they met at the first tee for their second round, the gallery had grown even larger as word spread about the tight match and the quality of their golf. Their battle resumed. Each win of a hole was immediately answered, and the lead changed hands several times.

At the tee of their twenty-first hole, George and Newton stood all square. They waited while some boys who had been sent down from the clubhouse with pitchers of ice water poured large mugs of water for the men and their caddies. As they refilled their glasses, George broke the silent barrier that had formed between them as competitors.

"Do you come from a military family, Mr. Newton?"

Puzzled, Newton replied, "Not really. Our family had a few brushes with service, but nothing to speak of. Why do you ask?"

"I served for a spell with Canada's Queen's Own Rifles when I was younger, in my twenties. But my service was nothing compared to that of my grandfather. He was from Scotland and served with General Wellington against Napoleon during the Peninsular War in Portugal."

"Good Lord. He fought Napoleon?"

"Not just fought. Defeated. And then his regiment was moved on to Canada, first to Quebec City and then to Niagara, Upper Canada, to defend the colonies and to fight you Yanks in the War of 1812." He shook his head and laughed at the thought. "My grandfather would no doubt be scowling, knowing that his grandson was playing golf of all things against the bloody Yanks."

"That was a long time ago, Mr. Lyon. Thankfully behind us." Newton turned to his caddie and asked for a fresh ball.

As the boys took the water pitchers away, the two men refocused, returned to their match, and battled on. After twenty-seven holes, George and Newton were still tied. If George won a hole, Newton answered on the next. If Newton got himself one up, George would answer. But, as they approached the thirty-first hole of their match, No. 13, Echo, Newton stood one up, and perhaps he thought for a moment that any lead at all in such a tight match might be enough to win. There were six holes to play, and if Newton could just stay one up he might be able to hang on for a victory. Both men knew that Glen Echo's closing holes could be a stretch of steady pars for Newton. He was playing well, and George understood that if he were in Newton's muddy shoes, his strategy would be to force George to halve or win holes just to stay in the match.

Newton seemed settled on his strategy for the closing holes and finally turned to George. "War of 1812, you say? I think we licked you in that one, didn't we?" he teased.

"Not quite, my friend, not quite." George chuckled.

Newton, still with the honors, raised his eyebrows slightly with a playful air of disbelief and turned to hit his drive down the right side of the fairway. He would have a good angle to the green from there.

"Steady," George thought. "He's very steady." Yet he felt confident as he stepped up to his ball and crushed his drive across the lake, cutting through the fairway. His ball rolled down the middle of the 317-yard par four.

A few minutes later, after two excellent approach shots, they stood on the green assessing their putts. George was away, lying two but facing a long forty-five-foot putt across a wet and very slow green. Newton was lying two and faced a straightforward ten-footer. George stepped over his putt and glanced at the hole. Thanks to all his practice and the advice of Walter Travis, the hole suddenly looked as large as a paint can. The considerable gallery hushed. Newton turned to his caddie for a towel to dry his putter grip, assuming George would simply try to lag his putt up for a two-putt and from that distance be grateful. But George had other ideas. He rolled his putt with a solid stroke. It crawled across the soggy green, broke left, and without a wasted revolution, dropped in for a three. The crowd roared, and Newton turned in disbelief at the amazing putt that George had conjured. He now had to make his ten-footer just to halve the hole. Rattled by George's incredible putt, he backed off his original assessment and took another look at the line. He consulted his caddie. George could see that he was second-guessing himself. Finally, Newton stepped into his stance and, with a tense, jerky stroke, pushed his putt three feet past the hole, and then without pausing to consider his next stroke, rolled his next putt three feet past the hole in the other direction. The spectators let out a gasp. When he finished, he had four-putted for a six to George's three. The match was all square again with five holes to play, and George had a spring in his step.

Even though he had lost the hole, Newton turned to his caddie, shook his head, "You have to give that man credit. That was quite a putt he just made. Beating him will call for more than pars over the next few holes." He had formed a grudging respect for this Canadian. And there was no denying that the crowd enjoyed his play. There were constant cheers of encouragement from the crowd and shouts of support for both golfers. It was a match, and the spectators loved it.

As the two men walked across a muddy path to the next hole, George, ever the talker on the course, took up his story. "I remember my grandfather telling me the story of the Battle of Chippawa near Niagara Falls in that war. On a hot and humid fifth of July in 1814, your Yankee commander Winfield Scott made very effective use of his six- and twelve-pound field guns—cannons, really. It was a short but nasty—and bloody—battle. After Scott's Yankees and the Brits—and of course the native warriors who fought with each side—were done with each other, nearly two hundred men lay dead in the Chippawa fields and hundreds were injured. But Scott's first brigade carried the day, because of that cannon."

"I was right then, we did win that war," exclaimed Newton, slapping George on the back and warming to his gregarious, irresistible personality.

"Steady, my friend." George smiled and wagged his finger at him. "Your men did win that battle, I'll grant you. It was a huge victory for a relatively young army—in fact, it was the first time that an American army had defeated the British in an open engagement. The Brits had underestimated you Americans in that battle, but credit where credit is due, Scott had whipped his soldiers into shape, so they were trained and motivated. That was quite an achievement to defeat the Brits. Your countrymen's pride in their army swelled after that battle. They'd conquered the Brits that day, no argument on that point." George, now with the honours, prepared to tee off but then turned to Newton with a smile. "But eventually it was us Canadians who won the war." And with that, he drove his ball far down the middle of the soggy fairway, again.

A few muddy shots and soggy putts later, an invigorated George had won the hole with a four to Newton's five, and now stood one up. But Newton, undeterred, bore down and answered on the thirty-third hole with the same score, so that after thirty-three holes of golf, the two men stood locked in their struggle. The match was, again, all square. The crowd loved it as each man battled for the win.

Now, George and Newton stood on the sixteenth tee, Punch Bowl, for their thirty-fourth hole of golf. The crowd, growing by the minute, crowded around the tee box. It was called Punch Bowl for a reason: the fairway was straight, but it rolled downhill into a bowl, with an elevated green near the lake. George remembered this hole well, recalling that the approach to the two-tiered green was more difficult because the green did not hold a shot easily, even if it was wet.

To George's surprise, as they stood at the tee, Newton looked out over the fairway and remarked casually to himself and his caddie: "As many times as I have played this hole, I can never quite recall the best approach." He turned to his caddie and seemed to be trying to replay it in his mind, trying to remember.

Overhearing his remark, George commented quietly, "My grandfather used to say, 'Sometimes what we cannot forget is more powerful than what we cannot remember.'"

Newton looked at George puzzled, turning the interesting statement over in his mind. *"What we cannot forget." I wonder what Lyon means.*

As they considered their club selection for the 430-yard hole, a young boy approached waving his hands. "Egan has defeated McKinnie, four and three! Egan's in the final!"

Within minutes behind the boy came a crush of new spectators. Only Newton and George remained on the course in an Olympic match. The noisy gallery swelled to several hundred as Newton and George looked intently at each other. They knew that whoever won this match would face the golden boy, Chandler Egan. George smiled at Newton knowingly, as if to say, "I am ready to play. Are you?" Newton nodded. He was ready.

The caddies called for quiet, and Newton, having regained the honors, made his steady stroke of a mashie and again drove the ball down the middle. He turned to George and smiled. Without missing a beat, George answered with a booming drive that rolled twenty yards past Newton's. He smiled back at Newton as he handed his driver to his caddie. They walked off the tee side by side in silence to inspect their respective lies. But after a few steps, his curiosity got the better of him and Newton broke the silence. "And what of your grandfather in that battle at Chippawa?"

Grateful for more conversation, George resumed his tale of war. "He was a lieutenant at that point with the British Grenadier Company. The fire from Scott's field guns tore his company to pieces. Those types of cannons fire canister rounds, which are basically containers about the size of a can of peas." George held up his hands to show the size. "Each one would hold about 3,200 lead bullets, and the can itself would disintegrate as it left the muzzle. The bullets would easily blow through a line of men."

Newton winced at the thought of the carnage as he broke off to find his ball. He faced a 130-yard shot to the two-tiered green. He took his stance and hit a smooth iron to the center of the green. The crowd burst into applause, but their satisfaction would only last for a moment because Newton's ball suddenly started to roll back, slowly at first, but then it gathered speed and eventually rolled off the green. The crowd let out a collective mournful groan.

George stepped over his ball, facing a 110-yard shot to the green. He settled into his stance, and with his favorite Forgan iron, delivered his unique coal heaver's swing. The ball landed in almost the exact same spot as Newton's initial shot. There was no applause as the crowd waited. *Will it move?* No! George's ball bit where it hit and the crowd roared their approval.

Newton called over, "Well done, Lyon. Well done."

George tipped his hat and began to hum a song to himself as he walked to the green, putter in hand.

Newton, facing a difficult uphill lie, struggled to get up to the hole while George calmly made his two-putt for a four and advanced to the thirty-fifth hole: one up with two to play. The crowd had reached into the hundreds now, and men and women surged forward to surround the tee and lined both sides of the fairway, three deep in places.

The seventeenth hole at Glen Echo, Old Hickory, had originally been a 365-yard par four, but with the advice of Walter Travis it had been lengthened to 400 yards for the Olympic competition. And not only had it been lengthened, but it also had the unusual layout of sharing the same fairway as holes fifteen and sixteen. Lyon smiled as he recalled the early days of Rosedale with its golfers crisscrossing fairways with dairy cows.

Newton and George crossed paths with Colonel McGrew and Albert Austin. The presidents were on their way to the fourteenth green. George tipped his hat to the two golfers and gave Albert a wink. Albert could tell from George's step that he was in the lead. And George could see from Albert's face that he was in trouble in his Presidents Cup match.

As they headed for the tee area, the two men paused again beneath a tree to allow the huge crowd to settle, and the caddies called for more water. George, seeing the short delay, picked up his story as if nothing important was underway and they had all the time in the world. The water pitchers arrived, and although both men were soaked to the bone and their shoes a muddy mess, they downed glass after glass of water.

"This will need to do for now," Newton said with a smile.

"Aye. For now." Lyon knew what he meant.

"What happened next? Was your grandfather killed?" He had become quite taken in by George's story of this battle long ago.

"The battle was not going well for my grandfather's company and his sergeant rode over to my grandfather and ordered him to lead a charge. But before he could comply, my grandfather was cut down by bullets from one of those nasty canisters. They tore through his right thigh, here, just above his knee. From the ground, he saw two friends killed before his eyes. They could not advance and they could not retreat, so for three and a half hours, the battle raged on over and around him. He lay there on the battlefield. This bloody chaos lasted until about six thirty that night."

"I had no idea your grandfather was there on the frontlines. I'm so sorry..."

"Oh, there is more... I see they are ready for us." George stepped out from beneath the tree and looked at the sky. "The weather looks like it may turn against us."

The caddies waved the men to the tee as dark clouds moved in and rain threatened again. Like soldiers themselves, they marched to the tee, and their caddies pulled their favorite clubs from the golf bags. Driver for Lyon. Mashie for Newton. It had been a long day, but each man mustered every ounce of energy, and they struck their balls far down the fairway. When they arrived to find them, the two balls lay side by side and the gallery swarming alongside applauded their effort. Two approach shots to the seventeenth green followed. The balls again lay equal distances from the hole. Two tense putts each and both men, tired and worn from their battle, walked away from Old Hickory with a par. They climbed to the eighteenth tee. George still one up. There was one hole to play.

The eighteenth, Sweet Home, was a 405-yard finishing hole that ended beside Glen Echo's classic Victorian clubhouse. The hole, with its dogleg, had originally been 355 yards, but again, Walter Travis added fifty yards for the Olympics to make it a challenging uphill hole to a large green. It could be a difficult finishing hole. Par was never a certain outcome. And Newton knew he needed to win the hole just to extend the match. A half was of no use.

George, still with the honors, stepped to the tee and once again crushed a powerful drive out to the fairway. On his final few holes, his drives had been lengthy, but this one was clearly more than three hundred yards. Uphill. The crowd let out a roar of approval. The excited chattering of the gallery after George's huge drive must have been especially loud in Newton's ears, because after he had pinched up a solid mound of sand for his ball, he reached for his driver. All day he had used nothing but his mashie from the tee. Now he needed as much distance as he could muster. He dug the toes of his shoes into the muddy turf with extra determination, took the driver back sharply, and then gave a mighty swing. A gasp and then a groan swept through the huge gallery. Newton had topped his drive. At this most critical juncture in the match, he had advanced his ball no more than thirty yards. He leaned on his driver and stared at the ground in frustration.

After a few seconds, Newton composed himself and walked forward from the tee to his ball. He stared at it for a moment, selected his mashie, and then, with a swing more akin to his usual gracefulness, stroked his ball up closer to the green, not ten yards from George's drive. He was in trouble and knew it. As both men stood in the fairway assessing their next shot, the crowd streamed past them and began to gather around the green, spilling onto the practice putting area. The entire green would be surrounded in minutes by a throng of hundreds, and George and Newton would be forced to wait.

George turned to Newton. "While we wait, I must tell you, Francis, of what happened at Chippawa, if you care to know."

"I am sorry, I assumed that your grandfather fell in that battle."

"He was badly injured, but as he lay on the plain surrounded by the dead and moaning wounded, stretcher parties were sent out by each side to collect the fallen. A Yankee stretcher party, thinking he was dead, passed him by. But he watched as a young U.S. soldier stopped and bent over a fallen British soldier. The U.S. soldier had noticed the unusual brass belt plates on the dead British soldiers—engraved with the image of the Sphinx and the word 'Egypt'—to commemorate the regiment's service in 1802 fighting Napoleon in Egypt."

"Good Lord." Newton lifted his vest to reveal the belt buckle. "I had no idea."

"Even though the stretcher parties had been told not to do so, some American soldiers took the belt buckles of fallen soldiers as souvenirs. My grandfather's was among them."

"And what became of your grandfather?"

"He was carried off to a makeshift hospital where his wife, my grandmother, worked as a nurse. His leg was badly injured. By October of that year, he still had not recovered, and sometimes he could not walk for two to three days at a time. But he remained active in the service until 1818, and then retired from the army at the ripe old age of twenty-nine. Imagine that. He was still only twenty-nine. And he went on to have sixteen children."

Newton ran his hand over the buckle as he walked to his ball. Lying two, he was still away. Newton asked his caddie for his trusted mashie again. He moved into his stance ready to hit, but at the last moment stepped away. He looked up to the huge gallery that now stood silently around the green, waiting for these important shots. The match rested on what happened now. Newton turned and looked at George, who stood with his young caddie. Newton returned to his caddie and put the mashie away. He pulled an iron instead. The green was uphill and he would make no mistakes leaving it short. He stepped back into his stance, drew the club back, and struck. Although it was covered in mud, the ball could be seen sailing to the green, where it bit and held. The gallery roared its appreciation for the shot. Newton had stuck his approach seven feet from the hole. Now, lying three, Newton faced a do-or-die putt if he hoped to even extend the match.

"Well done, Newton. Well done." George gripped his favorite iron one more time, and the coal heaver hit a solid approach shot that settled near the edge of the green in thick grass that had been trampled by the gallery. He was lying two but facing a difficult downhill chip onto the green. George was away. He looked at his line and the hole. He carefully chipped on to the green but the ball refused to release. It sat some 20 feet from the hole. Both men were lying three. George rolled his ball to within two feet and stepped aside. Newton needed to make the putt and again hope that Lyon missed.

Newton stalked his putt from every angle, and then stood over his ball a long, agonizing minute. He hesitated. He second-guessed himself. The weight of needing to make the putt just to have a slim hope of extending the match settled on him. A hush fell over the throng that surrounded the two men who stood alone on the green. And then, as if the silence itself had turned his hands to stone, he rolled his putt past the hole. He tapped it in for five. George tapped in for five and being one hole up after thirty-six holes had the victory. The crowd exploded and flooded onto the green around them.

Newton removed his hat and broke into a wide smile as he shook George's hand. "That was a golf match to remember. You played extremely well, George. And I enjoyed every minute of our conversation. I have a feeling Chandler Egan will have his hands full tomorrow."

"You played a fine match as well, Francis. You have been by far the greatest challenge to date. It was quite a battle."

As they left the eighteenth green, it was after six o'clock and the crowd of men, women, and children pressed in around them, shouting their appreciation. Newton and George, smiling broadly, pressed through the crowd, their arms around each other's shoulders. The crowd, now standing in a light rain that had begun to fall, showed no signs of losing their enthusiasm for the golfers. Dozens of men and women reached out to shake their hands. The spectators parted as they walked to the clubhouse but still cheered them on, calling out, "A great match," "Best match yet," "Well done, Lyon," "Great match, Newton," and "You both gave your best!" They knew that they had seen a classic match.

Although disappointed, Newton shared one last thought over the happy din: "Your grandfather sounds like he was quite a man."

"He was, and I had the honor to be named after him. I thought you should know the provenance of that beautiful belt buckle. Please wear it knowing that the man who wore it until July 5, 1814, had a proud history of service to his country."

Newton ran his hand across the buckle and nodded. "I will. I will indeed." The power of what we cannot forget. Newton now understood what Lyon had meant by those words.

As they approached the clubhouse, George could see a young man standing on the veranda, watching the finishing hole. It was Chandler Egan. He turned and walked away.

"Let me buy the Scotch Wizard a drink," George said.

"Anything but water," Newton laughed.

And so, George and Newton retired to the clubhouse grill to replay every single hole and every single shot to the delight of the members who crowded around them.

George Lyon was in the final, and tomorrow he would face none other than the golden boy, Chandler Egan.

17

Equal Footing

FRIDAY'S MATCH HAD been a very long, challenging, and exhausting round of golf. The socializing, storytelling, and singing in the clubhouse after the round had been a tonic to George, but now he needed rest. When he finally made his way upstairs to his room, he sank into a waiting steaming tub with a mug of hot tea in hand. It was a good time for some reflection on the week but his thoughts turned briefly to the next day and his final match against Chandler Egan. *This time tomorrow there will be an Olympic champion.* After five consecutive days of intense competitive golf, it was time for a bit of physical accounting.

His body was tired like he could not remember. He felt a dull, sore stiffness in his right shoulder and recalled uncomfortable nights twenty years ago as a young soldier with the Queen's Own Rifles as he struggled to sleep during a bone-rattling three-day trip on a troop train from Toronto to Battleford. His shoulder had never been quite the same after that adventure.

He lifted his left foot from the water and considered it, turning it from side to side. It looked swollen. He had sprained it seriously one cold January night while playing hockey on the Jock River in his youth. The sharp twinge he now felt always followed some athletic endeavor. Today's full thirty-six holes of competition with Newton had inflamed it. "Clambering up those muddy hills and trekking through those soggy valleys has not helped. It's a miracle my ankle isn't—" he thought, as he lowered it back into the hot water "—maybe it is better left unseen at this point."

He looked at his weary hands now: red, worn, and wrinkled. He tried to count the number of holes of golf he had played since Sunday's practice round. He lost track at two hundred. "Perhaps all these calluses will be a help tomorrow."

He took a sip of tea and thought back to his days with the Civil Service League and a baseball game at the Old Jarvis Street Lacrosse Grounds in Toronto a few years ago. "A few years ago? What am I thinking? It was *twenty* years ago," he realized, shaking his head in disbelief. In that ballgame he had hit a double, but the bat had stung sharply in his hands as he made contact with the ball. When he finally scored, he sat on the bench staring at his still-stinging hands. His teammate Cannonball Crane had laughed and told him the feeling was called "bees in the hands." That same sensation when hitting a golf ball was usually bad news, and he had felt it a couple of times when his club struck a few snarly roots while he was playing Lambert on Thursday. He made two fists, flexed his big hands and powerful forearms, and lowered them back into the comforting water.

He began to wonder if this young boy Chandler Egan even *had* calluses on his hands, but he quickly caught himself. "Who am I to underestimate this young man? He has spent his entire life golfing. He has trained with James Foulis, bested Walter Travis in the U.S. Amateur, and beaten as many men in this competition as I have. And his matches haven't even been close. He sailed past Harold Fraser of Inverness Club, eight and six; Nat Moore of Lake Geneva Golf Club, seven and six; and even Harry Allen of the Field Club, six and five. His toughest match was the semifinal, but he dispatched the music teacher Burt McKinnie of Normandie Golf Club, four and three. And Westlake's newspaper articles about the tournament insist that Egan wasn't even playing his best golf..." George tried to put aside those dangerous confidence-killing thoughts.

As he stood to climb out of the tub and reach for a towel, his stiff back now gave a pointed reminder that he was, after all, forty-six years old, and that tomorrow he would face a young man who had just turned twenty.

George cast his mind back. *What was I doing when I was twenty?* There had been all that baseball, hockey, curling, football, and cricket, but his mind settled on something very early. *There had been the pole-vaulting record I set at nineteen: ten feet, six inches.* He recalled that first medal he had ever won—still had it tucked in a drawer somewhere. *I must look for it when I get home.* He had seen in the St. Louis papers just a few days earlier that the winner of the Olympic pole-vaulting competition—a Mr. Dvorak of the Chicago Athletic Club—won with a vault of eleven feet, six inches. In all these years, pole-vaulters had added exactly one foot to George's record. But pole vaulting could hardly be compared to Olympic golf championships. A day of vaulting was not the same as a full week of golf. And in this weather. From everything he saw, read, and heard about these Olympic Games, it was becoming clear that this was a different generation of athletes and sports were changing. *Egg whites, rat poison, and brandy? Just to win a race? Madness.*

Wrapped in a thick white towel, George padded about his well-appointed room and replayed the day's round, hole by hole, shot by shot. He thought about the slippery Glen Echo course. And his right knee. Oh, it had burned at times as he climbed that nasty hill at the ninth hole. With each round, that hill seemed harder to climb. McGrew had said that the forecast called for rain again tomorrow. As much as the grounds crew labored to make the course playable, it couldn't handle much more water. With the mud, the water, the rain, it would be a tough trek tomorrow.

And the crowds. Goodness, the crowds. George had been in matches before that were followed by spectators. When he played Vardon at Rosedale, the players had been followed by a crowd of nearly three hundred. But this was different. And tomorrow was Saturday. With people off work and with visitors to the World's Fair making the journey to see the final match, the course would be crowded and noisy.

He looked at his wool suit that hung by the door and hoped it would be dry by the morning. It was a hardy suit, and it had taken some punishment this week. Thanks to Albert, a young woman had brought a freshly laundered shirt and underclothes to his room. They would be welcome tomorrow. George wanted to look his best. The papers had been unkind about his form again. That Westlake fellow would not let it drop. He was a proud man, and he knew that he represented his friends and fellow members at Lambton, Toronto—and all of Canada, for that matter. "God forbid my wife and children see some horrid photograph of me looking like a drowned rat on the front page of the *Toronto Daily Star*."

A knock at the door brought a telegram. It was from Annette. She must have heard that he made the final round and that brought a smile to his face. As he opened the telegram, he thought how glad he was that they had had a chance to celebrate their thirteenth wedding anniversary a few days before he left. It was a special day for them each year.

Dearest George,

The papers are filled with the wonderful news. The finals! Congratulations, my love. I thought of what you will face tomorrow and recalled something I had read once. So I pulled down our copy of Lady Troubridge's Book of Etiquette and thought you might note her advice at page 98: "One reason why golf is so popular is that it is a sport in which old and young can join on equal footing." Equal footing, my love. Be easy on that young fellow, Egan. You have made us proud.

Love,
Annette and the children

He folded the telegram and tucked it into his suit vest pocket for the next day. Knowing it was there washed away his pains. Tomorrow, it would give him the strength of ten men.

18

The Duel

SATURDAY MORNING at 7:30 a.m., George, Albert, and Bert sat down to enjoy a hearty breakfast of eggs, toast, and sausages (plus two helpings of pancakes for George). When they finished, George pushed his plate aside and turned to Bert with a question.

"Bert, I've had some second—and third—thoughts about the young fellows who have been caddying for me this week. They have been good lads, but frankly, they haven't offered much advice about the course, and they are as quiet as mice. I don't think any one of them has uttered more than ten words over thirty-six holes, other than, 'Yes, Mr. Lyon,' 'No, Mr. Lyon,' 'Good shot, Mr. Lyon,' 'We'll find that one, Mr. Lyon.' I need a little companionship out there, Bert. I would be greatly appreciative if you would caddie for me today."

Bert was stunned. He hadn't expected to be asked. "Mr. Lyon, I'm honored, but I'm not sure I'm ready to... caddie. Really?

If you had asked me last night, I could've prepared a bit... Done some thinking..."

His father, who knew that George had planned to ask Bert, jumped in with a laugh. "If he had asked you last night, you wouldn't have slept a wink, and you know it."

Bert looked a little sheepish, knowing his father was correct, but still considered George's request. "That's probably true."

"It would be a great help to me," George pressed him gently.

"All right, I'll do it, but I... I'm not sure I'll be much help, Mr. Lyon—"

"All I expect is your friendship and a little conversation along the way."

"I think I can manage that much."

"And—this is of the utmost importance..." George frowned, put his elbow on the table, and pointed one of his thick fingers at him. Bert hesitated; perhaps he had agreed too quickly.

"There can be absolutely no complaining about my singing."

Bert smiled, relieved. "There will be no complaints, Mr. Lyon."

"Good. Now I have a pretty good sense of the course and my club selection. I fear the weather is going to be a factor, though. Would you put a few extra towels in the bag? We may need them to dry the club grips. Check the supply of balls. I should play fresh ones."

"I'll head out and check your clubs and bag now." Bert tossed his napkin on the table in excitement and went to the front porch to inspect George's clubs.

Albert finished his coffee and turned to his friend. "Thanks for including him. I think it'll be a wonderful experience."

"And he'll be good company. I hope that you'll walk along with us as well, Albert."

"I'll try to not get in the way." He reached out solemnly to shake George's powerful hand. "Good luck, George, we're proud of you."

"I wouldn't be here were it not for your friendship and encouragement, Albert. I shall do my best today."

"In that case, Mr. Egan certainly has his hands full." Albert brightened. "I shall see you at the first tee. I have a little business with Colonel McGrew to attend to first."

George, left alone at the breakfast table, reached into his vest pocket and touched Annette's note. He didn't need to read it; he recalled her words: "Equal footing, my love."

He felt a hand on his shoulder and turned to see the waiter standing by to take his plate. "Good morning. It's been quite a week for you folks, hasn't it?" said George, looking around at the busy dining room. "You'll be grateful to see the end of us and get back to normal, I suspect."

"It's been a busy week, that's true, but we've so enjoyed meeting you and the other Canadians. You've been real gentlemen, and we all wish you good luck today," he said spiritedly. But then he hunched down and lowered his voice to a whisper: "You probably shouldn't spread this around, but we'll be pulling for you." He stood back up and continued removing dishes as if nothing had happened.

George was tickled at this genuine gesture of support.

"And Mr. Lyon, I know that you sometimes get hungry out there, so I packed a sandwich for you, just in case. And a fresh apple," he continued, handing George a carefully wrapped package.

"How thoughtful. You and your staff are too kind," George called out as the server returned to the kitchen.

It was nearly 9:45 a.m. when George stepped onto the porch. The rain was relentless. It was cold and the wind was blustery. It looked like it might be the most difficult day yet. He glanced over toward the first tee to see a mass of hundreds of black umbrellas: a scene that looked more like a funeral than a golf match. With a flip of his collar, a tug on his tweed cap, and a quick pop of his umbrella, he headed for the first tee.

As he made his way through the crowd of men, women, and children, a few of them patted his back or applauded. Others called out: "Well done, Lyon!" "Congratulations, Mr. Lyon," "Good luck in the final."

To stand there in this downpour, George realized, these were people who truly appreciated golf. He acknowledged their applause, waving to them as he passed. "Thank you for coming today... Thank you for your support... Let's pray that this rain stops soon... What has Missouri done to deserve this treatment?"

A nervous-looking Bert was waiting for him under an umbrella with a firm grip on George's golf bag. He stood as if reporting for duty. The wind seemed to gust even harder at the tee.

"How are we doing, Bert? Ready for some golf? Tuck this sandwich and apple into the bag somewhere, would you?" George could see that Bert was anxious.

"All ready, Mr. Lyon. I stuffed extra towels in the bag, too." George smiled as he looked at the bag. It was twice its normal size. "But I'll be grateful when we're off this first tee. I hadn't expected such a huge crowd." Bert looked around at the noisy, soaked gallery.

"It's a good crowd, indeed. We shall see how long they last in this rain and cold." As George looked through his clubs, making sure each was in order, he searched for a way to help Bert relax and said matter-of-factly, "Bert, this may seem like an odd question, but do you know why it is called a tee?"

Surprised, Bert looked up from under the umbrella and smiled. How could George Lyon be so relaxed and ask him questions when he was about to tee off for the Olympic championship? "No, Mr. Lyon, I don't know. I've never even thought about it."

With a thick, comical Scottish brogue loud enough for anyone nearby to hear, Lyon said, "Well, laddie, in Scotland we speak a language called Scottish, and in Scottish, a small pile of sand is called a *teay*. So when we pinch up a bit of sand for a *teay* shot, we are putting it on a *teay*." He laughed as he said it. "But I really wish I had a cup of hot *teay* right now." Bert and nearby members of the gallery laughed at Lyon's humor. It helped to take a bit of the tension away, and Bert relaxed his grip on Lyon's golf bag. A little.

Enjoying the moment, Lyon turned to some young men in the crowd as they waited for Chandler Egan and said, "We've had quite a challenge this week with the rain washing out our sandy tees. I wish someone would invent a better way to tee a ball. I imagine something perhaps like a wooden peg of some kind." One of the young men, a dental student from Boston who had traveled to St. Louis for the World's Fair and the golf competition, made a note to himself.

It was five minutes past ten, and Chandler Egan was nowhere to be seen. Another ten minutes passed and still no Chandler Egan. Colonel McGrew stood huddled under a shell of umbrellas with Albert Lambert and Tom Bendelow. They were engaged in an animated discussion. George hoped they weren't thinking of canceling the round because of the weather or, even worse, disqualifying Egan as a no-show. Suddenly, the group broke apart, and McGrew climbed onto his stool, speaking trumpet in hand.

As he did, the crowd parted and Chandler Egan finally arrived under a canopy of umbrellas, as if nothing were wrong, his cousin Walter in tow as caddie. George had heard gossip that Egan had been using such playing tactics throughout the week. A late arrival, Chandler thought, might throw off an opponent and make him anxious. Such tactics, he would discover, had little impact on George Lyon. He watched as Chandler and his cousin set up under their umbrellas and waited for McGrew to speak. Neither man looked at George. He, however, watched them closely.

Remarkably, although George and Chandler had been at Glen Echo all week, on the same course for several rounds of golf, and stayed in the same clubhouse, the two of them had never met. George had met virtually every other golfer over the week. Yet here they stood, for the final Olympic match, as strangers. "How odd," George thought. "Had it been deliberate?"

He looked at Chandler and realized that he was not just young, he looked almost like a teenaged boy: clean shaven, slender, and tall—almost willowy—and dressed in cotton pants, vest, Harvard tie, and stylish jacket. These were the clothes of a younger generation. For some reason, at that moment, looking at the young man, a pang of disappointment shot through George. He remembered how much he had anticipated meeting Walter Travis—the Old Man—in the final match. Instead, he faced this boy wonder.

George reached his hand into the pouch pocket on the side of his golf bag for a fresh ball, his finger felt something sharp and he withdrew it almost immediately. He reached in again and pulled from the pocket a brass buckle engraved with a Sphinx and the word "Egypt." He smiled and searched the faces in the crowd for Francis Newton. He found him standing near Colonel McGrew and tipped his hat. Newton, in return, gave a little bow. George turned the buckle in his hand and slipped it into his vest pocket with the note from Annette.

"Ladies and gentlemen, if I could have your attention," McGrew called out over the steady drum of rain beating on hundreds of umbrellas. "We are about to get underway with this final match, the match that will decide the 1904 Olympic golf champion." It suddenly seemed to start raining a little harder, and a cold wind blew an umbrella across the tee. McGrew pressed on, mustering as much enthusiasm as he could. "It gives me great pleasure to introduce the finalists in this match: Mr. George Lyon, of Lambton Golf Club in Toronto, Canada, and Mr. Chandler Egan, of Exmoor Golf Club in Chicago, Illinois. Mr. Lyon is the 1903 Canadian Amateur champion and Mr. Egan is the current 1904 U.S. Amateur champion."

Even though they huddled close together and clutched umbrellas, the thick crowd managed to give an enthusiastic round of applause for both golfers.

"Each man has defeated four of this country's top golfers in thirty-six holes of match play each day this week. That, ladies and gentlemen, is a great deal of golf!" McGrew could not resist some praise for his course. "Let me add that our course, Glen Echo, has presented an admirable challenge." Nor could McGrew resist a dig at de Coubertin. "Dare I say, this Olympic golf event has greatly exceeded the events held in Paris just four years ago. We have had many more golfers, tougher matches, and our magnificent course. We have also had you as a devoted gallery, and now we have the final challenge of a lifetime. If we could just get a little sunshine, it would be perfect." McGrew broke off, tilted his huge black umbrella, and looked up at the black clouds a bit annoyed. Sunshine was nowhere to be seen in the entire State of Missouri. "Please join me now in acknowledging the achievements of these two gentlemen." Another round of applause followed from the gallery.

George stepped forward with a broad smile from under the umbrella into the rain to acknowledge the applause and tipped his hat. Chandler—hatless—simply raised his hand and waved to the crowd.

George walked across the tee and reached his hand out to Egan. "Good morning, it's a pleasure to finally meet you, Mr. Egan. Congratulations on reaching the final. Too bad about this weather." George could feel the strength in the young man's grip. That explained his remarkable shot-making ability.

Chandler turned to select a club. "Thank you, Mr. Lyon. Play well."

McGrew announced that the coin toss had given George Lyon the honors and called for quiet.

The two men had stood at this first tee ten times already throughout the week; each knew Lilac Way was 276 yards, a par four. It wasn't a particularly difficult hole, but starting well always made a difference. After teeing a ball, Lyon spread his feet wide, drew back his club in cricket-bat style, and proceeded to hammer the ball. "Smote" was the word that occurred to George Westlake as he took notes on George's swing that wet morning.

Aside from the rain drumming on the many umbrellas, there was silence as George's ball sailed out over the fairway, and then a burst of applause as someone called out, "He's driven the green!" Chandler and Walter looked at each other in shock.

Chandler Egan stepped up to the tee, pinched up some sand, and sent his ball well down the center of the fairway. He held his finish as if posing for a textbook sketch of the model swing. George smiled and recalled his first lesson with John Dick at Rosedale. John had posed the same way as Egan did now. The crowd applauded Chandler's effort as the ball settled about forty yards in front of the green.

"Well done, Mr. Lyon!" Bert was beaming as he took George's driver, dried it, and returned it to the bag. "I think you shocked Mr. Egan with that one."

"Thank you, Bert. Shall we be on our way?" George was off like a shot down the fairway; Bert ran to keep up as Chandler and his cousin walked slowly, well behind. George was on the green in one. Chandler would need to work a miracle to win the first hole now.

A few minutes later, after no miracles from Chandler Egan and a routine two-putt, George stood one up.

They slipped and slid their way with the huge gallery across a path to the second hole, a 432-yard par four, The Valley. After their drives—one elegant and one not—George and Chandler were lucky to find their balls in the soggy fairway that sloped hard from left to right. Egan hit a fine shot to the green, but George nearly holed his second from the fairway, and with a one-putt, was now two up.

They moved on to the third hole, Spooks—so called because it was nestled next to the local cemetery. It was a difficult par three, and even harder as the wind blew brisk and cold across their path to the green. Each man would settle for a four.

Long Drive was the first par five of the course. Glen Echo had accepted Travis's recommendation and lengthened the hole to 538 yards with a cross bunker at the 500-yard mark. Still with the honors, George stepped to the tee and drove his Haskell long and hard down the right side of the fairway. Even with all the rain that morning, the ball rolled another twenty yards and settled at the foot of the slope on the right side. He was in a good position to think about clearing that bunker and going for this green in two.

Chandler, still taken aback by George's consistently huge drives, dug in his feet and gave a powerful swing. At the finish, though, his shoulders rolled up, along with his head and eyes, and he watched in desperation as his ball sliced sharply into the rough on the right side of the fairway. He slammed his driver to the ground in frustration.

The two men set off down the fairway, the noisy Saturday crowd close behind, pouring along the edges of the fairway. George was used to friendly chatter and socializing as he played golf. But so far, the two men had not said ten words to each other over the previous three holes. So, as they walked, George called out, "Not to worry, Chandler! We'll find that one. I'm sure it's in play."

Chandler smiled weakly at George, because finding the ball was not certain at all. His mind was already in turmoil; he was angry with himself. This old man's huge drives were forcing Chandler out of his usual game. He knew it was happening, but each time he stepped to the tee, he couldn't stop himself trying to match George drive for drive.

"We will have quite a duel today, Mr. Lyon," Chandler replied flatly.

"Ah, a duel? That's an interesting description." George considered it for a moment and perked up suddenly. "I should tell you about my great-uncle Robert. He fought a duel."

Chandler broke into a suspicious grin. "A duel?" he said doubtfully. "Really?"

Bert suddenly chimed in from beneath his umbrella too. "Really, Mr. Lyon? A duel?"

Delighted that someone finally showed interest in a little conversation, George leapt into his story: "My great-uncle Robert was my grandfather's younger brother—a Scotsman who came over to Canada when he was just a lad of sixteen. His brother, my grandfather, was a much older and established retired soldier who had started a sizable family."

Chandler suddenly realized that perhaps he shouldn't have asked about the duel and now he would need to hear George out.

George walked over beside Chandler. "When Uncle Robert arrived, he took a position apprenticing in law at an office in the Ottawa Valley—in a lovely little town called Perth. Have you been to Canada?" George turned to Chandler.

"No," he said, drifting to the side of the fairway as George talked.

George followed after him. "Well, you must come for a visit and play golf at my club, Lambton. It's a fine course. I don't suppose you curl, do you?"

"Curl? No. I've never even heard of it," he said. "Is it a sport?"

"Indeed. Interesting winter sport. You might enjoy it. Anyway," George continued brightly, "one day, he got into a quarrel with a fellow law student, a Mr. John Wilson, who was actually his friend. As it turns out, they were both enamored with the local schoolteacher, Elizabeth. Do *you* have a young lady in your life?"

"No, I don't. I've been busy with Harvard and competing in the U.S. Amateur last week and now these Olympics." Where is this going? Chandler must have wondered.

"Of course. Of course. Well, when the right one comes along, you'll find you have all the time in the world for her. Now, where was I? Ah, yes. My great-uncle made some unflattering remarks, shall we say, about Elizabeth and Wilson that, of course, got back to Wilson, and they ended up in fisticuffs on the steps of the courthouse of all places. Imagine that, two law students." George shook his head and laughed to himself. "It was a few years ago, 1833, I think, so he would've been around your age. Twenty-one." He paused and smiled at Chandler.

Chandler stood with his hands on his hips in silence. "I'm twenty."

The crowd had now surged along each sloppy side of Long Drive's fairway, and a group of young boys had dashed ahead with Walter Egan to see if they could find Chandler's ball. While they searched, George carried on his tale. "So, my great-uncle Robert challenged Wilson to a duel. His friends thought him mad and suggested they both calm down. But Robert wouldn't hear of it, so they agreed to meet the next day. Each came with a second to assist him." George stopped suddenly. "Oh, it looks as if they found your ball." George pointed to the rough, where the crowd of boys stood. "Let's have a look. I see mine over there, so you are away. Take your time."

Chandler put his head down and strode purposefully over to the rough, hopping over puddles as he went. The crowd parted when he was near the edge of the fairway. His cousin Walter stood in the middle with his hands on his hips, staring at the ball. It sat nestled, almost wedged, between the roots of a small tree and a bush. Sitting on hardpan dirt—no grass— it would be a very difficult shot. Chandler's frustrations were mounting. Head down again, he turned on his heel, walked back, and stood beside George in the middle of the fairway for a better view of the hole's layout and a possible escape from his dilemma.

They both looked up, surprised to see Tom Bendelow with a broom, sweeping large puddles of water from the green.

"Good Lord! Is that Tom Bendelow?" They said it in shocked unison, turning to each other and laughing. Chandler's reserve receded briefly.

The Scotsman Tom Bendelow, well-known and prolific golf course architect, had, at the request of Colonel McGrew, taken on the duties of managing the gallery for the Olympic golf events at Glen Echo. There he was, in a long slicker and a hat in the pouring rain, with a broom he had borrowed from a streetcar conductor, pushing the rainwater off the green with military efficiency. He stopped and waved to them as if to say, "Give me a minute." He bent and continued to brush streams of water off into a ditch.

With the conversational ice unexpectedly thawed a little between them, Chandler turned to George, hesitated slightly, and said, "So, your great-uncle. What did he do then?"

Bert's voice came again from under his umbrella. "Yes, Mr. Lyon, what did he do?"

"Ah, yes." George returned to his story. "My grandfather told me that they selected pistols, stood back to back, walked twenty paces, turned, and fired." George paused for effect. He could see that Bendelow had moved off the green to the edge of a water-filled bunker. He waved them on. "It looks like the green is as ready for us as it will ever be. You are away, Chandler."

"And?" Chandler urged. "The duel? What happened?"

Bert had been hanging on every word as he held the umbrella for George. "Yes, Mr. Lyon. The duel. What happened?"

"Oh, they missed each other," George said matter-of-factly.

"Ha! Some duel!" Chandler snorted.

Walter called Chandler back over to examine his lie again. George could see Walter looked frustrated, pointing dramatically at the green and muttering advice to his cousin. Chandler, instead, held his arm up in a different direction and pointed back out to the fairway at ninety degrees, looking for the safest approach. It was perhaps a wiser, more cautious approach. He was, after all, only down two. There was a lot more golf to play. Walter saw matters in a different light and shook his head. He pulled out the scorecard and pointed at the score. After only three holes, Chandler was down two already. Walter wanted Chandler to make a move, assert himself in this match. Press him, he urged.

Chandler looked out to the fairway where George stood waiting. He pulled a club from his bag, and the crowd stood back to make room for his swing. A few shouted encouragement, while others held their breath. It was clearly a difficult shot. He set up, dug into the soft turf again, and swung hard. The ball appeared to hit the root and popped up directly into some low-hanging branches, where it then deflected and fell into long grass at the edge of the fairway. It sat not more than ten feet from where they stood. The crowd groaned at Chandler's misfortune, and Walter looked to the heavens in frustration. Now they were in even more trouble.

George, seeing that he was now away, took a freshly dried iron from Bert, stepped up, slowly took his club back, and stroked his ball to the center of the soggy green, where it landed with a splash about eight feet from the flag.

Walter turned to Chandler. "Good Lord, 550 yards and he's on in two."

Chandler did his best to get on with his third shot, but when George sank his eight-footer for a three—his first eagle of the day—it made no difference. George was three up after just four holes, and Chandler Egan walked to the next hole shaken to the core. *Who is this old man with the powerful drives?*

But if Egan was shocked after four holes, he was reeling after five. The fifth hole was called Roadway, a short 277-yard par four. George rolled in a fifteen-foot putt to go four up after five holes. He was a man on a mission.

Chandler needed to get ahold of himself. The match was slipping away hole by hole. He conferred with his cousin at the edge of the green. He was playing well, striking the ball well, but George's huge drives were making it almost impossible for him to keep up. Winning the driving contest last Saturday seemed laughable to Chandler in retrospect. Had George been there, he would have won it in a walk.

As they headed to the next tee surrounded by the crowd, George broke the silence again. "There's a lot of golf to play yet."

"Indeed. Thirty-two holes to be precise." He sounded angry, perhaps a little overwhelmed, yet determined at the same time.

"But back to the duel," George rubbed his hands together as he spoke.

"I thought they missed each other," Bert said. Chandler leaned in under his umbrella to hear if there was more to this wild story.

"Oh, they missed, all right, and when they realized what had happened, Wilson suggested to my uncle that they now shake hands and quit the duel. Everyone's honor was intact. But my uncle's second—a French army veteran named LeLievre—egged him on. Robert, I assume, was filled with doubts and thought twice about continuing, but as the story was told by my grandfather, his friend would not let it drop. And at his insistence, the rivals reloaded, paced off twenty steps again, turned, and fired."

"Fools!" Chandler exclaimed.

"He had a chance to walk away!" Bert cried.

"Indeed. Wilson's second shot went through my great-uncle's heart . . ." He pointed at his chest. "And he died on the spot. And Monsieur LeLievre ran away, afraid that he would be blamed."

Chandler and Bert stared at George, aghast. What a story.

George carried on matter-of-factly. "Wilson was charged with murder, but he was acquitted. It was self-defense, after all. Actually, he went on to become a judge, and my great-uncle went on to be buried in the town of Perth at the age of twenty-one."

"How terrible." Chandler seemed genuinely moved by the tale.

"Yes, I think about him from time to time, especially when someone asks me to do something that I doubt in my heart. I think that if I, alone, must live with the result, then I, alone, must live with the decision."

Standing there in the pouring rain, Chandler looked squarely at George and nodded. This old man was no ordinary opponent. He would take no more advice from his cousin Walter that day.

They moved on to the sixth hole, The Glen, both men struck solid tee shots. As Bert dashed ahead to locate George's ball, Albert, who had already headed down the fairway, greeted him from under an umbrella. "George won't like this one." They stared at the muddy ball that had settled against a decayed stump.

George arrived at the stump. "Thanks, Bert. Hello, Albert. What have I got myself into?"

"I'm afraid this old stump is trouble. You're stymied. It shouldn't be here on a course like this during an Olympic match."

"Yes, but it is here," George said calmly, as he took off his hat and scratched his head. "I know what will help. Bert, go into my bag and get me ..."

Bert pulled the bag closer. What did he have in mind?

"Would you get me that fine apple we tucked in there this morning." Bert wiped the apple with a clean towel and handed it to him like a nurse hands instruments to a surgeon. George took a few bites and looked at the green. "As we sometimes must admit, I cannot get *there* from *here*. Do you know the origin of the word 'stymie,' Bert?"

Bert smiled at the prospect of another Scottish lesson. "No, I do not, Mr. Lyon."

"George, forgive me, but this may not the best time for language and history lessons for Bert. It looks as if Chandler has found his ball. He is in good position to go for the green." Albert could not believe that George was so relaxed.

In a thick, comic brogue, George gave forth as he surveyed the situation from under the umbrella and the rain fell even harder. "Bert, in Scotland the word *'styme'* refers to a person who is blind or partially blind. So if you cannot see the hole from where you lie, you are stymied. And you know what?"

"What?"

"Your father is correct. I am stymied." He handed Bert the apple and pulled his cap back on to select a club. George played the only shot he could chipping his ball out to the fairway, still away, he then left his next shot short of the green. Egan, finally seeing an advantage, hit a beautiful mashie. He posed watching as his ball lofted over the water that had gathered in front of the green and settled softly near the flag. He claimed his first hole with a four to George's five.

"Well done, Chandler," he called. He did not acknowledge the compliment, and George assumed that he had not heard it as Egan retreated into solitude. They had played six holes, and Chandler was having no more of George's conversation now. *Is this another of his tactics?* There was no camaraderie as there had been with Francis Newton and Lambert. It appeared that this match would be all work.

And so, with Chandler still down three holes, they battled on, halving Boomerang and Alps. Then on the ninth hole, Fountain, in a brief respite from the rain, Chandler struck his tee shot to within fifteen feet of the flag. George answered by sticking his ball just inside Chandler's, not nine feet from the hole, but had to watch as Chandler rolled his putt in for a two. George's ball limped and wobbled across the green, missing the hole by inches. Chandler had cut George's lead to two.

The rain continued to pour down as they halved Hard Scrabble and Hillside. On Westward Ho, the 496-yard par five, George was in trouble and could not reach the green after even three shots, so with the rain now nearly torrential, he conceded the hole. They had six holes to play before lunch, and George's lead was now only one. Bit by bit and hole by hole, the match was turning slowly in Chandler's favor.

On the fifteenth hole, The Lake, Chandler found the water, and George pounced on his mistake; he was two up again. But Chandler struck back on Old Hickory to cut George's lead back to one up. Both men were soaked to the bone and grateful to halve the morning's final hole—Sweet Home, indeed—and head to the clubhouse for lunch.

The rain continued to pour down, and the winds whipped the large U.S. flag that hung from a flagpole in front of the clubhouse, but the crowds had not diminished. They knew that the match they were witnessing was special, as two very different generations were battling for the gold medal. Although George was one up, as Westlake reported to his readers "there was no clear winner from the morning's round." Lyon had been four up at one time, but Chandler, with steady golf, climbed back into the match.

As they came off the eighteenth green, Bert looked at the scorecard, did a quick tally, double-checked it. "Mr. Lyon you shot eighty-three, and Mr. Egan, eighty-three."

Lyon nodded. "A tight match, indeed."

The *Associated Press* sent the news out over the wires, and in Toronto, the *Daily News* reported the match on the front page, with a hole-by-hole account of the scores and a description of the harsh weather, the difficult course conditions, and the slow erosion of Lyon's lead. Thousands of people across North America followed the Olympic golf battle through detailed newspaper accounts. Westlake described George Lyon as "a veteran whose sinews are of iron, and with a temperament as phlegmatic as an Algonquin Indian." His column, however, concluded with a question: "But can he last?"

In Toronto Annette opened the paper and read Westlake's words. She too wondered. "Can he last?"

— 19 —

The Wandering Spirit

THE MORNING'S ROUND had been a long, hard, rainy eighteen holes of golf. At six thousand yards, and with its numerous hills and valleys, Glen Echo had become a soggy physical and mental endurance test, not just for George and Chandler but for the spectators as well. Umbrellas in hand and many in rubber boots, they slogged in the hundreds alongside the two golfers as they did battle in the rain. They had completed the first eighteen holes of the match in three and a half hours. Both men were soaked to the bone and in need of a rest. The score stood George Lyon one up.

After they made their way to the dry warmth of the clubhouse, McGrew approached George and Chandler. "Dreadful weather, gentlemen. I'm so sorry, but there is promise of it clearing by the afternoon. A good lunch will be served in the dining room. You probably have time for a hot shower and dry clothes, if you wish. I'm sure neither of you have ever been forced to play through such dreadful weather in your lives, but I promise you a better eighteen this afternoon. Tom Bendelow has people sweeping the greens and draining bunkers as we speak." Then almost to himself he said, "Honestly, if we did not need to finish the competition today, I might have delayed the final round until the weather cleared."

"Not to worry, Colonel. We will be fine after a good lunch, won't we, Mr. Egan?"

"I'll have to beg off lunch gentlemen as I'm off to practice a bit. I need to sort something out." Chandler, without changing his clothes or having lunch, headed off in the steady rain to the putting area for practice.

"Have some lunch first, Chandler," McGrew called out, as if he were urging his own son to come in from the rain. But it was too late. Egan was out the door, his cousin Walter in tow.

George looked at McGrew and shrugged. "A hot shower sounds good to me, especially if I could get something fortifying with a touch of whiskey to go with it." He turned to Bert, "Bert, make sure you get some lunch and dry clothes as well. I'm not sure much can be done to dry those clubs, but at least they will be out of the rain for a while."

McGrew nodded and smiled. "I'll see that Bert here gets some lunch, and I will have that hot toddy brought to the members' change room immediately."

"I'll see you in the dining room in thirty minutes." George clipped his pocket watch closed and headed for the showers. In a few minutes, his now-familiar singing voice could be heard on the main floor of the clubhouse, loud and full throated: "There's a spot in my heart, which no Colleen may own. There's a depth in my soul never sounded or known ..."

When George finally crossed the dining room to join McGrew, Albert, and Bert for lunch, he looked refreshed and had a spring in his step. He acknowledged with a happy wave the applause from other members for his shower room performance.

"My God, Lyon, are you not worn out even a bit?" said McGrew with astonishment. "I can tell you that I'm exhausted just watching from the sidelines. I felt like a mule pulling stumps as I made my way around that course this morning. It was work. It's a real test of endurance for you and Chandler. I hope you will be fit for another eighteen holes."

George laughed. "Colonel, whenever I find myself physically tested as we were this morning, I try to recall some greater physical challenge that I have met and think to myself, 'Well George, if you met that, then surely you can overcome this.'"

"I don't know what could have been more difficult than the eighteen holes this morning." He nodded to a waiter to take their orders for lunch.

Albert smiled and commented quietly, "Oh, you have no idea, Colonel. No idea." He had heard the stories of George's adventures before.

George smiled at Albert, knowing that he would indulge another telling of a tale. "When I was about twenty-two or twenty-three, back around 1881, I joined the ranks of the Queen's Own Rifles in Toronto, hoping I was honoring my grandfather and a family tradition of military service. Frankly, I enjoyed the physical work and the discipline, and I was soon made a corporal. We marched and trained and drilled for a couple of years, never expecting to see any action. At times, I felt that we were almost pretend soldiers and when we were finally called upon to serve in 1885, it was unexpected, really. We couldn't believe it. Action. Finally. I'm not sure if you followed our bit of trouble with the Métis in Western Canada."

"I heard a little about some madman named Louis Riel who was stirring up trouble with your Indians and half-breeds. He was hiding out in Montana the last I heard of him."

The waiter set out in front of each of them a hot plate of roasted chicken, potatoes, and beets. Bert needed no invitation and dug in while George continued his story.

George bristled at the reference to half-breeds and tried diplomatically to clarify the situation in western Canada at that time. "As European men explored, traded, and moved westward in Canada, they met and settled in many cases with native women, and over time, entire communities of a new people were born. That was the origin of what we refer to in Canada as the Métis. It means mixed. And yes, it is true that Louis Riel, a Catholic, had fled to Montana after he killed a fellow settler, a gentleman named Thomas Scott. By the way, Colonel, this lunch is delicious. My compliments to your club for putting on such fine meals this week."

"I'm glad you are enjoying it. Please continue, I'm curious about this Riel chap."

"Well, Scott, the fellow he murdered, was a Protestant Orangeman. You can imagine the trouble it caused. And that death certainly inflamed our people back east in Upper Canada, and they wanted Riel brought to justice. Riel was, I think, of questionable mental stability at the end, but I have little doubt that he was devoted to his people, the Métis. At the time there were a little over 5,000 of them living in the area. They had settled along the North Saskatchewan River and were living a peaceful life until the Canadian Pacific Railway started cutting through their farms. I'm sure you've had similar troubles here as people pressed westward. Railways are wonderful things, but they certainly turned the countryside upside down for the Indian population."

"Yes indeed. I'm not sure if you know this, but Geronimo, one of their leaders, is at the World's Fair." McGrew took a bite of food and said this as if Geronimo deserved to be in jail.

George, Albert, and Bert flinched and glanced at each other with the fresh memory of the once-proud Geronimo sitting in a booth signing pictures of himself for a few nickels. They had been shocked to see Geronimo being treated like a sideshow in a carnival. Albert put his hand on Bert's arm to caution him not to say anything impolite. Bert stared at his plate instead.

George took a sip of strong tea and continued his story. "This was a part of our Northwest Territories, called the District of Saskatchewan. The Indians had signed land treaties with the government of Canada, but the Métis, their cousins, as the Indians referred to them, had nothing on paper. When surveyors arrived from the Canadian Pacific Railway, they wanted to see paper titles. But no one had papers. You can imagine the disputes as European settlors arrived and started setting up farms on what had long been considered Métis land. That was when Riel came back from Montana. I heard he had been teaching in a small school there. One thing led to another; he put together a small army of about 350 men, and the next thing we knew, the local government had a full-scale rebellion on their hands."

"Sounds like an awful mess." McGrew frowned at the thought of rebellion. He was a man who appreciated law and order.

"Oh, it was a mess, indeed. When the Indians—led by a fellow named Big Bear—got involved to support the Métis, matters degenerated into a terrible conflict. All the white people at the Hudson's Bay trading post at Frog Lake and Duck Lake were massacred that June. It was an ugly scene. Our North-West Mounted Police had to abandon two forts, at Fort Carlton and Fort Pitt. But they managed to get the rest of the settlors to the stockade at a place called Battleford. About 3,000 people lived in that area." George pushed his empty plate aside as a fresh pot of tea arrived. He turned to the waiter and with a wink said, "I thought I saw pie over there a minute ago."

The waiter smiled and said, "In fact, it is a fine peach pie, Mr. Lyon. I'll bring a healthy slice for you."

"Healthy slice. Oh, I like the sound of that. So here I was in Toronto, a twenty-two-year-old corporal. The government loaded my comrades and me on the trains with about 3,000 troops under a General Middleton and rushed us off to join 2,000 English volunteers and about 500 North-West Mounted Police. We were to provide relief for those poor souls at Battleford. I was with my good friend R.W. Rutherford—more of an artist at heart than a soldier. He and I were assigned to the same railcar. It took three days of travel on those trains, a lot of it sleepless, but we needed to get to that fort at Battleford before Big Bear."

Bert had heard none of this story before and now sat listening without touching his food.

"We had three columns of men; our column—about 760 of us—disembarked at Swift Current under Colonel Otter. A tough man. You know the type, I'm sure." McGrew took a bite of food and nodded. "Well, the fort at Battleford was still another two hundred miles away from where we disembarked. It was a hot May—very hot—and we were in full uniform, of course. Heavier than these fine suits, I can assure you." Lyon thumbed the still damp tweed lapels of his vest. "And with packs and rifles."

"You were two *hundred* miles from the fort?" McGrew wanted to make sure he had heard correctly.

"Aye. It was the closest the railway could get us to Battleford. We formed up and marched through the thick Canadian wilderness, battling vicious blackflies and mosquitoes as big as grasshoppers as we went. We started our march quickly and made good time, until we encountered a band of Cree Indians at Cut Knife Creek. This group was led by an Indian warrior named Poundmaker and with a fellow called Fine Day."

Albert looked at his son, whose jaw hung open. "Bert, don't forget to finish your lunch. You have a tough afternoon ahead of you."

Bert cut a small bite as George continued his story. But the food never made it to his mouth. "We engaged but managed to repel their assault to get past them. Quite a day that was. Some of our column set up and used a Gatling gun. Ugly weapon. I will never forget it. There were losses on both sides. Good men." George grew solemn at the memory. "I was promoted to sergeant that night for my work during the skirmish. It had been my first real action. There is much more to the story than I can tell you or than you wish to hear. In any event, my only point is this: we covered that stretch of two hundred miles in six days—thirty miles a day. We relieved the fort and then stayed on to help settle matters. We later caught Poundmaker, Big Bear, and even Louis Riel." George finished the last bit of his pie and settled back in his chair, satisfied.

McGrew was speechless. Bert was speechless. Albert smiled at their reactions. They were getting to see what kind of man they were dealing with.

"So, on a day like today, I think about those two hundred miles in full uniform and equipment. What I face on a golf course with a few clubs, well, it seems a task that is not only possible but considerably easier."

Bert spoke first. "Mr. Lyon... I had no idea that you fought Indians. I wish you had told me that story before... I cannot believe my ears. You need to tell me all about this again—all of it, from start to finish." Bert packed up the rest of his lunch and rose from the table, still staring at George. "I need to get your clubs ready, Mr. Lyon." He said it with an even deeper respect for the man. On the way out of the dining room, he pocketed another apple to tuck in Lyon's bag. And one for himself.

McGrew had sat back and was staring at this man across the table from him. "George, when you said you had some military service, I did not realize the extent of it. Your story is like something from an adventure novel. It is extraordinary. So much about your fortitude out there in the rain and mud now makes considerably more sense."

"Thank you, Colonel. It was a test of endurance, but it was many years ago. I was a young man then. Of course, if those memories of marching through the wilderness don't do the trick, I have another thought that will always help me overcome a challenge."

"What is that, pray tell?" McGrew could not imagine anything more motivating.

"I just pretend that my children are watching me, and then I do my best. Works every time." George pushed his chair away from the table to stand up. "Colonel, I believe I have some more golf to play. I should be getting to the first tee. It was a pleasure having lunch with you. I will see you on the course. Looking forward to the afternoon." As he stood, he saw Chandler Egan enter the dining room, still soaking wet from the morning round and his practice.

McGrew looked at his watch. "Goodness! Indeed, it is time. Nearly three o'clock." George's tale had made lunch pass in a flash.

George, chipper and refreshed, stopped Chandler Egan as he passed. "Mr. Egan, does the weather look much better for the afternoon? Shall we head to the first tee?"

"Just need a bite of lunch, Mr. Lyon. I shouldn't be more than fifteen or twenty minutes. I will be there as quick as I can." He raised a hand to get a waiter's attention.

"I shall see you there then." As George headed to the porch to check on the weather he stopped to chat with Francis Newton and thank him for the generous gift of the brass belt buckle. As he talked Bert stood on the veranda drying each of Lyon's clubs.

McGrew overheard Chandler's remark about taking extra time for lunch and frowned. He was painfully aware of the complaints about his repeated tardiness. He decided to have a word with the young man and took him aside. "Mr. Egan, you and Mr. Lyon tee off in ten minutes. If you are not standing on the tee ready to proceed, I will have no choice but to disqualify you. I hope we are not witnessing some unseemly gamesmanship. Mr. Lyon has been a gentleman throughout, and I intend for these Olympic matches to be held to the highest standard. Is that understood?"

"It is indeed, Colonel, but I was working on my putting and my driving over the lunch period," said Chandler, a little embarrassed.

With that bit of business taken care of McGrew marched to the veranda only to be stopped by Westlake and his ever present notebook. "Colonel, it took awhile for Mr. Egan to find his game this morning. But it seems he has settled down now. My money's on the young man to take it this afternoon. As tough as Lyon is I'm not sure the old fellow can handle another eighteen holes in this weather. That wind and rain cuts right through a man out there. I'm exhausted following them. Do you not agree?" He held his pencil ready to record his answer.

Both men turned to see Bert listening as he dried George's clubs.

Westlake sputtered, "Not to take anything away from Lyon, he has fought well. But... really. Can he last?"

Bert looked at the two men, dried a club and slammed it into the bag with such force he surprised even himself.

McGrew walked over and put his arm around Bert's shoulder. He turned to Westlake. "Bert, I do believe that Mr. Westlake has no idea what he is talking about or what Mr. Egan is up against. Would you agree?"

"No. I don't suppose he does, Colonel. Please excuse me, I have to meet at the first tee the golfer who leads this match."

McGrew let out a laugh and said simply, "These Canadians!"

Five minutes later, Chandler and his cousin stood, sandwiches in their hands, ready to begin the final eighteen holes of the championship round. Thankfully, the rain had finally let up, and the crowd had swelled again to more than four hundred.

George was one up and had the honors. He stepped into his stance, took a deep breath, exhaled, winked at Bert, and proceeded to drive the green of Lilac Way for the third time that week. The crowd let out a roar of approval. George was giving their national champion a match to remember, and they loved him for it.

Bert was quiet as they headed down the fairway. George noticed that he seemed troubled. "Everything all right, Bert?"

Bert snapped to attention. "Yes, I'm fine but..."

"But..."

"But I cannot imagine you fighting Indians when you were a young man, and... and, well... my life seems so... boring compared to what you have done. You had all that excitement and adventure when you were young like I am now. What will I do that is exciting?" The World's Fair and George's tales had lit his imagination.

"Bert, I didn't have an opportunity to finish that tale over lunch. It was an adventure, I'll give you that, but not without its troubling moments. There are matters that still gnaw at me sometimes."

"There is more?" Bert could not believe it. "You have to tell me. Everything."

"Everything? You are quite sure?"

"Everything."

Realizing that Chandler Egan would not be offering much conversation in the afternoon's match, and seeing Bert's enthusiasm, George promised to finish the story over the next few holes—whether Bert liked what he heard or not.

George certainly showed a preference that day for the first six holes of the Glen Echo course. Perhaps fortified by the excellent lunch, after halving the first hole with fours, George promptly won the second hole, halved the third and fourth, and then won the fifth and sixth. Within an hour and a half of teeing off, he stood four up and in control of the match. Despite his practice over the lunch hour, or perhaps because of it, Egan continued to be wild off the tee as he struggled to match Lyon's drives. He was in desperate straights again.

The path to No. 7, Boomerang, their twenty-fifth hole of golf that day, was an unholy mess from the morning's rain. The crowds could barely manage the slope to the tee area. A group of men rushed to help a woman who slipped from the top of the hill to the bottom and landed in the mud. Covered from head to toe, she still would not leave the course, insisting that she would continue to follow the match. The crowd, laughing and cheering, gave her a round of encouraging applause for her fortitude. Thinking that this was as good a time as any, Bert asked for more details about George's adventures out west many years previous.

"After we reached Battleford and relieved the fort, they soon found more work for us. There were more engagements, and ugly ones at that. Women and children were caught in the conflict. We were often a superior force in men and firepower, but the Indians proved able—and noble—fighters. Although it is difficult to be noble in the face of a Gatling gun. Eventually the Indians that had been captured were going to be tried and sentenced, so the local government had brought in a pretty tough-minded judge, Judge Rouleau was his name, to take charge of the trials. He was furious one morning when he found out that a prisoner he had sentenced to be executed, this fellow named Pa-pa-meck-sick, also known as Round the Sky, had escaped, slipped away in the night."

To Bert this tale was as captivating and as exciting as any adventure novel he had ever read back home in the cozy comfort of his father's mansion on Spadina, and he repeated the name as if he were another Geronimo. "Pa-pa-meck-sick. I wonder what that meant."

"Well, it could have meant 'I'm not staying round here,' because he was never recaptured. The soldiers who were supposed to be guarding him had been enjoying a little too much whiskey the night before, and I guess he saw his chance. They were all punished accordingly, I assure you." Seeing a gap in the crowd, George felt a little impatient. He needed to keep moving. He had momentum. "Are they ready for us up there yet? That young lady seems determined to follow the match to its conclusion."

Bert clambered up the hill to find Chandler Egan waiting at the tee. He waved George to the top of the hill.

With the honors, George wasted no time pounding his drive 200 yards to the center of the fairway. Chandler quickly stepped to the tee, and with a graceful swing, matched it. When the two men arrived at their balls, they were side by side not ten feet apart. It was the first time Chandler had matched one of George's huge drives, and he was clearly pleased with himself. Both faced 130-yard shots to the green.

George looked at his ball. "Bert, we have a little problem here—a cuppy lie." Bert looked at the ball and saw that it had settled into a deep soggy divot. He looked at Chandler's ball. Perfect lie. George looked at the lie again and could not imagine getting a solid stroke on the ball. He selected a mashie, swung, but topped it. The ball scuttled along the fairway not ten yards. Chandler, seeing his chance, hit a beauty to the fat of the green. He was on in two. George pulled his midiron and attempted a half stroke to the green but, to everyone's surprise, left it short. He pitched on and one-putted for a five. Chandler two-putted and cut George's lead to three.

Bert toweled off George's putter and said, "Perhaps we shouldn't be discussing the Indians, Mr. Lyon." Bert felt he had been a distraction and perhaps cost George the hole.

"Nonsense. Those kinds of troubles are all part of the game. We must play the ball as it lies—whether we like it or not. Besides, I have not even told you the worst part of my story."

As they marched on to the twenty-sixth hole, No. 8, Alps, George carried on his tale. "Judge Rouleau wanted a reliable detail to round up more of the accused Indians, and my unit was assigned the task of bringing Big Bear and others involved in the original massacre to trial. We did our job, as assigned, and I still recall escorting a very proud and defiant Indian, Papamahchakwayo, known as Wandering Spirit, to Rouleau's court."

"Well done, Mr. Lyon. How exciting!"

"After the very quick trial, my unit was assigned another task."

"Capture more Indians?"

"No. We marched Wandering Spirit to the gallows, where he was hanged."

Stunned, Bert said nothing.

"And we did it seven more times for seven more hangings of the Indians who had fought alongside Riel and the Métis. It was the largest mass hanging in our country's history."

Bert fussed with the clubs at the tee. His face was ashen.

"Bert, are you all right?"

He stayed silent as he pulled the driver from the bag, toweled the grip, and handed it to George. "They hanged eight men?"

George took the driver and pulled a ball from his pocket. "No, Bert. We hanged nine."

Chandler Egan had the honors now and took little time hitting an excellent tee shot to the fairway. He seemed to be finding his form. George stepped to the tee and hammered his drive down the center. Without a word, he handed the club to Bert and made his way down the fairway alone this time. Feeling he had the advantage now, in his haste, Chandler sliced his approach to the par five. George, suddenly off form, hit his approach into the rough. Both men found the green with their next shot but arrived to discover an unusual situation. Lyon had laid Chandler a half stymie. George's ball was between Chandler's ball and the hole, partially blocking its path. George looked at the tight alignment. *Could Chandler manage to get his ball past mine without hitting it?* Chandler sized up the line, gave his ball a firm tap, and watched as it trickled passed George's. No more than a hair's width had separated the balls as Chandler's passed, and the gallery let out a collective sigh of relief. George rolled his ball close, and both men then tapped in for a five. George was still three up.

On they walked in silence to the tee for the par three, Fountain. Egan had taken that hole with a two in the morning round. Still with the honors, he drove the ball close to the edge of the green. George again, seemingly distracted, sliced his tee shot. He hit an uphill mashie but left the ball well above the hole for a difficult downhill putt. Chandler calmly pitched to within a yard and made his putt for a three. George two-putted, and Chandler won the hole for the second time that day and cut his lead to two.

Bert decided that this was a time for silence. In three holes, Chandler had shown strong form and momentum, whereas George was making uncharacteristic mistakes. *Is he tired? Is the week finally catching up with him? Something seems off.*

The two golfers joined battle on the par five, Hard Scrabble, and par three, Hillside, with Chandler making extraordinary long putts to halve the holes and stay in the match. But then George, finding his form, answered with a long putt of his own to halve the par five, Westward Ho. There were six holes to play and Lyon was two up. Egan's supporters were becoming vocal, cheering his every shot. Bert had not said a word in the last three holes, afraid he might have upset George's good nature with awful memories.

George finally broke the silence. "Bert, do you not want to know about the ninth man we hanged."

"I was too afraid to ask, Mr. Lyon. I'm worried about the match. I think all this talk of hangings has brought you bad luck."

"Nonsense. You should know about these things. Grab my clubs and I will finish this story before we get to the next tee.

Where are we headed? Ah, yes, Echo, par four, 317 yards. We halved it this morning."

"You can tell me later, Mr. Lyon. Really."

George put his head down and talked as they walked. "I was on a train back to Toronto when they finally brought the last man to trial. Louis Riel himself. They rushed in a no-nonsense judge, Judge Richardson. Within a few days, Riel was convicted of murder and sentenced to hang. No recommendation for mercy. The country was in an uproar— Catholics and Protestant Orangemen, in particular. Quebecers pleaded with Prime Minister John A. Macdonald for mercy. At least commute his sentence, they begged. Of course, others were only too happy to remind him of the massacres. The pressure was enormous, until, they say, one day in a meeting he finally exploded and shouted, 'He shall die though every dog in Quebec barks in his favor!' And his colleagues sat in stunned silence. They had never seen him so angry."

"What happened?"

"November 16, 1885. The soldiers took him from the police barracks, marched him to the gallows, and hanged him."

"He was number nine."

"Yes, he was number nine, and I feel it has left an open wound in the country. I am not sure it was the right thing to do. We shall never know."

Bert may have been right about bad memories or bad luck, because within fifteen minutes and after a few errant strokes of George's club, they were standing by the green for Echo, and Bert was writing down a five for George and a four for Chandler. Chandler had cut George's lead to one. There were five holes to play. *What is happening?!* Bert vowed there would be no more talk.

The next hole was Dewdrop. At 136 yards, it was a short par three, and the crowd pressed in around the men on the tee. Any mistake or heroic shot could be the difference now. It had not rained in hours and the course actually looked to be drying out in some of the higher spots. Both men struck their tee shots straight downhill to a very small green. On in two, Chandler was away. George, on in one, turned to wink at Bert, confident that he could win this hole, that he was back in form. As he looked back, he watched as Chandler, to a wild cheer, rolled in a twenty-foot putt to halve the hole. George could not believe his eyes and clapped to acknowledge another great putt from Chandler. George was one up with four to play. Bert watched as Westlake smiled and made a note for his story.

This match was not over by any stretch.

20

The Lake

BERT LOOKED DESPERATELY at George as they walked to the tee box for the fifteenth hole, The Lake. It would be their thirty-third hole of golf that day. "I don't know how you can stand it, Mr. Lyon. My heart is pounding. The tension is killing me! Can a sixteen-year-old have a heart attack?" He had watched in horror as George's lead slipped away over just a few holes. He knew that George wanted a little conversation while he played, but all this talk of hangings and politics seemed to have hurt his mood.

George smiled and put his arm around Bert's shoulders. "Don't you find it thrilling, Bert? This is why we compete. To face up to challenges and moments like this. If it were easy, we wouldn't want to be here. Well, *I* wouldn't want to be here." And with that, George began to sing "My Wild Irish Rose." And not just to himself. He fairly bellowed the words: "You may search everywhere, but none can compare to my-y-y wild Irish Rose."

Some members of the gallery who followed close by, hearing George's happy attitude, shouted encouragement: "Come on, Lyon, you can do it!" Another called out, "Bravo, Canadians!" One older man struggling along with a cane, perhaps a vicarious competitor, even joined in the song. George stopped to shake his hand and thank him. Bert, suddenly encouraged by George's positive attitude, lifted George's clubs onto his shoulder with renewed energy and marched on. What Bert hadn't noticed was a fire in the eyes of that old, dark horse. And as George turned away from the crowd, he slipped his hands into each of his vest pockets to touch Annette's note and a certain brass buckle. He would need all the help he could get to finish.

Upon finally making their way through the noisy now singing crowd, they saw Chandler and Walter conferring near the edge of the fifteenth tee of The Lake. The cousins seemed mystified that George could be relaxed, singing and laughing, and even chatting with the gallery. Chandler had just halved the previous hole, Dewdrop, in dramatic fashion. He was reenergized, having at last attained some momentum. The match had changed direction in favor of Chandler again. "Doesn't Lyon notice that?" Chandler thought.

George tipped his hat to the Egan boys, smiled, and switched to humming his favorite song. Bert even caught himself humming along with him.

But, in fact, for all of George's positive attitude, Bert had good reason to feel the tension. Chandler had certainly raised his game over the last few holes to the level that everyone—especially his many Chicago supporters—expected of him. Chandler was playing as he should. His putting was now electric; he was running down putts from all over the green. And it seemed he would pour it on to finish off this old fellow, just as everyone knew he could and should. Out of the corner of his eye Bert saw the ever present Westlake.

Waiting to tee off, George thought back over the last few holes. *Indeed, what has changed?* At 164 yards, the ninth hole, Fountain, had looked like an innocent par three over the water to a large green. Even in this overcast, rainy weather, Fountain was probably the prettiest hole on the course. Surrounded by flowers on its borders, and with the mist from the beautiful namesake fountain drifting across the fairway, it was a hole that, on any other day, might give a golfer pause to reflect on life. It was surrounded by bunkers, which today were filled with water, but the real challenge had been the wind that swirled above the green. The flagstick, topped like all the others on the course with a small American flag, had flapped furiously in the wind and bent to and fro. George and Chandler had both struck solid irons to the center of the green. But for the second time in the final round, Chandler had knocked in his putt at Fountain to win the hole. Putting. Putting. As Walter Travis had written: "For all the attention one may get for a powerful lengthy tee shot, this game comes down to which man can make the putt. Two hundred yards or two inches, each counts for one stroke."

This had certainly been the case at Dewdrop. George had felt confident that he could win that hole and go two up, but Chandler's heartbreaker of a twenty-footer downhill—breaking putt to halve it—stung like no other. George had glanced over at Chandler and seen, even before the ball had dropped, that he looked as if he suddenly knew in his heart that he could do it: win it all. In golf, confidence can be everything. A man may strike a thousand shots perfectly, but just one misplayed shot can lead to a questioning of the stroke that starts a tiny rip in his confidence and can tear his game apart.

The reverse was seemingly true for Chandler. A few excellent shots, and his confidence had been restored; thoughts of mistakes had been quickly erased.

But now, as they stood on the tee box of The Lake, a par four of 360 yards, George banished those thoughts. Nothing could be done about past shots; those holes were history now. He was one up, and for all of Chandler's putting fireworks, George reminded himself that in thirty-two holes of golf today, he had never lost the lead. So he waited, still quietly humming. Chandler was certainly taking his time. He seemed to be fumbling in his bag for a fresh ball, then he spent a few moments talking to his cousin. *Is this more gamesmanship? Deliberate delay?* Having won the thirty-first hole, Echo, and halving the last, Dewdrop, Chandler still had the honors for teeing off. "Why delay when you have momentum," wondered George.

The crowd stood quietly, waiting, until a small smattering of applause turned into an enthusiastic roar and shouts of encouragement to both men. The gallery appreciated the golf they were seeing. They wanted to see more.

Bert spoke up. "Why is he waiting, Mr. Lyon?"

George watched Chandler carefully, and his keen eye saw something that few others around the tee may have noticed. As he took a fresh Vardon Flyer from his bag, Chandler had turned to look at the choppy, dark waters that gave this hole its name. It had just been a glance, but George saw it. And now as he selected his driver from his bag, Chandler turned and looked at the lake again. Both he and George knew that Chandler had struggled on this hole during the morning round. He had found the water then, and George had gone two up. If one played this hole down the right side, it left only a short iron to the green. But the left side? Certain death in the water. That memory must have seemed fresh in Egan's mind.

After returning to his bag for a towel to dry his club, Chandler finally bent and pinched up sand for his ball and stood behind it, looking out at the fairway. His head turned ever so slightly to the left for a glance yet again at the dark waters and swollen banks of the lake. It was now clear to George that Chandler's delay was not, in fact, a tactic. It was hesitation. Deadly hesitation.

Chandler set up to drive, and as he drew his club back, his eyes unconsciously flickered for one last glimpse of the chilly waters. His driver arced beautifully, until the last fraction of a second, when fatal doubt crept in and tore through his swing like a knife. His ball started out to the right over the fairway but then turned gracefully to the left, as if predestined, into a watery grave to loud groans from the gallery. Any proverbial wind that had powered his sails disappeared in an instant. His head fell to his chest, and he stepped aside for George.

George set up quickly and, with his low, flat, awkward swing, hit his drive out well over the lake, down the middle of the fairway. Chandler stepped up to hit another ball and then, in a blur of shots, The Lake hole was over. Although it was a par four, George's five to Chandler's six had been enough to win the hole. George's mind flashed back to his first lesson about match play with Mr. McLaughlin in the summer of 1896 at Rosedale. *What score beats five? Four. What score beats seven? Six. Ah, match play.* George stood two up with three holes to play.

Chandler, clearly demoralized as he left The Lake's green, walked slowly to the thirty-fourth hole, Punch Bowl. This 430-yard par four, dogleg left, was one of the most challenging holes at Glen Echo. Half the battle still remained once one got onto its arduous green that sloped from back to front. Many a well-played shot would roll off if not stroked directly to the center of the green. But the difficulty of Punch Bowl's green would not matter this time. Although the rain had stopped, it was overcast, and a stiff wind still blew across the tee.

George had regained the honors. Bert handed him his freshly toweled driver, and George stepped to the tee. The ugly coal heaver's swing would not fail him now, and without a trace of hesitation, he crushed yet another powerful drive to the right side of the fairway. Even after all the rounds of demanding golf—in the cold, and the rain, and the wind—his swing never faltered. He had made the corner of the dogleg and was in perfect position to go for the green in two.

Chandler stepped to Punch Bowl's tee and stared down at his ball. He gripped his driver and shrugged as if trying to shake something off his back. He regripped the club and then suddenly stepped away from the ball, perhaps still unnerved by what had happened at The Lake. He was conscious of George's huge drive that he had just witnessed. With George two up, he knew he needed to win every hole. The crowd, knowing, too, of the pressure he faced, fell silent as he stepped into his stance again. A boy's voice called out from the crowd, "Come on, Chandler! You can do it!" The gallery laughed at the boy's obvious enthusiasm for Chandler and then broke into supportive applause for their favorite. But his focus cracked, and Chandler was forced to step away from the tee one more time. Someone called for quiet, and with a scowl, Chandler resumed his stance. He gripped and regripped his driver.

What followed was described by George Westlake in the Chicago papers the next day as "one of the weirdest displays of golf in recent memory."

Chandler, wanting to match yard for yard George's long drive, swung as hard as he could. His beautiful classic swing was nowhere to be found. Off balance, he fell out of his stance, sliced his tee shot, and it disappeared into the rough. A low, almost mournful gasp went through the crowd.

Chandler, with Walter close behind, bolted from the tee in a desperate hurry to find his ball. He had spent the entire day trying unsuccessfully to keep up with Lyon's huge drives. *It can't end this way.* He would do everything in his power to recover from this shot. When they located the muddy Flyer, Chandler quickly pulled a midiron and inexplicably rushed his second shot. George and Bert had not even reached his drive when they saw Chandler's second shot strike a nearby tree—still on the right side of the fairway—and drop to the ground. From there, he still had no shot to the green. But it didn't matter, as Chandler's third stroke was even more wild, striking yet another tree. A desperate panic set in as he struck his ball a fourth and fifth time.

All the while, George, waited in the fairway, and then patiently hit a fine second shot into position, thirty yards in front of the difficult green, and using his reliable mashie, he pitched to within two feet of the hole. Chandler putted and finally pulled his sixth shot from Punch Bowl's cup. He stepped aside to watch. George, lying three, calmly rolled in his putt. George four; Chandler six. George was three up with two holes to play. Chandler had run out of holes.

With the crowd in stunned silence, Bert reached into the cup, pulled George's ball from the hole, and handed it to him. "Mr. Lyon, you are Olympic champion."

21

Victory

SATURDAY, SEPTEMBER 24, 1904, EVENING

G EORGE LYON STOOD on Punch Bowl's green and stared at the Haskell ball that Bert handed him as the crowd suddenly surged forward. It didn't seem possible that it was over. Their cheers and congratulations sounded as if they came from another world. He had done it. He had won the Olympic championship and the gold medal. His mind flashed back nine years earlier to that crisp October day at Rosedale Golf Club on his first tee with John Dick.

"Tipcat, indeed," he said softly to himself.

As Albert rushed up and hugged him in a frenzy, calling out, "Olympic champion! Olympic champion!" George's eyes searched the crowd for Chandler Egan. He saw him at the edge of the green, leaning heavily on his cousin's shoulder. He was clearly devastated by the loss. George pushed his way through the crowd to reach him and gently pulled him away from Walter. The young man looked every inch a boy at that moment.

The crowd surrounded them again, and George put his arms around Chandler as if he were his own son. Standing there amid the noise from the gallery, and enveloping Chandler with the deep smell of sweat and wet wool, George said to him, "You fought a hard match, Chandler. It could have gone either way on many of those holes. Be proud of the match. You played well. Let's have a drink and some dinner. Goodness knows we've earned it."

But Chandler would have none of it. He pulled away, and George could see in his eyes bitter disappointment. He could see the worst form of anger: Chandler was angry with himself.

"I could have played better... I *should* have played better..." He was near tears. "I didn't play my best. I was too tired... I was stale after last week's Amateur... It was too much... I didn't... I *couldn't*..." He turned to walk away but caught himself for a moment, and then turned back to George and was suddenly a genuine and gracious gentleman. "Thank you, Mr. Lyon. I was simply out-classed by you today. Your powerful driving forced me off my game. You are one of the cleverest players I have ever met. I should have played my own game... Congratulations on a great victory. You have earned it." Overcome, Chandler leaned on his cousin Walter again and made his way toward the clubhouse. A small crowd of his friends gathered around him with consoling words. But none was sufficient.

Colonel McGrew was suddenly at George's elbow, shaking his hand furiously. "Congratulations, Mr. Lyon! An amazing feat!"

But before George could answer, the crowd moved forward and hoisted him onto their shoulders. He waved to the crowd of Americans and saw that it made no difference that he, a

Canadian, had defeated their best. They were recognizing an Olympic champion.

The soft rain that had been falling stopped, and the crowd carried him up the hill and through a grove of trees as far as the clubhouse steps. Colonel McGrew rushed ahead and now stood smiling and nodding. McGrew put his speaking trumpet to his lips one last time and asked for quiet. At his side stood Albert Lambert. He caught George's eye, waved, and winked, as if to say, "Enjoy the moment. You've earned it." The crowd finally set George down at McGrew's feet.

"Ladies and gentlemen, what a marvelous day." The crowd cheered. "What a magnificent match." They cheered again. "Mr. Lyon and Mr. Egan, please step forward and let these wet, weary but grateful spectators thank you for your performance today. Let them show their appreciation for you—" Before he could finish, the crowd roared its approval again. George stood at McGrew's right hand with Bert at his side and raised his wet wool cap in acknowledgment as McGrew searched the crowd for Chandler Egan. He leaned down to Mr. Lambert and asked, "Where is Mr. Egan?"

Lambert leaned in and whispered, "Mr. Egan has retired for the day."

McGrew frowned and muttered his disapproval as he returned to the crowd. "Ladies and gentlemen, a round of applause for our Olympic champion, Mr. George Lyon, winner by a score of three and two." And McGrew could not resist a few more comments about the course. "I think we would all agree that even with the unusual amount of rain we have had this week, Glen Echo has lived up to our expectations and given our golfers a true challenge." The crowd gave a mighty round of applause. "I want to remind all competitors and their guests that dinner will be served at seven thirty in the dining room, followed by the presentation of various trophies and medals, and there will be champagne, of course. But first, we have an important presentation to make inside, out of any more of this rain. Please join me in the clubhouse." The crowd surged forward.

George turned to Bert. "Bert, I couldn't have done it without you. I was so pleased to have you along for the journey today." Bert felt a swell of pride and for a moment enjoyed the glory, too. George handed his clubs to Bert. "I won't be needing these for a while."

Colonel McGrew turned to shake George's hand again. "I'm sure you want a hot bath and a cup of tea—if not something a little stronger—before dinner."

George laughed and threw his arm around McGrew's shoulder as if they were lifelong friends. "Nonsense! Join me for a drink." The men who had gathered around him on the clubhouse veranda now filed into the dining room. On the far side, George could see the magnificent Olympic cup on a table. Colonel McGrew walked over and stood beside it, beaming.

As he was about to enter the packed dining room, George stopped and, with a little help from Albert, removed his soaking wet tweed jacket and hat. The crowd and his fellow golfers parted as he started to walk toward the trophy. George stood thirty feet from the beautiful trophy he had dreamed of not six months ago. With a broad and mischievous smile, he raised his hands over his head and then suddenly pitched forward into a full handstand. The crowd roared and clapped as George Lyon, age forty-six, having just played thirty-four holes of golf in the cold rain and cyclonic winds on a hilly course of some six thousand yards, proceeded to walk—*on his hands*—across the dining room to accept his prize. With each stride, the crowd and waitstaff cheered and chanted his name: "Ly-on! Ly-on! Ly-on!"

Colonel McGrew, not knowing how to react, scratched his head and let out a belly laugh. He turned to his son-in-law and Francis Newton, who now stood by his side. "Gentlemen, we have a champion—a *true* champion."

George leapt back to his feet beside McGrew and accepted the trophy with a firm kiss on the etching of Glen Echo. It was time to celebrate.

Later that night Glen Echo's dining room had never looked more magnificent, with stiff white linen tablecloths, crystal glasses, gleaming silverware, and men in their finest. After a sumptuous dinner and plenty of good old-fashioned American hospitality, Colonel McGrew called the proceedings to order. It was time for the presentation of trophies and medals. The trophy table, laden with beautiful hardware, had been set up alongside the head table for all to admire.

One by one, McGrew called golfers forward for a presentation and a few words. Each was met with appreciative—and at times envious—applause. The western team, captained by Chandler Egan, was called up to accept a trophy identical to George's championship trophy—each trophy rumored to be valued at $500. Chandler wasn't present to accept it, having retired to bed early for the evening. So Walter Egan accepted on behalf of the team. Chandler's trophy for having won the driving contest was accepted on his behalf by his cousin Walter as well.

Burt McKinnie then stepped forward to accept the putting contest trophy. He declined to give a speech but held his trophy aloft to cheers, as if he himself had won the gold medal.

Walter Egan stepped forward once more to accept the trophy for winning the First Flight consolation round, along with Warren Wood of Homewood Golf Club, who won the Second Flight. W.W. Burton accepted the trophy for the Third Flight, but acknowledged to polite applause and laughter that he had probably only beaten Colonel McGrew in that flight because the Colonel had lost his ball. Albert Austin stood to acknowledge his victory of five and six over S.J. Harbaugh of Glen Echo in the Fourth Flight consolation round. He would have at least one good story to tell to his club mates back at Lambton.

Colonel McGrew himself stepped up and accepted, with a huge smile, the international Presidents Cup, having defeated Albert in their presidents' match.

E. Lee Jones of Lake Geneva accepted the handicap cup, having achieved a net score of seventy-six. To his credit, Jones took a few moments to acknowledge the controversy that surrounded his win over Dr. Shaw. The unfortunate Dr. Shaw, who had had such a miserable start on Monday in the qualifying round, continued to have bad luck when he handed in his scorecard with a four instead of the correct five on one hole. He was disqualified and, as such, missed a win for the handicap cup. However, good sportsman that he was, Dr. Shaw rose and proposed a toast to Mr. Jones with a good-natured comment: "My real handicap is that I cannot count!"

Francis Newton and Burt McKinnie stepped forward to accept trophies and medals for their achievements in reaching the semifinals. They were given a standing ovation.

The room fell silent as Colonel McGrew prepared to make the final presentation. He looked out over the fine dining room, now filled with happy men and clouded by cigar smoke.

"I would like to take a moment to say a few words about this next gentleman. He's a Canadian." Bert let out a whoop of support to the laughter of the men. "When I asked him if he was of Irish or Scotch descent, he replied, 'I'm a wee bit of Irish and a good bit of Scotch.'" Colonel McGrew drew a hearty laugh from the crowd and warmed to his speech a little more. "I feel I have come to know this man over the course of the week. He has shared with me some of his life experiences, and I feel I have come to understand a little of his deep character, his love of family, his love of this game we all cherish, but most importantly, his love of people."

Francis Newton called out, "Hear, hear."

"Someone said that the game of golf builds character in a man. I must respectfully disagree. In my view this game *reveals* a man's character. Mr. Lyon, or if I may call you George, you have shown us all great character this week—on and off the course. Now, I know that there were complaints by some golfers..." McGrew paused for effect, "that your singing was too much for them—on and off the course." A roar of laughter rose again. McGrew had the room in the palm of his hand. "But we can overlook that nasty habit given your remarkable swing, your skillful play, and your fortitude. Please step forward to accept this trophy and this gold medal—which I hope you like, as I had a hand in its design—and our warmest congratulations. I declare you, George Lyon, 1904 Olympic champion for Golf." The men rose to their feet to give him a hearty ovation.

George walked to the front of the room and stood beside McGrew, at first shaking his hand but then giving him a bear hug. They had become friends. He accepted his gold medal for golf as he stood again beside the magnificent trophy. With a broad smile, he held the medal aloft for all to see, and with a nod, George humbly acknowledged the prolonged applause.

The room fell silent as he prepared to say a few words. "Thank you so much, Colonel McGrew, for those kind words—

at least those about my golf. But be forewarned, if I have anything to do with it, there may be more singing later."

A few men called out, "No! No!" in jest.

"Thank you for your hospitality and your friendship. I must say that you Americans certainly know how to make a man feel at home. You have been most gracious in your hospitality in this magnificent clubhouse of which you should be very proud. If I could take a moment to acknowledge the fine play from *all* the golfers, in particular those I had the pleasure of crossing swords with along the way: Mr. Cady, Mr. Stickney, Mr. Lambert, Mr. Newton, and of course Mr. Egan. I enjoyed our matches immensely. Thank you, gentlemen."

He asked his Canadian companions, the Austins, to stand and be acknowledged as he thanked them for their support and friendship. "Colonel McGrew, Glen Echo is a very, very fine course and I commend you and your club members for the work you did to prepare it for these Olympics. I look forward to returning someday and playing it once again—perhaps with less on the line and no gallery! Maybe a little sunshine, too." And then, to everyone's pleasant surprise, George called special attention to Tom Bendelow for his talents managing the gallery "and his skill with a streetcar broom. It is nice to know he has something to fall back on if the architecture business does not work out." George thanked the course superintendent and his staff for their excellent work in preparing the course each day under very difficult conditions, as well as the fine staff of Glen Echo's clubhouse. The men rose again to acknowledge the sometimes forgotten work that goes on behind the scenes of every major golf tournament.

A voice called out, "You are world champion, Lyon!" Another cheer went up from the men as they held up their glasses to toast him.

George raised his hand and acknowledged the compliment but concluded his remarks by saying, "I do not think for a moment that winning this medal and trophy means that I am the best golfer in the world..." He paused for effect and looked about the room at the smiling faces. "But I do know that it means I am certainly not the worst!"

All those present rose in another standing ovation. He had won not only the Olympic Championship but their hearts as well. It was late—very late—before the celebrations ended that night.

George Westlake stepped away from the dinner and drinks onto the wide veranda that wrapped around the Glen Echo clubhouse. In the excitement and socializing, he had missed his deadline for the newspapers and needed a little bit of peace and quiet to compose the last few words of his special story describing Lyon's victory that day.

For all the rain that had fallen that week, the skies were now clear and it was a beautiful September evening in Missouri under a full moon. The electric lights were on over the practice putting green, and he could see a lone golfer there rolling putt after putt. From the dining room, he could hear the gentlemen golfers who—with full encouragement from George—had decided to strike up yet another chorus of song. Westlake could see through the window George Lyon standing on a chair, arms around the shoulders of Austin, Lambert, and McGrew, leading the group in a hearty version of his favorite song.

"The sweetest flower that grows
You may search everywhere
But none can compare with my wild Irish Rose.
My wild Irish Rose

The dearest flower that grows
And someday for my sake
She may let me take the bloom
From my-y-y wild Irish Rose."

Westlake knew that Colonel McGrew was right. In George he saw a man who not only loved the game of golf but who loved people and who loved life. The gold medal was in the hands of a true champion.

Westlake had his story. His article the next day would begin with the words, "The greatest golf tournament ever held in America concluded on Saturday..." and end with, "Lyon's golf was a revelation and his victory is a rebuke to those who say the boys now have all the best of it in the royal and ancient game."

The Champion
Returns to Toronto

MONDAY, SEPTEMBER 26, 1904

"WHY ARE WE slowing down, Albert?" They had departed St. Louis early Sunday morning and after so many hours on the train home to Toronto, George was ready to see Annette and the children and settle into his own bed at long last. It had been a long, arduous week, and this train ride was beginning to feel even longer.

"I'll ask the porter. We are still a good distance from Union Station." Albert stood and pulled on his jacket as if concerned, but he knew full well why and where they were stopping.

While Albert and Bert marched to the end of the railcar to investigate, George looked at the trophy that sat in the plush green velvet seat across from him and shook his head. It was a beauty, and he knew the children would be thrilled at the sight of it. George checked his vest pockets for what must have been the hundredth time. In the right-hand pocket sat the brass belt buckle from Newton and in the left, with

Annette's still-damp telegram, the gold medal. Austin had told him to pin it to his lapel, "Wear it home for all to see," but that was not George's style. It was safer in his pocket.

The train shuddered to a stop, and George, determined to see where they were, reached to pull back a heavy gold-and-red striped fabric curtain. Before he could take in a single landmark, men—dozens of them—began to pour into the car. The train was making an unscheduled stop at Lambton Golf and Country Club, courtesy of Albert Austin. George's club mates cheered as they gathered around him, and had there been more room, they probably would have tried to hoist him on their shoulders and carry their hero the length of the entire train.

Albert and Bert stayed well back and watched as the members shook George's hand, slapped his back, and marveled at the trophy. A few already-started bottles of fortification also made their way on board, and florid toasts were made as the train chugged out of the Lambton stop and continued on its way to Union Station.

Through it all, Albert watched his friend receive the good wishes and congratulations with his customary modest manner. It was hard not to admire such a humble man. Albert turned to Bert and noted, "There has been no change in the size of that man's hat." To the delight of his friends on this final leg of the journey, George answered their questions; recounted each match, hole by hole; and gave detailed descriptions of his opponents and their strategies. Without much prodding, he even led them in a song. But as the cheering, singing, and storytelling began to subside, Albert called out, "George, have you shown them the medal?"

The singing and chattering stopped completely, and they all turned in unison to George. Suddenly, the railcar was quiet.

The members had been so enthralled with the trophy and stories that no one had seen the medal.

"The medal, George. Where is the gold medal?" someone called out.

He reached into his vest pocket and pulled out a small silk pouch and tugged at its string. With a flourish, flashing his unmistakable smile, he held the medal aloft. It dangled before their eyes from a red ribbon, two linked, brilliant, shining gold pieces. Colonel McGrew would have been delighted at their reaction to his design. The members oohed and aahed as it was passed from man to man. Each laid it in his hand, turned it over and over, made a weighing motion as if judging the quality and quantity of the gold, and then ran a finger over the words "OLYMPIC CHAMPION, GOLF" and the image of a golf bag and clubs. It was passed solemnly from man to man, each saying, "Well done, George."

It was dark now, and as they rattled along the tracks approaching downtown Toronto, George could see the lights in the homes of the Junction neighborhood coming on one by one, and then streetcars inching along Queen Street, steamers of the Toronto Ferry Company out on the lake, and finally, the towers of Union Station at Front Street. He had missed his city and as he returned to it he felt a deep but tired satisfaction at what he had accomplished. He looked at Albert and his son chatting merrily about the week's events and made a note to do something special for both of them. He could not have done it without their help and support and looked forward to a day when he could play golf with George Jr.

A porter passed through, announcing the next stop: "Union Station, folks. Don't forget your personal items." At long last, the train slowly pulled into cavernous Union Station. George stood and took down his hat and coat; straightened his shirt, tie, and vest; and gave his moustache a quick brush. Even after this lengthy train ride, he wanted to look his best when he finally saw Annette. "I hope that I am able to get a cab home," George said softly as he bent to pick up his trophy.

"I don't think that will be a problem, George," Albert said with a laugh. "The problem will be getting *to* the cab."

George looked puzzled at the comment and leaned across the seats, shading his eyes to look out the window. "Oh, my Lord!"

Through the steam billowing out from the engine, he could see that the platform was overflowing with hundreds of well-wishers wanting a glimpse of their Olympic champion. When he finally stepped from Austin's private railcar, trophy in his arms, a cheer went up and down the platform, building to a steady roar as people chanted his name, "Ly-on! Ly-on!" over and over. Among the many smiling faces, George recognized dozens of friends from golf, curling, and cricket clubs across the city. There, in the midst of them, he saw a beaming John Dick. George smiled at him across the throng, shrugged his shoulders, and simply nodded as if to say, "Who could have imagined..."

Before he could do anything, his brother-in-law, Fritz, was at his arm, shaking his hand and patting his back. "Congratulations, George! You must be tired," he said.

"I am a little tired, but not too tired to dance," George replied.

"You shall have a lifetime of bragging rights after this victory, George. I hope you are satisfied that I shall never be able to enjoy a family dinner again."

"I don't think for a moment that I will win every one of our matches from now on, but you will need a thick skin for a few weeks at least, my friend. Are Annette and the children well?"

"Yes, everything is in good order. They wanted to be here, but the scene looked a little overwhelming, especially for the children..They are waiting for you at home."

"I cannot get home fast enough, Fritz. Can you get us a cab?"

A photographer approached George. "Mr. Lyon, would you have a moment for a photo? I have a spot set up over here for you."

"Go on, George. Let the gentleman take a picture of an Olympic champion," Albert urged.

"If you and Bert will join me in the photo, then, yes, by all means."

"I thought perhaps I would get a photograph of you and the trophy, and perhaps your golf clubs, Mr. Lyon."

"I have the clubs right here, Mr. Lyon." Bert, still his faithful caddie, passed the clubs to George.

The photographer arranged George, who was in his finest pinstripe suit, in a dignified pose with his right hand around his clubs, the other in his pant pocket, and the trophy at his feet. "Perfect, Mr. Lyon." In a flash, the only portrait of George Lyon and his trophy had been taken. And it *was* perfect.

George looked for Albert and Bert, but they had been swept away in the crowd of friends and colleagues. Exhausted, but grateful for the attention, and with a few more waves of his cap to the crowd, George, Fritz—and the trophy—were in a cab on their way to Rosedale. They would be up late that night, sharing stories, opening gifts from the World's Fair, passing around the gold medal, and trying in vain to find a place on the mantel for the greatest trophy ever awarded for Olympic golf.

The champion was home at last.

Before Tiger
There Was a Lyon

SEPTEMBER 24, 2015, was a gorgeous sunny day, probably not unlike that fall day that George Lyon stood on the first tee of Rosedale with John Dick—the day he fell in love with golf. It was the 111th anniversary of Lyon's victory, and to mark that day—and what would be the last year of his reign as Olympic golf champion—Lambton Golf and Country Club hosted an event to remember his role in founding Lambton, and to honor him and his victory. It was attended by Lyon's descendants: Mary Lou Morgan and Hume Martin, as well as his great-grandsons, Ross Wigle and Sandy Somers. Representatives of the Canadian Golf Hall of Fame were in attendance with another "guest of honor"—the original sparkling Olympic trophy. I was invited to participate in the day's events, and in addition to being asked to say a few words about George Lyon, I had the distinct pleasure of playing eighteen holes of golf with Lyon's great-grandsons—both of whom, I might add, seem to have inherited the golf DNA of George Lyon and Fritz Martin. Let's just say, I had to buy the drinks after our round.

It would be tempting to think of George Lyon only in the context of his Olympic win in 1904, but as I have tried to illustrate, there were other things that happened in his life that tell us as much about his character as that victory in St. Louis.

Others have spoken about George Lyon's trip to London, England, in 1908, for the next Summer Olympics. He was there to defend his golf championship. Sadly, infighting among the golf authorities in Europe, the Royal and Ancient, and others, resulted in golf being dropped from the Summer Olympics. Lyon, the only golfer who attended, was offered the gold medal by default. Anyone who knew George Lyon would understand his refusal to accept that medal and his return to Toronto empty handed. True athletes seek genuine competition, and they accept medals and trophies that acknowledge their victory or achievements. They do not accept medals or trophies because no one else showed up. I think Lyon's refusal says a lot about his character.

But there were other events too, even before the 1908 Olympics in London, which give us insight into his character.

As we golfed that day at Lambton, Ross Wigle told me a story of his great-grandfather's participation in a golf match. Lyon was ahead and preparing to putt, when his opponent noticed that the caddie had accidentally laid Lyon's golf bag on the green in breach of the rules. When it was the opponent's turn to putt, he rolled his ball not to the hole but over to hit Lyon's bag and tried to claim a two-stroke penalty. Lyon would have none of it, explaining that it was unsportsmanlike. If winning meant so much to him that he was prepared to engage in that type of low behavior, then Lyon would concede the match. So Lyon picked up his ball and left.

In 1906, the U.S. Amateur Golf Championship was held in New Jersey at the Englewood Golf Club. George Lyon, then age forty-eight, traveled to New Jersey to compete. Who was the favorite to win that championship? None other than defending champion Chandler Egan. The two men met, to do battle once again, in the second round. This time, there could be no excuses from Egan as he was at the height of his game. He had successfully defended his Amateur championship in 1905 six and five over David Sawyer. Any fan of golf at that time knew of their history at Glen Echo in 1904 and of Lyon's unexpected victory. Was Egan there to seek revenge? To even the score? A huge gallery followed the golfers around Englewood to find the answers to those questions. Once again, George Lyon came in for ridicule about his style of golf. Who was this old man with the odd swing, competing against America's favorite yet again? After twenty holes, the spectators knew the answer—Lyon was the victor, again.

But it was in the next round that things got interesting. Eben M. Byers, runner-up in 1902 and 1903, had defeated Lyon's hero Walter Travis to advance to the finals and meet Lyon. More than three thousand spectators followed Byers and Lyon for thirty-six holes of match play in ninety-degree weather. After thirty-five holes, Byers was one up. They halved the thirty-sixth hole, and Byers won the match. James A. Barclay in his book *Golf in Canada: A History* noted the following quotation from the *New York Tribune,* "Young Byers, trim in knickerbockers and with a style modeled on the methods of classic St. Andrew's and Sandwich, was in contrast in every way to the stocky, gray-haired, old time amateur cricket player, who stood in flannel trousers and white shirt as if to bat or bowl. He golfs as a baseball player does, hitting and poking, instead of swinging with freedom and follow-through, but Lyon made shots with fine results. 'He reminds me of a baby elephant,' said one stickler for style." Elephant, indeed.

On the final green, spectators swept not toward the victor, Byers, but toward Lyon in a spontaneous show of affection. They loved his style of golf; they loved the man and his spirit. Although he did not win the U.S. Amateur Championship, he had won the hearts of American golf fans again that day.

We all know that our abilities on a golf course must fade with age. George Lyon suffered wrist injuries that inhibited his golf as he got older, though he shot his age for many years. But his action on the course was not the end of his impact on golf, as he went on to contribute to golf course architecture and to write about golf. He was an honorary member of more than twenty golf courses in Canada. He served the Canadian Seniors' Golf Association as charter governor and chairman of the tournament committee, and was captain of international teams.

Lyon would have read about the passing of Walter Travis in July 1927 and of Chandler Egan in April 1936. At Christmas in 1937, at the age of eighty, George Lyon suffered a stroke and died the following May 1938. He is buried under modest stone at Mount Pleasant Cemetery in Toronto. I have stood there and thought about his contribution to golf and his life as a Canadian. I wondered: Have we done enough to remember this man? I don't think so. Should his face be on a Canadian coin? A stamp? Should he be acknowledged in some way at the Summer Olympics in Rio in 2016? Yes, of course.

There have been many great golfers. Tiger Woods and Jack Nicklaus tower over the others by virtue of the number of majors they have won, and I would say, in Nicklaus's case, the number of times he came second and third in majors. They are in a class by themselves. Other golfers such as Arnold Palmer, Gary Player, Tom Watson, Nick Price, Sam Snead, and of course Ben Hogan also rank among the greats. Before them, there stands the iconic Bobby Jones. Some say Canadian Moe Norman (Canadian Amateur champion in 1955 and 1956) was the greatest ball striker of all time. That is a story for another day.

I hope that in telling the story of George Lyon, readers will appreciate that before all of them there was another generation of golfers who ignited this sport in North America. George Lyon was one of them. As I like to say, before Tiger, there was a Lyon.

Postscript

Where Is George Lyon's Gold Medal?

A

MAZED AND CERTAINLY confused—this was how I felt back
in 2013, as I stood in the pro shop at the Rosedale Golf
Club, staring at what I thought to be the original (and
only) Olympic gold medal for golf. Unfortunately, as it
turns out, what hangs in their magnificent new clubhouse's
rotunda is not only *not* George Lyon's medal it is not even
a replica of Lyon's gold medal. George Lyon's family had
once corresponded with the Olympic Committee in Paris,
seeking a replacement gold medal because the original had
been lost. The Olympic Committee advised the family that a
replacement medal was not possible, but after some further
correspondence, they agreed to provide a replica medal. What
was provided to them resembles more the gold medal awarded
for a track-and-field event and is not identical to the original
medal awarded for golf.

George Lyon returned to Toronto from St. Louis, Missouri,
victorious on September 26, 1904, with his beautiful trophy
and his gold medal. In reference to them in an interview

shortly after his return to Toronto he said, "I finally won by three up and two to play, and thus came into possession of one of the finest—if not the finest—trophies ever given in a golf tournament. I also got a very pretty gold medal." Unfortunately, to this day that pretty medal remains unaccounted for.

Having thought about the matter of the missing medal for a few years now, I have speculated on a number of theories about what may have become of George Lyon's medal. Perhaps the medal was simply misplaced and is in the hands of someone who does not understand the medal's significance; it's in a jewelry box or memory chest, waiting for someone to identify it correctly. If this is the case, then I guess the golf world must simply wait until it is identified and shared. Or maybe the medal was stolen and is in the hands of an individual or private collector who cannot reveal the fact of its ownership. Again, this could involve a long wait before the medal is shared, if at all. Would a reward and promise of amnesty after 111 years help?

George Lyon or his family could have sold the medal for its gold value or intact to a private collector, perhaps during the Great Depression that stretched from 1929 to 1940 in Canada. This theory seems plausible. Why? Between the time of his victory in St. Louis, in 1904, and the end of the Depression, in 1940, the world saw innumerable and tumultuous economic changes. George Lyon was not a rich man. A title search of the property at 13 Dunbar Road reveals that before the Lyon family faced those difficult times in Toronto they had purchased their modest home in April 1901 for $4,350 in the name of Annette Lyon alone. They put down only $600 and financed the balance with a Mary Montgomery. In the dark days of the First World War, in November 1911, that mortgage was extended.

In 1915, their son, George Seymour Jr., volunteered for duty and went off to fight in the Great War. Tragically, he was injured in the third bloody battle of Ypres that occurred between April 24 and May 3 of that year. He and his fellow Canadians had inflicted heavy casualties on the enemy during those horrific battles. However, the Germans, for the second time at Ypres, answered their assaults by sending clouds of green-and-yellow gas across the battlefield. One thousand men died, and another 5,975 were injured by the dreaded, deadly gas. George Seymour Jr. was one of them.

He returned home a different young man. Eventually, he recovered sufficiently from his injuries, and he was able to play golf. He even worked with his father to raise funds for the Red Cross through exhibition tournaments. This was hardly what George Lyon had dreamt about on his train ride home from St. Louis. A few years after the war, in June of 1925, George Jr. married Evelyn Mary Robinson. However, he finally succumbed to pneumonia related to his war injuries just six months later, on October 20 of the same year. He was only twenty-seven years of age. What a blow that must have been to George and his family.

In the meantime, on August 17, 1923, the Home Bank of Canada closed, after twenty years of business, suffering from "bad and doubtful debts" that had been brought on by the world financial crisis. And then, in 1926, a few months after George Seymour Jr.'s death, their home mortgage was replaced by a further $5,000 mortgage to a James Cosgrove. Only four years later, in October of 1929, the stock market crashed, and the world entered the Great Depression that would last a decade. Canadian author Barry Broadfoot later called those days Canada's "ten lost years." Were the times so hard that the medal was lost as well?

George Lyon would have read about the Summer Olympics that were held in Amsterdam in August 1928 and probably felt a pang of disappointment that, again, golf was not to be an event. However, the fact that Canadians brought home four gold medals, four silver, and seven bronze that year—the best showing ever for Canada to date—would have brought a smile to his face, especially the showing by Canadian women. It was the first time that women had been allowed to compete in track-and-field events, and the Canadian women set a world record in the four-hundred-meter relay. George would have experienced the same feelings in August 1932, as the Summer Olympics were held in Los Angeles and he read of Cornwall, Ontario, native Duncan McNaughton's gold medal win in the high jump.

On January 30, 1933, George Lyon probably felt renewed sadness for his lost son as well as a sense of dread for the world when he heard of Hitler's appointment as Chancellor of Germany. The world was sliding toward world war once again during his lifetime.

And then, on April 6, 1933, it was announced that President Franklin D. Roosevelt had signed an executive order forbidding the hoarding of gold coin, gold bullion, and gold certificates within the United States. Of course, the usual effect of telling people that they cannot hoard something is that they immediately begin hoarding. His presidential order made it a crime to possess gold, whether as an individual or a corporation. This order extended his use of a wartime statute that had also prohibited the hoarding of gold, silver, or currency. The purpose of the order was to allow the U.S. Federal Reserve to increase the supply of money to deal with the Depression. Any significant amounts of gold coin, gold bullion, and gold certificates had to be exchanged for the equivalent of $20.67 (USD) per ounce, or an estimated $350 (USD) per ounce by 2015 standards. Small amounts were exempt, as were artistic items, and gold that was used in industry, for example, by dentists or artists. Individuals were also allowed to own up to one hundred dollars in gold coins, and rare and unusual collector coins were exempt. Certainly, medals such as Lyon's or any of the medals awarded at the 1904 Olympics would have been exempt as well. However, gold is gold, and during the Depression, times were certainly hard enough that the gold medal whether in Canada or the U.S. could have been sold for its value.

Whatever the case, after two extended mortgages, the Lyon home was sold for $6,000 that same month in 1933, with a mortgage back to George and Annette in the amount of $1,600. It is difficult to know what was going on in their lives at this point, but times were changing. Was the medal sold during these desperate times? We don't know.

I had another thought as I read about his later life. George died on May 11, 1938. Perhaps the gold medal is buried with him, tucked in his vest pocket (along with that note from Annette?). A part of me hopes this theory is true.

And then again perhaps George Lyon gave his medal away. You may ask why he would do such a thing. Well, actually there was a precedent. John Ball, the famous English golfer and contemporary of Lyon (Lyon was sometimes described in Canadian papers as "Canada's John Ball"), was known to give his many medals away. Ball won the British Amateur a total of eight times. In one of his most famous wins, in 1899, he came from five back to win the British Amateur at that fine Scottish course, Prestwick, home of the first British Open. He was the first to win the British Amateur *and* British Open in the same year. Years later, Ball was reportedly contacted about lending his collection of nine gold medals to an exhibition of sporting trophies in London. When asked, Ball replied, "I'm sorry but I don't know where they are. I think I've given most of them away to friends." Compare that attitude with the fact that today's professional golfers often pay enormous sums for replica trophies. As Padraig Harrington once said, "I think the trophies mean everything now... You're playing purely to get the trophy." After he won the British Open he ordered the maximum two replicas of the Claret Jug, but claimed he would have ordered eight if allowed. Rory McIlroy grew up coveting the silver medal awarded to the leading amateur at the British Open. (He finally won it at Carnoustie in 2007.) Replicas of the trophy awarded at the U.S. Open are nearly $20,000. Graeme McDowell paid that much for his, while Jim Furyk's replica cost $14,500 minus the cost of hand engraving.

Was George Lyon as generous as John Ball? Perhaps. By the time George Lyon retired, his trophy case was full of silver and gold, and much of his hardware was passed on to family. For example, he had among other items a silver tray from the members at Lambton in 1910; a silver cup to celebrate his win in the Governor's Match, July 14, 1914; a silver fruit bowl presented to him by the City of Toronto on the occasion of his Olympic victory; and many others. As James A. Barclay points out in his marvelous book (dare I say, Canadian golf bible) *Golf in Canada: A History*, George Lyon's record in amateur golf has not been equaled to this day by any Canadian male golfer. So consider the following achievements and the trophies that would have come with them: Canadian Amateur champion as a Rosedale member in 1898, 1900, and 1903, and as a Lambton member in 1905, 1906, 1907, 1912, and 1914; U.S. Amateur champion in 1906 (runner-up);

Canadian Seniors' Golf Association champion from 1918 to
1923, and again in 1925, 1926, 1928, and 1930 (he was both
the Canadian and U.S. Seniors' champion in 1923, 1930,
1931, and 1932).

In light of these many victories, is it difficult to imagine that a small Olympic medal might be overlooked as an
important heirloom by its original owner? Unfortunately, we
may never know the answer. A few years ago, a group tried
to raise funds to make a film about George Lyon and his lost
medal in the hope it would spur a successful search. They
were unsuccessful on both scores.

I have a beautiful replica of the gold medal, courtesy of
Lambton Golf and Country Club and Glen Echo Country Club.
Both clubs have taken great pride in their respective roles in
those Summer Olympics in 1904: Lambton as Lyon's home
club and Glen Echo as the host of the competition. They have
maintained a wonderful relationship, alternating a Ryder
Cup–like event between their clubs' members each year.
In 2016, their match returns to Glen Echo. To honor these
events and the memory of the 1904 Olympics, Glen Echo had
replica medals struck and presented them to participants.
They are identical to the one George Lyon received. Unfortunately, they are not gold, but I value mine as if it were.

Do you have a theory about George Lyon's gold medal? If so,
consider sending me a message at http://www.georgelyon.ca.

Chronology

Some Interesting
World and Golf Events

1754   First recorded rules of golf are published by St. Andrew's Scotland golfers.

1759   Golf is reported to have been played on the Plains of Abraham outside Quebec City by soldiers of General Wolfe having taken the fort.

1789   George Seymour Lyon Sr.—George Lyon's grandfather—is born in Scotland.

1812   The War of 1812 is declared by George Washington on June 18. George Seymour Lyon Sr. arrives in Canada with the 100th Regiment of Foot.

1814   George Seymour Lyon Sr. fights and is injured in the Battle of Chippawa in July.

1815   Jane Austen publishes her novel *Emma*.

1818   George Seymour Lyon Sr. settles in Richmond, near Ottawa, Ontario, after discharge.

1820   The game of poker is developed by sailors in New Orleans.

1823 The Royal Society for Prevention of Cruelty to Animals is founded in London, based on law introduced by "Humanity Dick" Martin, an Irish ancestor of Annette Martin, George Lyon's wife.

1824 The Glenlivet becomes the first licensed Scotch distillery.

1825 Ottawa has its beginnings in Bytown.

1827 The Lucifer, the first friction match, is invented, and soon, British golf matches are called "lucifers."

1833 Lyon's great-uncle is killed in a duel in Perth, Ontario.

1848 The gutta-percha ball is invented and replaces the feathery.

1857 The first book of golf instruction, *A Keen Hand,* is published by H.B. Farnie.

1858 George Lyon is born in Richmond, Ontario.

1862 Walter Travis is born in Australia.

1865 The American Civil War ends.
   · The Royal Wimbledon Golf Club opens in London, England.

1867 George Lyon's uncle is mayor of Ottawa, and Canada celebrates its Confederation.
   · *Das Kapital* by Karl Marx is published.
   · The typewriter is invented.
   · The curveball is invented by Brooklyn pitcher William Cummings.

1869 Young Tom Morris wins first of four successive British Opens.

1873 The Royal Montreal Golf Club is founded as the first golf club in North America.
   · The population of Canada is 3.8 million.

1876 The Toronto Golf Club is founded, the third golf club founded in North America.

1879 Brantford Golf Club is formed but later fails because of the latest craze—lawn tennis.

1881 Niagara Golf Club is founded.
   · There is a shootout at the O.K. Corral by Wyatt Earp and his brothers.

1884   Chandler Egan is born on August 21.

1885   Banff National Park is established around hot springs at
        Lake Louise.

1887   Royal St. George's Golf Club in Sandwich, England, opens.

1889   The Eiffel Tower is completed for the Universal Exhibition
        in Paris.

1890   Cy Young signs with the Cleveland Indians.
     • Canada Dry ginger ale is invented by Toronto pharmacist John
        J. McLaughlin.

1891   Basketball is invented by Canadian James Naismith.
     • Shinnecock Hills is founded.
     • George Lyon marries Annette Martin.
     • Royal Ottawa Golf Club is founded.

1892   *Toronto Star* begins publication.
     • Spalding begins making golf clubs and balls.
     • Vancouver Golf Club is formed.

1893   The first Stanley Cup is presented to the winner of an amateur
        hockey match by Lord Stanley.
     • Toronto becomes the first city in North America to have
        two golf clubs.
     • Chicago Golf Club opens the first eighteen-hole golf
        course in the U.S.
     • The first Ferris wheel is constructed at the Chicago World's Fair.

1894   Niagara Falls Power Co. transmits the first commercial
        electric power.
     • The X ray is invented.
     • Colonel R.W. Rutherford (who fought with Lyon in 1885)
        paints *Putting Green*. A copy of the painting graces the cover
        of Kavanagh's *History of Golf in Canada*. Rutherford's painting
        The Surrender of Poundmaker hangs in the library of the
        Canadian House of Commons.

1895   The U.S. Open is instituted.
     • Rosedale Golf Club is founded in Toronto.
     • Tom Harley wins the first Canadian Amateur Championship.

- The use of a pool cue as a putter is banned.
- The Breakers is completed at Palm Beach, Florida, by Henry Flagler.
- Walter Travis buys golf clubs while on business in the U.K. and returns to the U.S.
- Oscar Wilde's libel trial proceeds in London.
- George Lyon plays golf for first time, in October, at Rosedale in Toronto.
- Lake Geneva Course, Wisconsin, opens.
- First U.S. Amateur Newport.
- Royal Canadian Golf Association is formed.

1896 Canadian prime minister Wilfred Laurier elected and takes office July 1.
- In August, the gold rush begins in the Klondike.
- The Olympic Games are revived in Greece by Pierre de Coubertin.
- The world's first public golf course opens in New York's Van Cortlandt Park.
- Tootsie Rolls, Cracker Jacks, and Michelob beer are introduced.
- H.G. Wells writes *The Invisible Man*.
- Walter Travis plays golf for first time.
- Chandler Egan plays golf for first time at age twelve.
- Stuart Gillespie wins the Canadian Amateur.

1897 The Boston Marathon is established.
- W.A.H. Kerr wins the Canadian Amateur.

1898 The Spanish American War breaks out on February 15.
- The Battle of San Juan Hill occurs on July 1 and 2, and Teddy Roosevelt and the Roughriders become famous.
- Aspirin is first marketed.
- George Lyon wins his first Canadian Amateur Championship.
- "My Wild Irish Rose" by Chauncey Olcott becomes popular, and Scott Joplin's *Maple Leaf Rag* sheet music is published.
- Cleveland golfer Coburn Haskell invents the liquid center of the gutta-percha golf ball.
- Missouri becomes the "show me" state.

1899 Vere Brown wins the Canadian Amateur.

1900 Albert Lambert wins the Paris Olympics for golf (no medals or trophies are awarded).
- Walter Travis wins his first U.S. Amateur, playing at Garden City, New Jersey.
- A.G. Spalding begins marketing the Vardon Flyer.
- Harry Vardon tours the U.S. and Canada, breaking club records wherever he plays. He also wins the U.S. Open at Chicago Golf Club.
- Harold Hilton wins the British Amateur for the second time at Royal St. George's. Harry Vardon is the first to win both the U.S. Open and British Open in same year.
- George Lyon wins the Canadian Amateur.
- There are an estimated fifty golf clubs in Canada.

1901 On January 22, Queen Victoria dies and Edward VII is crowned.
- President William McKinley is assassinated on September 6, and Theodore Roosevelt becomes the youngest president in U.S. history at age forty-two.
- Leon Czolgosz goes to the electric chair for assassinating President McKinley, claiming he was inspired by Emma Goldman.
- Nobel Prizes are awarded for the first time.
- Crayons are invented, and the "Teddy" bear is named for President Teddy Roosevelt after he spares a mother bear on a hunting expedition.
- The rubber core golf ball is introduced.
- W.A.H. Kerr wins the Canadian Amateur.

1902 The Haskell golf ball is used by Sandy Herd to win the British Open and by Laurie Auchterlonie to win the U.S. Open.
- Lambton Golf Club is founded in Toronto.
- Bobby Jones is born in Atlanta, Georgia, on March 17.
- Fritz Martin wins the Canadian Amateur.

1903 The Harley Davidson motorcycle is introduced.
- Walter Travis wins his third U.S. Amateur in three years while playing at Nassau Country Club in Long Island.
- George Lyon wins his third Canadian Amateur.
- The Oxford and Cambridge Golfing Society tours the U.S.
- Willie Park Sr., winner of the first British Open, dies at sixty-nine.

- The first World Series baseball championship is held between National and American leagues. Boston beats Pittsburgh five games to three.
- In November, Roosevelt is re-elected.
- The term "birdie" is first used, and "eagle" follows shortly thereafter.

1904   Walter Travis, playing at Royal St. George's, is the first overseas golfer to win the British Amateur. He uses the Schenectady putter. It is immediately banned in the U.K.

- The St. Louis World's Fair and Summer Olympics open in St. Louis. George Lyon wins the gold medal for golf. He loses the Canadian Amateur to Percy Taylor at the Royal Montreal. Etienne Desmarteau of Montreal wins the gold medal for hammer throw, becoming the first Canadian to win an individual gold medal at the Olympics. The Shamrock Lacrosse Club from Winnipeg wins the first team gold medal for Canada. The Canadian soccer team from Galt, Ontario, wins the Olympic gold medal.
- J.H. Oke wins the first Canadian Open.
- On October 6, Toronto celebrates George Lyon's Olympic win with a dinner at Lambton Golf and Country Club.
- In October, the World Series is canceled because New York refuses to play Boston.
- On November 19, the Summer Olympic sports program ends in St. Louis.
- On December 12, Eaton's department store in Toronto opens its first escalator.

1905   Fred Lorz wins the Boston Marathon—the same man who rode in a car at the 1904 Olympic marathon and accepted the medal from Alice Roosevelt before being disqualified.

- Chandler Egan retains his U.S. Amateur title in a victory at Chicago Golf Club.
- George Lyon wins the first of three successive Canadian Amateurs (1905, 1906, 1907).

1906   Eben Byers defeats George Lyon in the final of the U.S. Amateur at Englewood, New Jersey, but Lyon wins his fifth Canadian Amateur in Ottawa.

- Robert Trent Jones is born in England.

- Mount Vesuvius erupts in Italy, so the Summer Olympics are moved to 1908 in London.

1907 John Ball, playing at St. Andrew's, wins the British Amateur for the first time since returning from the Boer War. It is his sixth title.
- Jerry Travers, at the age of twenty, wins the U.S. Amateur at the Euclid Club in Cleveland.
- Tom Longboat wins the Boston Marathon, setting a record.

1908 The London Summer Olympics are held. Golf is decreed unsuitable for the Olympics. Canada wins three gold medals (one for lacrosse, again), three silver, and nine bronze.

1910 Steel shafts for clubs are patented by Arthur Knight.
- Fritz Martin wins the Canadian Amateur for the second time.

1911 Harry Vardon wins his fifth British Open at Royal St. George's after having a bout of tuberculosis.

1912 John Ball wins the British Amateur for the eighth time.
- George Lyon wins the Canadian Amateur.
- Ben Hogan and Byron Nelson are born in Texas.
- The fifth Olympiad is held in Stockholm, Sweden. Canada's George Hodgson wins two gold medals for swimming.

1913 Frances Ouimet, age twenty, is the first amateur to win the U.S. Open, defeating Harry Vardon and Ted Ray in a play-off. (Walter Hagen, also twenty, makes his first appearance at a U.S. Open and finishes three shots back.)

1914 George Lyon wins his last Canadian Amateur.
- World War I begins.
- Harry Vardon wins his sixth British Open at age forty-four, the first Open to be covered by newsreels.
- Karl Keffer wins his second Canadian Open in Toronto. It will not be won again by a Canadian until 1954 with Pat Fletcher's victory.
- Francis Ouimet wins the U.S. Amateur at Ekwanok, Vermont.

1915 Jerry Travers wins the U.S. Open, but the British Open and Canadian Open are canceled because of the war (1915–1918).
- George Seymour Lyon Jr. is injured in a gas attack at Ypres, France.

1916 U.S. professional golf tour implements Caucasians-only policy.

1917 J. Barnes publishes the first golf instruction book using
      photographs.

1920 Dr. William Lowell develops the Reddy Tee, a small wooden
      peg with a concave top and a pointed bottom.
  · There are more than one hundred golf clubs in Canada.

1921 The Royal and Ancient rules limit the size and weight of golf balls.

1925 George Seymour Lyon Jr. dies on October 20.
  · Steel-shafted clubs are permitted.
  · Don Carrick wins the Canadian Amateur.
  · There are more than three hundred golf clubs in Canada.
  · Lambert Airport is established in St. Louis.

1926 Bobby Jones wins the British Open.
  · Harry Houdini dies of a ruptured spleen from a punch to the
    stomach delivered by a McGill student.

1927 Walter Travis, called the Grand Old Man, dies on July 31.
  · Don Carrick wins the Canadian Amateur.
  · Charles Lindbergh—a pilot recruited and financed by Albert
    Lambert—flies the *Spirit of St. Louis* from New York City to Paris
    on May 20–21.

1928 The Summer Olympic Games are held in Amsterdam.
  · James Foulis dies.

1929 Moe Norman is born on July 10.
  · George Lyon lays the cornerstone for St. George's Golf Club
    in Toronto.
  · The stock market crashes and the Great Depression begins.

1930 Bobby Jones completes the Grand Slam.
  · George Lyon wins both the Canadian and U.S. Senior
    Championships.

1931 Maple Leaf Gardens opens and the Leafs lose two to one to
      the Chicago Black Hawks.

1932 The Summer Olympic Games are held in Los Angeles.
  · Sandy Somerville wins the U.S. Amateur.

1933 Augusta National Golf Club opens.

1934 Marlene Stewart Streit is born on March 9 and goes on to become Canada's most successful female amateur golfer.

1935 Gene Sarazen hits the "shot heard round the world," a double eagle on No. 15 at Augusta National Golf Club, and goes on to win the Masters.

1936 Chandler Egan, called the Grand Old Master, dies on April 5.
· The Berlin Summer Olympics are held.

1938 George Lyon, called the Grand Old Gentleman of Golf, dies on May 11.
· Superman makes his first appearance in action comics.
· Kristallnacht rages through Berlin on November 9.

1939 Canada joins World War II.

1946 Albert Lambert dies.

1951 Marlene Stewart Streit wins the Canadian Women's Amateur Championships.

1963 Marlene Stewart Streit wins the Australian Women's Amateur and becomes the only person in history to have won the Canadian, U.S., British, and Australian Women's Amateur Championships.

1971 George Lyon is inducted into the Canadian Golf Hall of Fame.
· Marlene Stewart Streit is inducted into the Canadian Golf Hall of Fame.

1974 Fritz Martin is inducted into the Canadian Golf Hall of Fame.

2004 Marlene Stewart Streit becomes first Canadian inducted into World Golf Hall of Fame

2014 Toronto declares November 16 Louis Riel Day.

? Toronto declares George Lyon Day.

For a more comprehensive chronology of Canadian golf, see James A. Barclay's book *Golf in Canada: A History,* Appendix A, page 598.

Bibliography

Armstrong, Frederick H. *A City in the Making: Progress, People and Perils in Victorian Toronto.* Toronto: Dundurn Press, 1988.

Barclay, James A. *Golf In Canada: A History.* Toronto: McClelland & Stewart, 1992.

Barrett, Ted. *The Complete Golf Chronicle.* London: Daily Telegraph, 1994.

Batten, Jack, ed. *Canada at the Olympics: The First Hundred Years, 1896–1996.* Toronto: In Fact Publishing Limited, 1996.

Bennett, Carol and D.W. McQuaig. *In Search of the K&P: The Story of the Kingston and Pembroke Railway.* Renfrew, ON: Renfrew Advance Limited, 1981.

Berton, Pierre. *Marching Us to War: Canada's Turbulent Years, 1899 to 1950.* Toronto: Doubleday Canada, 2001.

Browning, Robert. *A History of Golf: The Royal and Ancient Game.* New York: E.P. Dutton and Company, 1955.

Buckingham, William and the Hon. George W. Ross. *The Hon. Alexander Mackenzie: His Life and Times.* Toronto: Rose Publishing Company, C.R. Parish Co., 1892.

Cruickshank, Tom and John de Visser. *Old Toronto Houses.* Richmond Hill, ON: Firefly Books Limited, 2003.

Darwin, Bernard. *British Golf.* Wellington, NZ: Adprint Limited.

Ellman, Richard. *Oscar Wilde.* New York: Penguin Books, 1987.

Filey, Mike. *Toronto Album: Glimpses of the City that Was.* Toronto: Dundurn Press, 2001.

———. *A Toronto Album 2: More Glimpses of the City that Was.* Toronto: Dundurn Press, 2002.

Flaherty, Tom. *The U.S. Open (1895–1965): The Complete Story of the U.S. Championship of Golf.* New York: E.P. Dutton and Company Inc., 1966.

Goodner, Ross. *Golf's Greatest: The Legendary World of Golf Hall of Famers.* New York: Golf Digest Inc., 1978.

Graves, Donald E. *Redcoats and Grey Jackets: the Battle of Chippewa, July 5, 1814.* Toronto: Dundurn Press, 1994.

Guillet, Edwin. *Early Life in Upper Canada.* Toronto: Ontario Publishing Company Limited, 1933.

Hall, Roger and Gordon Dodds. *A Picture History of Ontario.* Edmonton: Hurtig Publishers, 1978.

Harper, Stephen J. *A Great Game: The Forgotten Leafs and the Rise of Professional Hockey.* Toronto: Simon and Schuster Canada, 2013.

Howell, Nancy and Maxwell Howell. *Sports and Games in Canadian Life: 1700 to the Present.* Toronto: Macmillan Company of Canada Limited, 1969.

Johnson, Paul. *The History of the American People.* London: Orion Books Limited, 1997.

Kingwell, Mark and Christopher Moore. *Canada: Our Century.* Toronto: Doubleday Canada, 1990.

Kluckner, Michael. *Toronto: The Way It Was.* North Vancouver: Whitecap Books, 1988.

Labbance, Bob. *The Old Man: The Biography of Walter Travis.* Ann Arbor, MI: Sleeping Bear Press, 2000.

Lapierre, Laurier L. *Sir Wilfrid Laurier and the Romance of Canada.* Toronto: Stoddart Publishing Company, 1996.

Larson, Erik. *The Devil in the White City: Murder, Magic, and Madness at the Fair that Changed America.* Toronto: Vintage Books Random House, 2001.

Lavallee, Omer. *Van Horne's Road: An Illustrated Account of the Construction and First Years of Operation of the Canadian Pacific Transcontinental Railway.* Toronto: Railfair Enterprises Limited, 1974.

Lears, Jackson. *Rebirth of a Nation: The Making of Modern America, 1877 to 1920.* New York: HarperCollins, 2009.

Lee, James P. *Golf in America.* Montreal: St. Remy Media Inc., 2001.

Legrand, Jacques. *Chronicle of Canada.* Montreal: Chronicle Publications, 1990.

MacMillan, Margaret. *The War that Ended Peace: The Road to 1914.* New York: Penguin Canada, 2013.

Martin, John Stuart. *The Curious History of the Golf Ball: Mankind's Most Fascinating Sphere.* New York: Horizon Press, 1968.

Matthews, George and Sandra Marshall. *Images of America: St. Louis Olympics, 1904.* Mount Pleasant, SC: Arcadia Publishing, 2003.

McCord, Robert R. *Golf: An Album of its History.* Ithaca, NY: Burford Books, 1998.

Mott, Morris K. *Sports in Canada: Historical Readings.* Mississauga: Copp Clark Pitman, 1989.

O'Driscoll, Robert and Lorna Reynolds, eds. *The Untold Story: The Irish in Canada* (vols. 1 and 2). Toronto: Celtic Arts of Canada, 1988.

Official program, Olympic golf championship, Glen Echo Country Club, September 17–24, 1904.

The Queen's Own Rifles of Canada website, www.qor.com.

Redmond, Gerald. *Some Aspects of Organized Sport and Leisure in Nineteenth-Century Canada.* Mississauga: Clark Pitman Limited, 1989.

Rust-D'Eye, George H. *Cabbagetown Remembered.* Toronto: Stoddart Publishing Company Limited, 1984.

Stephenson, James A. *Curling in Ontario, 1846 to 1946.* Toronto: Ontario Curling Association, Ryerson Press, 1950.

Stevens, Peter F. *Links Lore: Dramatic Moments and Neglected Milestones from Golf's History.* London: Brassey's, 1998.

Strungnell, Bill. *A Great Canadian Sportsman: George Seymour Lyon.* A paper for physical education, Prof. Kevin Jones, based on interviews with Fred Lyon, son of George Lyon, provided to the author by Mary Lou Morgan.

Toronto Star: A Voyage across the Years, 1894 to 1960. Toronto: Toronto Star Newspapers Limited, 1994.

Trager, James. *The People's Chronology: A Year-by-Year Record of Human Events from Prehistory to the Present.* New York: Henry Holt and Company, 1992.

Troubridge, Lady. *The Book of Etiquette,* vol. 2. London: Associated Bookbuyers Company, 1926.

Wallace, W. Stewart, ed. *The Encyclopedia of Canada,* vol. 5. Toronto: University Associates of Canada Limited, 1948.

Warner, Oliver. *With Wolfe to Québec.* Glasgow: William Collins Sons and Company Limited, 1972.

MICHAEL COCHRANE is a Toronto author and lawyer. He has published a number of best-selling books about Canadian law and is frequently featured on television and radio as an expert. He was the host of BNN television's national legal affairs program, *Strictly Legal*. An avid golfer, and a lover of the match play format in particular, he was the 2007 Lookout Point Country Club (B Flight) Match Play champion, the Cedar Springs 2009 Match Play champion (eighteen and over), and 2014 and 2015 Cedar Springs (Senior) Match Play champion. He has three holes-in-one to his credit, including an albatross—but that is a whole other story.